AF386685

No Experience Necessary

No Experience Necessary

Why Betting on Yourself in Your Twenties Is the Best Decision You'll Ever Make

Ronnen Harary

CROWN CURRENCY
NEW YORK

CROWN CURRENCY
An imprint of the Crown Publishing Group
A division of Penguin Random House LLC
1745 Broadway
New York, NY 10019
currencybooks.com
penguinrandomhouse.com

Library of Congress Cataloging-in-Publication Data is on file with the publisher.

Hardcover ISBN 979-8-217-08700-6
Ebook ISBN 979-8-217-08701-3

Editor: Kevin Doughten
Editorial assistant: Jessica Jean Scott
Production editor: Sohayla Farman
Text designer: Andrea Lau
Production: Christopher Andrus
Copy editor: Laurie McGee
Proofreaders: Janet Renard, Alissa Fitzgerald, Jacob Sammon, and Mads Dunn
Publicist: Tara Gilbride
Marketer: Mason Eng

Illustrations by Kris Jackson, David Sarrafo, and Suzanne Reeves

Manufactured in the United States of America

1st Printing

First Edition

The authorized representative in the EU for product safety and compliance is Penguin Random House Ireland, Morrison Chambers, 32 Nassau Street, Dublin D02 YH68, Ireland, https://eu-contact.penguin.ie.

For my late grandmother, Sophie Levy,
who modeled curiosity and an
openness to learn from all people

Contents

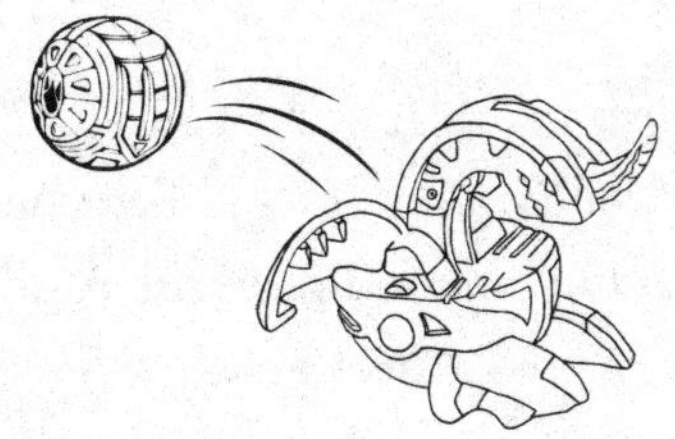

Prologue

A few months ago, when I was on vacation in Cape Town in South Africa, I hired a tennis pro to give me some lessons. He was a young guy, just twenty-one years old. In between rallies and working on my backhand, we sat down for a drink of water and started chatting. He asked me what I do for a living, and when I told him I was the CEO of Spin Master, the toy company that created PAW Patrol and Bakugan, he almost fell off his chair. "Bakugan?" he said. "I *loved* Bakugan. That was my *favorite* toy growing up."

At our next lesson, he showed up with a box. When he opened it, I saw that he'd brought me his whole collection of Bakugan. He had about thirty of them, and as he went through them, showing them to me and telling me stories about each one, he got very emotional. What hit me square between the eyes was that he knew Bakugan better than I did. Because these toys were a lived experience for him. He was the one who grew up playing with them for hours on end with his friends, fantasizing about how these characters grew to a hundred feet in size. My partners and I had brought Bakugan into the world, but for this kid, for a few magical years, Bakugan had become his world.

I had always known that Bakugan was a great toy and a successful product. It had generated more than $1 billion in sales and launched several seasons of a hit TV show syndicated around the world. At the peak of its popularity, it outsold both Transformers and Star Wars toys. It was our marquee product for several years, surpassed only by the success of PAW Patrol, which debuted in 2013 and would go on to gross more than $14 billion in global revenue. Spin Master itself now has twenty-eight offices around the globe, with over three thousand employees generating more than $2 billion in annual revenue. We started with nothing and grew, year by year, toy by toy, to become what we are now: the fourth-largest toy company in the world, behind Hasbro, Mattel, and Lego. The toys and animated shows we've produced over the past three decades have fueled the imaginations of millions of young children, giving them countless hours of play.

Whenever I stop to think about the scale of what my partners and I have accomplished, it fills me with pride, but when I think about the look on that young tennis pro's face, it fills me with joy. I had given this young man the opportunity to lose himself in a fantasy world of adventure, to be a hero in his imagination. I had inspired this kid so much that he spent years collecting these toys, and they meant enough to him that he was still holding on to them more than a decade later as a young adult.

Everyone who goes into business, everyone who dreams up a bold new idea, hopes to have that kind of impact on the world. Yes, you want to achieve a measure of financial success, but more than that, you want your vision and your passion to be seized and embraced by the public. That's the win. That's the goal. And that is why stories like mine, the journey from start-up to success, are more or less the main subject of half the how-to books that line the shelves of the business section at Barnes & Noble. But this book is not one of those. This book is not a how-to. Because if any aspiring entrepreneur out there wants to learn from and emulate my success, the important thing to know is not how I did it.

What's important is *when* I did it.

I cofounded the company that would become Spin Master when I was barely two years older than that young man I met in Cape Town. I was twenty-three, less than a year out of college, and living at home with my mother. My partners, Anton Rabie and Ben Varadi, hadn't even graduated yet. We didn't have much money, and we had no real experience to speak of. What we did have was the excitement that came with venturing out on our own for the first time. We had the promise of a road yet to be traveled, the wide-eyed eagerness of three guys too young to be cynical about the world. We had brains like sponges, soaking up tons of new information every minute.

What I remember most from that time is being driven by a deep sense of passion and wonder. Everything around me felt exciting and new. I felt like time would stretch on forever. I felt like the world was a blank canvas, and I could do anything with it that I put my mind to. I'd work and work and work, all day long, my body running on nothing but adrenaline and Tim Hortons coffee. Finally making it home around midnight, I'd realize I was starving because I'd forgotten to eat since breakfast. I'd grab a slice of bread, wolf it down, then get up the next morning and do the same thing all over again.

I remember the joy that came with pursuing my dream. I was doing the thing that everyone says they want to do but that so few of us ever actually do: I was becoming the person I wanted to be. I was becoming myself. Still, if you asked me to build Spin Master again, to do it all over from scratch, I couldn't. Not in a million years. Even with all the capital and experience I've accrued, it wouldn't be possible, because I no longer have the one thing I had then: my youth.

The power of youth is an incredible, magical thing, and I'm always encouraged by the many young entrepreneurs I see taking advantage of it. And yet, out of the thousands of students who enroll in business school every year, most of them incredibly bright and talented, the number who actually go on to start their own businesses is not nearly as high as it could be. Why? Every year, thousands of young people come out of community colleges and, despite having a great deal of grit and determination, aren't always given the same opportunities as their peers at four-year institutions. And, as important as a college education can be, there are thousands of others who simply don't have the resources to go after one. Who's to say that those people don't have considerable talents and remarkable insights from having joined the workforce at a much younger age than most of their peers? At a certain point, we have to step back, look at all these twentysomethings, and ask ourselves: How many brilliant ideas are going unrealized? How much creative potential is going untapped? And is it good for society that we let all that youthful energy go to waste?

The idea of starting a business when you're not even old enough to rent a car might seem crazy to some, but for me it always made perfect sense. In fourth grade, when I was about ten years old, my teachers noticed that I was falling behind. They tested me and determined that I had a learning disability, dysgraphia. Dysgraphia is a condition in which your hand isn't able to keep up with your thoughts. As you write, your hand cramps up and your handwriting becomes illegible, not only to the teacher but to yourself. You have to keep going back over your sentences and rewriting them and thinking to yourself, *What did I mean to say here?* You lose your train of thought. Your ideas get bottlenecked in your mind. You've got all these things you want to say, all this information that wants to come out, but you can't express it properly, and few things are more frustrating than being unable to make yourself understood.

It wasn't just handwriting either. Reading and spelling were a challenge for me too. Even typing. To this day, anything moving through my hands comes out slower and not as clear. (Voice-to-text technology has been a lifesaver.) Then, on top of the dysgraphia, I was also diagnosed with spatial awareness issues. If you gave me a thousand-piece puzzle, I don't think I could finish it. If I did, it would take me months.

As a result, school was difficult. It was hard for me to keep up in lectures. I struggled to take notes. If a test had to be done in an hour, I'd need at least two, and I endured a great deal of shame as a result. I hid my diagnosis from my friends. Anytime I had to go to a different room to write my exam, I would make up excuses as to why. I didn't want anyone to know I was a special-ed kid.

But the thing about a learning disability is that it's really, as I call it, a learning gift. It isn't a lack of intelligence; it simply means your brain takes in and expresses information in a different manner, which forces you to develop a different and in many ways stronger set of abilities to get by. To get my thoughts on the paper, exam after exam, essay after essay, I simply learned how to grind it out. During one of my undergrad business courses, the class had to do a four-hour case study. It took me eight hours to get through it. By the time I'd finished, all my friends had gone to the bar, gotten drunk, and stumbled home. To this day I've got a grit and a determination that have served me well. Dysgraphia also gave me my creativity. I learned how to see the world differently. I'm creative not in terms of being able to draw or write music, but in coming up with ideas and solutions, in bringing people together to collaborate and manifest the thoughts that I have in my mind, which is exactly the kind of creativity you need in business.

Given my struggles with a pen and paper, it was painfully clear to me early on that I would never be something like a lawyer or a doctor.

I could never sit in a cubicle and do what other people wanted me to do, simply because there are so many standard office tasks that I have trouble doing; in the real world, nobody gives you eight hours for a four-hour job. I might have done well in sales, possibly in real estate, which has always been a passion of mine. But more than anything, I knew I wanted to be my own boss. I wanted to create a career for myself that was custom-tailored to my strengths. I wanted to build something that was my own and have all the freedom and independence that came along with it, to be able to be and live in the way that felt right to me. I was a dreamer filled with ideas, and I wanted my shot at making them come to life. So I chose to go into business.

I offer the example of my learning disability simply to illustrate the fact that all people have major challenges to overcome and unique circumstances to navigate. We all have our own lived experience. Yours will be completely different from mine. Maybe you grew up in a low-income family and you're coming out of college saddled with student debt. Maybe you're interested in an industry that's being threatened by major technological change. And by the time you're reading this, who knows what state the economy will be in. It could be booming, or it could be in recession, as it was when we were starting Spin Master in the early 1990s. We all have our own time in history, and we don't get to choose it.

And it doesn't matter. It doesn't matter what you've gone through, and it doesn't matter how daunting the world in front of you might seem. Because the one thing no one can take away from you is your lived experience, and no one can stop you from turning that lived experience from a negative into a positive. No one can take away the gifts that you're endowed with that are innate to you. We are all unique, far more so than we realize, and at the end of the day, if you're here on earth and you're breathing, you have the agency to choose the path that you want for yourself.

So, what should that path be?

There are plenty of young people for whom a stable, conventional career is the right one. Going into law or medicine or working for a large corporation suits them just fine. And that's great. But at the same time, all across the world, there are young people who have the capacity to do something different, something extraordinary. They have ideas that animate them, passions that call to them. But when they graduate from college, they fall into a pattern. They're told that starting a business is too risky, that they're too young, that they need to first get established.

THESE WELL-MEANING BUT OFTEN MISGUIDED messages come from everywhere, from parents and schools and even from broader society. Young people are encouraged to get exposure to the business world on someone else's dime, maybe get a few years' worth of savings in their bank accounts. Having that foundation, they're told, will give them the tools they need to take the leap to start their own endeavor later in life. So in this seemingly rational pursuit of "experience," all too often these potential entrepreneurs set out to do the opposite of what they ought to be doing. They take jobs that don't particularly interest them. They work diligently for someone else and put off the day when they'll work for themselves. After four or five years, feeling a bit stagnant, they decide to go to graduate school in hopes of breaking the inertia and finding a way to alter the trajectory of their careers. Thereafter, it's anyone's guess. Their twenties are quickly fading, they're starting to settle down with families, and life has almost certainly thrown them all sorts of unexpected twists and turns.

I believe it would be better if future entrepreneurs were given a different message, preferably while they're still young enough to take advantage of it. I want their minds to be opened up to the near-infinite possibilities that lie ahead of them if they're confident enough to take a leap into the unknown. I want them to know that their youth, far from being a disadvantage, actually gives them singular benefits that can enable them to succeed.

In your twenties, the energy you're able to tap into isn't just jet fuel. It's rocket fuel. Compared to the average forty-five-year-old, you have the stamina of a professional athlete, and you can go and go and go. It's practically limitless. The same thing goes for your time. Time is a paradox. It's the one truly zero-sum resource we have; you can't buy more of it, and it isn't for sale. At the same time, in your twenties, time *feels* infinite. The days stretch on forever, and it seems like a lifetime can happen in less than a month. If you start a business young, you'll have that infinite sense of time at your disposal.

At that age, you've also got the right brain. From the moment you're born up to the age of twenty-five, your brain is still elastic. Your neurons are firing like crazy, exploding with ideas, dreams, and possibilities. Most importantly, your mind is still open. Age and wisdom are invaluable in many respects, but aging also works like a kind of plaque; you develop set ways of doing and seeing, and being able to peel those layers back to see the world anew becomes a task in itself. But in your youth you're able to see the world with fresh eyes and seize something new before anyone else has a chance. You live closer to the zeitgeist, steeped in the culture of what's happening now and what's waiting right over the horizon. You still have the same sense of wonder and possibility you did as a child, only unlike a child, you have the ability to turn your dreams into action. You've got your ignorance too. Lots of it. And that's a good thing, because it means you don't know your limitations, enabling you to push yourself further than anyone else ever imagined you could.

These are just a few of the superpowers that the young possess; as the following chapters will demonstrate, there are countless others. And with all those advantages at your disposal, if you have a dream and a vision, starting sooner rather than later will bring compounding rewards and benefits down the road. Being a young entrepreneur will give you ownership, equity, a stake in the upside—financial and otherwise—of everything you create. It will give you control—control over your own destiny, control over your time and your environment, control over how you work, when you work, and with whom. It will give you a blank canvas to express yourself and share your vision of the world. It will give you the opportunity to build a career that's in total alignment with your talents, your sense of purpose, and your values. Most importantly, more than anything, it will give you the ability to be independent and self-reliant, allowing you to live a life in which you remain true to yourself. Make no mistake, there are many, many risks involved in starting a new business or any other endeavor. But you only get one life, and the single greatest risk of all is to look back at the end of that life and realize you didn't live the one that you wanted.

ONE MORNING IN MY APARTMENT in Tel Aviv, as I was starting to sketch out the ideas that would become this book, I spotted two young guys sitting in the window of an apartment across the way, hovering over a couple of laptops. I have no idea what they were actually doing. Maybe they were two guys working in fintech or cybersecurity, or maybe they were just scrolling through Facebook. But my sense of it was that they were hammering out something they were excited about. They had that air about them, like, *Hey, I've got this great idea we should work on!*

In my imagination, I was looking at the next Steve Jobs and Steve Wozniak, the next Bill Gates and Paul Allen. This was going to be one of those legends you hear about, a great business that started up in a garage or a basement, only instead of a garage or a basement it was the window of this tiny apartment looking out over the Mediterranean Sea. I kept thinking how these future titans of industry had no idea what life had in store for them, how they would create something out of nothing and one day have an operation employing thousands of people and making a huge impact on the world. Seeing them made me reminisce about my own start-up days. Building something from the ground up was the most grueling, taxing experience I've ever had. It was also the most magical time of my life. I was stretching myself and growing as a person, constantly doing things I never imagined I'd be doing, meeting people I never imagined speaking to.

At one point in our journey with Spin Master, I thought we would run out of innovative ideas for toys. It's never happened. We have always found new materials to play with, new mechanisms, new hardware and new software to push us to new horizons. The same is true in every other industry as well. Which is why we need a culture that encourages youth innovation. More people taking more risks is better for everyone. Good ideas that lie fallow are a missed opportunity to grow and move forward. New companies bring innovative products and services that are healthy for communities, healthy for driving the economy, and indispensable for breaking monopolies and creating a more dynamic society. New companies mean more opportunities for all. Because there is no limit to the amount of innovation in the world. It truly is boundless.

In the pages ahead, I have laid out my story, how my partners and I, three twenty-three-year-old middle-class kids, built the fourth-largest toy company in the world. In Part I, I'll show you how we started the company, using our early successes to illustrate how the powers of youth put the wind at our backs and gave us advantages that our better-established competitors lacked. In Part II, I'll take you through the early years of our company, product by product, showing you how we used the powers and advantages of youth to build a profitable, successful, self-sustaining enterprise. Then, in Part III, I'll step back and look at the big picture, detailing the incredible rewards our efforts have given us in return, rewards that have compounded greatly over time, simply because we started as young as we did. When you get to the end of the book, you'll find an appendix that outlines and summarizes the core ideas and arguments of each chapter, which can serve as a reference for you as you begin your own journey.

But as I said before, this book is not a how-to. It is not a road map. It's a manifesto, an inspiration, and a call to arms. And why am I the guy to make that call to arms? Why is my story one that people should pay heed to? Because my story could be anyone's story. My story could be your story. There's nothing special about where I came from or who I am, and the same thing is true of my partners. We're three kids from working middle-class families, products of the public education system available to everyone. We were never the smartest kids in class. We definitely didn't have the best grades. At the same time, despite that very typical upbringing, all three of us were deeply eccentric and nonconformist, so much so that the system wasn't really built to let us in. We all knew we had to find a unique path to succeed in life, and if you've picked up this book, odds are you feel the same way about yourself.

Becoming an entrepreneur is not a job. It's a calling. It's less about the specific idea you have or the product you want to make. It's more about the life you plan to lead. It's about wanting to create your own world and control your own destiny. And in that regard each of us is unique. We all have individual points of view, different talents, different temperaments, and our own idiosyncratic quirks. Your path to success may not look exactly like mine. Your definition of success may be completely different from mine. So my goal in writing this book is not to give you some copy-and-paste template on how to succeed in business. My goal is to illustrate the fundamental truths and universal principles that made my life possible, so that you can understand those principles and apply them to your own hopes and dreams.

The first of these universal principles you're going to have to face is risk: assessing the downsides and potential pitfalls of taking the leap that you hope to make. Myself, I believe that risk—especially the ways in which young people should assess and think about risk—is poorly taught in schools and widely misunderstood. Which is why it's the subject of the very first chapter you'll read in these pages. But there is a far more important idea that young people should be think-ing about as they set out on their life's journey, and that is the inverse risk. If risk is the potential downside of taking an action, the inverse risk is the opposite. It's what you stand to lose by *not* taking that ac-tion. It's the upside that will never materialize if you don't take a chance, if you don't make the affirmative choice to live the life you believe you're destined to live—and as you will see by the time you get to the final chapter of this book, the cost of not betting on your-self may turn out to be truly staggering.

The principles you'll read about in these pages aren't just true for entrepreneurs. In fact, this isn't really a "business" book at all. It may seem that way at first glance, simply because business was the field I chose to enter and so those are the examples I have to share. But the reality is that what I have to say about the power of youth and the ability to chart one's own path can apply to any young person pursu-ing any endeavor. Today we find ourselves in a turbulent, ever-changing world. It might feel like a time to play it safe. It might feel scary to strike out and face that world on your own. But the truth, I believe, is that having agency and control and the ability to chart your own path is now more important than ever.

As I write this, the world is in a moment of transition, similar to when we transitioned from an agricultural economy to an industrial economy. Transition shakes things up, and as a result of shaking things up, creates opportunity. Over the past few decades, computers and the internet have transitioned us into a knowledge-based economy. Now, artificial intelligence, or AI, promises to take that revolution even further. It is too early to say precisely what the impact of AI will be, but what we can say for sure is that AI is offering us a new set of tools. From the invention of the steam engine to the invention of the microchip, access to new tools gives us the opportunity to do things that have never been done before. As a result of that change and disruption, young people especially have a huge amount of white space opportunities before them and chances to bring new things out in the universe. Because of that, I honestly feel that this is an incredibly exciting time to be alive.

I've written this book because I want to see more kids like the ones I saw outside my window, brainstorming in coffee shops, tinkering away in garages and basements. I've written this book because not everybody is as lucky as I was. I didn't leave college lost and aimless and needing a nudge in the right direction; I had a passion and knew exactly what I wanted to do. I didn't have parents discouraging my dreams and telling me to play it safe; my parents believed in me and supported me every step of the way. Not every young person has those blessings. Maybe you have the idea and the dream and the aspiration, but you're still stuck in neutral. Maybe you're surrounded by parents and peers who don't share your enthusiasm and excitement. If you don't have that support, this book can be that support.

It can help you make your case to the naysayers you encounter. It can help you vanquish the last, nagging bits of doubt from your mind and give you the missing piece of confidence that you need.

I've written this book because I want young people to have a better understanding of what their twenties can bring them. I want to give them clarity, a different way of seeing their future. I want to help them expand the realm of the possible, to understand just how much they are truly capable of doing. I want young, idealistic, thoughtful entrepreneurs to see business as an opportunity to make a defining statement about who they are and what they believe. I've written this book for you, because society will be a better, more interesting, more dynamic place as soon as you start investing your boundless energy and creativity in your own world-changing ideas. More than anything, I've written this book because I'm excited to see what you create once you're done reading it.

And since none of us are getting any younger, let's get started.

PART I
Start

1.

Risk

I n April of 1994, I found myself sitting at my mother's kitchen table. It was nearly a year after I'd graduated from college. In that time I'd spent a few months working for my girlfriend's father, who'd given me my first job, and at that moment I was busy ramping up for the new season of Campus Faces, the business I'd started with my best friend and partner, Anton Rabie.

Anton and I were committed to making something of ourselves in business, in part because we loved it and were passionate about it, but also because we both knew that, despite our talents, we weren't employable in any conventional sense of the word. We both struggled with learning disabilities and we both had our own idiosyncratic, nonconformist temperaments. Anton, who was preparing to graduate that May, was interviewing with Nabisco about a position. In the end, they told him that he was the most qualified candidate for the position, but they could tell he was too ambitious for it; if they hired him, he'd be gone within a year. So they turned him down in favor of the less-qualified person who was sure to stick around.

Given our situation, Anton and I both knew we couldn't just

wander through the college job fairs and wait to see what opportunities were offered to us. Which is why we'd already started one business and were actively looking to capitalize on the momentum we'd built up. We were working, doing. We were in the flow, so when an opportunity did come our way, we'd be ready to grab it and keep moving.

Which is exactly what happened that morning at my mother's breakfast table. Sitting across from me, my mom was flipping through *Yedioth Ahronoth*, the Israeli newspaper she liked to get. She noticed an article and showed it to me, translating the gist of it into English for me as well. It was about these odd, cute little things called, in Hebrew, *Rosh Desheh*, which translates to "Grass Head." The Grass Head was about the size of a softball. It was made out of pantyhose stuffed full of sawdust and grass seed, and it had a face painted on it. You'd put the Grass Head in water for a few days, and by the time you took it out, grass would be sprouting from the top, making it look like it was growing hair.

The idea for the Grass Head had originated from somewhere in Turkey. Nobody seemed to know who'd come up with it first, but now they were being made and sold in Israel and they were a huge hit with kids and grown-ups alike. Like the pet rock, they were a perfect novelty gift: low-end, inexpensive, and yet kind of amazing. People loved to put them on their desks and watch them grow; it was something they'd never seen before. According to the article, six major companies in Israel were already manufacturing their own versions of the Grass Head, and several hundred thousand of them had been sold. For a country as small as Israel, a fraction of the size of North America, that wasn't just a big number. It was an insane number.

The spark hit me right there. This one article gave me all the information I needed. As far as manufacturing the Grass Head itself, all you needed was sawdust, seed, a nylon casing, and decorations for the face. Several different companies were already selling competing versions, which meant it wasn't a patented, proprietary product. No one even knew who the original inventor was. It was an open-source idea, just sitting there, and since nobody in Canada was making them yet, we had a chance to be the first. I felt like the universe was serving up an opportunity and asking me, *Hey, are you interested?*

Luckily, a few weeks later my grandmother, whom I loved dearly, was coming on a long-planned visit from Israel. Knowing that I was curious about these Grass Heads, she brought me one so I could see what they were all about. As soon as she gave it to me, I already knew what to do with it. I soaked it in water and within a few days it started sprouting hair. It was both totally predictable and utterly magical at the same time.

I told my mother and grandmother that I wanted to start up a company to make Grass Heads in Canada, and what followed was a good conversation about risk. We talked about the cultural differences between Israel and Canada and whether that would have any impact on its popularity here, and we agreed that it probably wouldn't. Where we disagreed was on the issue of making them. They both suggested ordering a bulk shipment from one of the Israeli companies that was already manufacturing them, but I intuitively felt that buying the product from someone else entailed too much risk. We would lose the ability to control our supply, the shipping and delivery timeline would be too long, and it would require too much capital. My mom and grandmother felt that the risk ran the other way, that I'd be investing too much of my time and money getting a manufacturing operation up and off the ground.

It was fun having that talk with them, and it was also a classic example of exactly the kind of risk analysis one should engage in before starting a new business: Listen to what everyone has to say, keep an open mind, debate the issues in a kind way, but know that in the end only you can decide; it's your vision and your internal knowing that will need to make the call. And that's what I did. Going with my gut, I said, "No, we need to manufacture it ourselves and have control over what we do."

Once I decided that, I called Anton and I told him I had something amazing to show him. I drove over to his place and—in what must have been an unbelievably anticlimactic moment—I put the Grass Head on the table in front of him.

"Let's manufacture and sell these," I said.

Anton stared at this bag of grass and sawdust for a moment. Then he looked up at me and said, "That is the most ridiculous idea I've ever heard."

"Is it?" I said. "They've already sold a few hundred thousand of these in Israel. It's so popular that half a dozen companies are making them, and they're doing it at scale. It can't cost that much to produce, we already know that it works, and nobody in Canada is doing it yet. It's an open market. Why would we not give it a try?"

||

I have always been comfortable with risk. It's never made me nervous. I've always been naturally curious about what's possible, and I have a deep faith that things will work out one way or another if you apply enough effort. It's partly an attitude that's innate in me, and partly one that was shaped by my family's experience.

As Bulgarian Jews living in the shadow of Hitler's Germany in the 1930s, both of my grandfathers had good, stable jobs. My dad's father operated a currency exchange, and my mom's father, having gone to university to become a doctor, had gone into the picture-frame business to support his family. With the outbreak of World War II, rather than face a destructive invasion, Tsar Boris III of Bulgaria sided with Hitler and the Third Reich, and nearly fifty thousand Bulgarian Jews, my family among them, were corralled into forced-labor camps. They managed to survive the war thanks to the king and thanks to their fellow countrymen, who rose up to protest the deportation of Bulgarian Jews to the death camps in Poland. But it would only be a temporary reprieve. After Hitler's defeat, the Communists took over, and Jewish persecution only got worse. All Jewish property—personal effects, homes, businesses—was confiscated by the government, and in 1948 every living relative on both sides of my family boarded the boats leaving for Israel. Both of my grandfathers were broken men, forced to start over in their forties running small shops. Israel was a poor country then, and they were just surviving, essentially. My grandmother on my mom's side had to wake up at four in the morning to pick strawberries and then trek to the market in Tel Aviv to sell them. Not having any time to care for her own daughter, she put my mom in a kibbutz, where she lived from ages seven to fourteen.

My father, meanwhile, started working at thirteen, finishing high school at night. At twenty-one, fresh out of the army, he met some Jewish guys visiting from South Africa on the street in Tel Aviv. They stopped my dad to ask for directions, and since my dad's a friendly guy, they all started chatting and hanging out together. "If you ever come to South Africa," they told him, "look us up." So he did. In 1962, he moved down and, after initially finding work as a traveling salesman of transistor radios, he wound up becoming a partner in a business that sold Persian carpets. Five years later, he met and married my mother on a return trip to Israel. He brought her down to Johannesburg, which is where my sisters and I showed up, first my older sister, Michelle, in 1969, then me in 1971, and finally our youngest sister, Maskit, in 1973. Then, when I was barely four years old, South Africa's political instability had us on the move again. The Afrikaner apartheid regime wouldn't fall for another fifteen years, but what had always been a deeply immoral situation was increasingly becoming an untenable one as well, and it was not the best place to raise kids. So we packed up everything we owned and emigrated to Toronto, Canada.

At the end of my parents' long, hard road, I was lucky enough to grow up in a place of safety and stability, a land where anything was possible and opportunity was everywhere. We lived at 15 Ames Gate in the suburb of York Mills, one of those idyllic middle-class neighborhoods with great schools where the kids all ran around outside until we got called home for dinner. Thanks to the stories passed down around the table, the scars of my family's experience were etched into my subconscious, I'm sure. But the fact that they made it through their ordeal and even managed to thrive taught me that change and risk are manageable and normal parts of life. You can change jobs, cities, or even continents, and things will work out somehow.

Still, even within the safety and security of that nice suburban environment, I was forced to confront risk for an altogether different reason: Most of the time, I was on my own. My parents always took care of my sisters and me in terms of making sure we had food on the table and a roof over our heads. In that respect they were wonderful parents who did everything they could to give us the best chance in life, and I am grateful for that. But for all their logistical and functional support, emotionally speaking, my parents could only give me what they got from their parents, which wasn't much. They weren't equipped to relate to their kids on that level. In fact, I'd go so far as to say they were emotionally absent. My parents never read to me as a kid, never helped me with my homework, never talked to me about any problems I might be having with anything. My parents never even acknowledged my learning disability. There was never a single conversation about it. It was my teachers who helped me.

Years later, after my parents had divorced and after I'd become an adult myself, my mother would open up and be much more engaged in my life, particularly when the idea for the Grass Head came along. But growing up, I was that kid at hockey practice who was always stuck trying to find a ride home because no one was there to pick me up. There was one hockey match and one tennis match that I can remember that they came to. Otherwise, they weren't around. They were busy. They were working, because that's what they knew how to do.

Naturally, being left at hockey practice isn't a life-or-death scenario. But trying to navigate that circumstance is an exercise in assessing the potential pitfalls and upsides of a difficult situation. Who can I ask for a ride? Whose parents won't mind driving me out of their way? Who can I trust? Do I have money for the pay phone if everyone leaves without me? That's more risk analysis than most kids have to calculate on a typical school day. And I never had any choice but to figure it out, because I had to get home one way or another.

With my mom and dad, over time I learned to stay quiet and not ask for much, which is not a great trait to develop. I conditioned myself to figure things out and do them on my own. Being the poorest kid in a middle-class neighborhood, if I wanted to keep up with my friends and do the things they were doing, I had to make my own money. So I started shoveling my neighbor's driveway. I got a paper route. I did everything I had to do to be self-sufficient from an early age.

There were certainly dangers and risks to being a twelve- or thirteen-year-old kid out navigating the world by himself, but for whatever reason I didn't see them. Either I was oblivious to them, or I was willfully ignoring them because of the benefits that were accruing to me in spite of them. Being out in the world earned me money. It made me good friends. It taught me that, once I got over any initial fear, I could find the upside and the opportunity in anything. I was naturally an active, curious kid, but necessity made me even more so, because it gave me so much practice at it. Necessity forced me to take risks. My home life drove me to be independent, and independence forced me to be creative and look for opportunities rather than downsides. I wouldn't say it's the healthiest way to train a future CEO, but there's no denying the fact that my parents' absence instilled in me the tenacity and resilience my future job would require.

What I learned from my family is that in a world where there is so much that you cannot control, the greatest possible risk is to not have control over your own destiny, to be unable to make your own way and do for yourself. Is there risk in starting a business? Sure, but given my family's history, I was far more comfortable with that kind of risk than with the risk of leaving my fate in someone else's hands.

In the fall of 1990, I enrolled at the University of Western Ontario, which is the equivalent of a good flagship state school in America. It's the big campus in the small town, like the University of Michigan in Ann Arbor. I got wait-listed at first; because of my dysgraphia, my test scores weren't as high as they might have been. But that turned out to be an opportunity to learn yet another good lesson from my parents. My mom and dad were both big doers. They'd built their lives through a long process of trial and error. When you hit an obstacle, you tackle it head-on, and that's what my mother encouraged me to do when I was wait-listed. She told me to drive two hours to the admissions office and then sit there in the waiting room until someone let me explain my situation: how I had a learning disability and how I'd worked so hard to overcome it and that's why I deserved a spot. So I did, and they decided to give me a chance.

Because I wanted to go away for school, which was more expensive than living at home, my parents said they would only cover my university fees. It was on me to get jobs or loans to cover my room and board. Anton was in a similar situation, and by the end of freshman year, we both wound up with the same gig: selling fertilizer door-to-door, trying to get people to sign up for service contracts to have their lawns fertilized. And if you've ever sold fertilizer door-to-door for any length of time, you won't be surprised to learn that we were looking to do something else, *anything* else, as quickly as possible.

That something else was inspired by a business some other guys were already running when we showed up at school. It was called Campus Faces. Every fall, as hordes of college students were joyously making their way back to campus for the new semester, these two upperclassmen would go around with cameras and capture the excitement. This was before the internet or cellphones or selfies or any of that; it was just two guys with old-school film cameras taking pictures of friends seeing one another again, new kids going to all the orientation parties, or students hanging out in the hallways of their dorms. Then they'd make posters with collages of all the photos and hang them up around campus. Then everyone would cluster around these posters trying to find themselves in the pictures. What made this a business was that the Campus Faces guys sold ads around the edges of the posters to the local businesses that served the student community, everything from McDonald's and Coca-Cola to small local businesses and restaurants. Students loved Campus Faces, and the advertisers did too.

For the whole of my freshman year, I had the thought in the back of my mind that something like Campus Faces was the kind of great idea I wanted to pursue. Then, right at the beginning of that summer, as we were going door-to-door selling fertilizer, we found out that the guys who'd started Campus Faces had graduated and weren't coming back to do it again. "Screw the fertilizer," we said, and we jumped on it immediately. We didn't have a grand business plan. We didn't know the first thing about photography or commercial poster printing. I don't think we even spoke to those two upperclassmen to ask them how they did it. We saw that there was a market, knew people liked it, and realized there was a great opportunity waiting right there in front of us.

And how much were we putting at risk? Practically nothing. Just our time and our effort. We didn't have to build a prototype. We didn't even have to put up any capital to get it going. We knew who the advertisers were from the previous year's posters, so we went around to those businesses, plus some new ones we thought of, and took in about $4,000 in deposits—half of which I took to go to Europe for the summer. We found a boilerplate one-page advertising contract, and we had the advertisers sign that. In other words, we didn't overthink any of it.

When we came back for the start of school, we went around taking the pictures. Then we laid out the photo collages at my mom's house with my sister and a bunch of her friends, took them to the printer and had about nine thousand copies made, which we handed out to students for free. They then went and hung them up in their apartments and dorm rooms around campus. Once we were done, we went back to our advertisers to collect the balance of payments that they owed us.

That first year we grossed $12,000, and out of that Anton and I each took home around $3,000. The following year we had the idea to expand our operations to a second school and grossed about $30,000. The third year we did five different schools and grossed more than $100,000. Most of what we netted after our film and printing costs went right back into paying for school, which allowed us to graduate with no debt. We were left with some money that we used to travel, plus around $10,000 we kept in reserve for whatever our next venture might be. Because we'd already decided that there would be a next venture. We knew we were going to build a business, and we were open to whatever might come our way.

I ended up graduating in three years and took the job working for my girlfriend's dad while I waited around for Anton, who was in a four-year program and would finish a year after me. I needed him to graduate as well so we could build something together. We'd named our company Seiger Marketing, because "marketing" is such an open-ended word it left us plenty of room to do whatever we wanted. Maybe it'd be scaling up Campus Faces. Maybe it would be something else. The "something" didn't matter, so long as it was a business. Then my mom passed me the article about Grass Heads in her newspaper and my grandmother walked off the plane with the prototype of the same.

I FELT LIKE THE GRASS HEAD was an ideal venture for where Anton and I were in life. It represented a challenge, certainly, but not one that was beyond our reach. And it didn't feel risky to go for it, as we'd already made the macro commitment to tackle the next big opportunity that crossed our path. It felt like another chance to leap into the unknown and see what would happen. That is where risk entered the equation for us: What was the downside risk to us at that moment in time? We'd decided that we wanted to be business partners, and we knew our Campus Faces business was somewhat niche. We needed to expand, and as much risk as there might be in trying, it was riskier not to try. It was riskier to possibly miss the boat while waiting for a better opportunity to come along. Whether we succeeded or failed, we would be building a base of competence and knowledge to serve as the foundation of a future business. With all that in mind, the Grass Head made perfect sense.

Or it made perfect sense to me, at any rate. Then I drove the two hours to Western Ontario University to show the Grass Head to Anton, only to hear him say, "I don't get it." In his defense, what would you say if someone told you that a bag of sawdust that sprouted hair was going to be your golden ticket? But in my mind, Israel had proven that there was a big market for these things. It was just up to us to execute, and I was convinced that if we didn't seize the opportunity, someone else would.

For the next couple days, even with my impassioned pleading, Anton stayed on the fence. That moment was our first real glimpse into how our future partnership was going to take shape. It was the moment we began to see that Anton is not a product guy. He wasn't then, and he still isn't to this day. Anton—as you'll see in subsequent chapters—is the relationship guy. He loves sales, and he loves people. He couldn't see the future of the Grass Head as clearly as I did. But that was okay. He didn't need to see it. I did. I was more the vision and strategy guy, in addition to being the manufacturing and operations guy. He needed to trust that my instincts on that front were good, same as I would need to learn to trust him on relationships and sales and people. To Anton's credit, even if he didn't have complete faith in the idea, he did have faith in us, and after a couple weeks he came around and said, "Okay, let's give it a shot."

Once he was in, he was in. He switched channels quickly, and his brain immediately started firing on what we needed to do to make this happen. Step one was doing the R&D to reverse-engineer a prototype. First up was an epic trip to Kmart where Anton and I bought a whole shopping cart full of different brands of nylon pantyhose while the cashier and all the other customers stared at us, like, *Why are these two college dudes buying all these ladies' pantyhose?* Then Anton was off to Michaels craft store for the plastic eyes and the stuff to draw on the lips and the eyebrows. Meanwhile, I went to a couple different nurseries and bought varying types of grass seed. Then I went to a lumber mill to get sawdust. I used my mother's car to pick it up, and there is still sawdust in the back of that car today; you can't get sawdust out of a car. Luckily, she didn't care. Indeed, she was completely supportive of us taking our shot, offering up not only her car and her house but every idea or friend or connection she thought might be useful.

It took a ton of trial and error. Over about ten days we made forty different prototypes. One upside of growing grass seed is that you can tell straightaway if it's working or not. Some of them looked awful. But eventually we started to understand how to make them. We found the right nylon casing. After about ten different types of grass seed, we finally found the exact one, for a perennial rye grass. It also turned out that the Grass Head needed a specific kind of sawdust, a fine grain with the right texture and consistency, and I ended up going to a school-supply company to get the kind of sawdust that schools used to clean the floors back in the day.

Spending our days stuffing seed and sawdust into pantyhose was actually fun. There was something empowering about it. We weren't waiting around for someone to give us a job. We weren't beholden to anyone. We were figuring out how to do something by ourselves and we had our destiny in our own hands. We changed the name from Grass Head to Earth Buddy. And where the Israeli versions we'd seen all came in a closed box with a full-color picture on the front, we decided to package ours in an environmentally friendly corrugated box with a cutout window so you could actually touch the Earth Buddy itself without opening it. We brought on my sister Michelle, giving her a 5 percent profit share for designing the packaging, as well as her husband, my brother-in-law Austin, giving him the same for helping with the engineering and the manufacturing.

With the packaging and product nearly complete, it was time for production. For our first run, we'd decided to make five thousand Earth Buddies, a number we arrived at because five thousand units was the smallest order we could place with the printer for the packaging. The number was big enough to be ambitious, but not so big as to put us in a deep hole if everything went belly-up. But to produce that many Earth Buddies, we would need someplace other than my mom's kitchen table to work. We would also need more workers to produce them. That's where Anton really stepped in, taking charge on the personnel and sales side of things.

A friend and classmate of ours had a father who was in the Toronto real estate business. He saw a chance to do a favor for some young people who were just starting out, and he agreed to rent us space at 40 St. Clair Avenue West, a nice office building in the heart of downtown Toronto, at an insanely cheap rent. Once we had the space, we needed workers. Since we knew nothing about hiring a manufacturing staff, we decided to try a local homeless shelter. "We need workers, and they need work," we figured, somewhat naïvely. Some of the people we brought in were great. They were hardworking folks who were down on their luck, and they took the opportunity to turn their lives around. (Two of them stayed with us for years and ended up in management, one of them running our manufacturing center, the other our shipping department, and I'm forever grateful that Earth Buddy changed the course of their lives as it did mine.) That said, for the most part it turned out that the reliability of the homeless was low.

Our other problem was that our fancy new office wasn't the kind of place where you typically had people manufacturing things out of grass seed and sawdust. At first we sectioned off part of the office with a plastic tarp that we thought would prevent the sawdust from floating out into the ether. It didn't work. Plus we had a bunch of homeless people smoking in the stairwell. The landlords were not happy. In the end we only manufactured there for two days. We started on Saturday, and by Monday morning we'd received a warning from the building: "If you don't stop this, we're going to kick you out." So we scrambled to find a proper manufacturing warehouse, and we did. Then we scrambled to find a more reliable labor pool, eventually making our way to employment agencies and immigration centers, where we found recent arrivals from Eritrea, Vietnam, India, and Sri Lanka who were eager, dependable, and capable. Once we brought them on board and started working out of the right space, the whole operation started to move. Less than three weeks after deciding to dive in with the Earth Buddy, with about $10,000 of our Campus Faces money invested in materials, labor, and other costs, we were ready to go to market.

We didn't have a sales plan other than the fact that Mother's Day was coming up and we thought it was a great time to sell it. We priced the Earth Buddy at $10, picked eight locations around Toronto, and set up tables on the street to sell them to pedestrians and drivers stopped at traffic lights. My younger sister Maskit and my grandmother even pitched in to run a table for us for free. We never thought to ask permission from the city; we just did it.

Despite our best efforts, it didn't go as well as we'd hoped. After a weekend of making our sales pitch at intersections all across town, we'd sold only seven hundred of them in total. In hindsight, knowing what I know about the toy business, those were really good numbers. Nearly a hundred units per location in only two days? That's unbelievable. But relative to the number of units remaining in inventory, it felt disappointing and made us realize how much work we had left to do.

Fortunately, Anton and I both knew this was going to be a process of trial and error, and it was our mission to figure it out. It took us less than five minutes to look at each other and say, "Okay, selling these on the street isn't going to work. Let's pivot and see if we can find some other ways to get them out." The fact that we'd already produced five thousand units, instead of a few prototypes, turned out to be a blessing. We couldn't give up. We were committed, and we had to move fast and improvise.

Our first move was going door-to-door to flower shops. Like the street corner, that met with limited success too. But we kept calling around, trying to piece it together. Eventually we found a gift distributor who took part of our inventory. Then we connected with Zellers, a large Canadian retailer with an "As Seen on TV" program that sold items on late-night infomercials. They decided to give us a shot as well.

Then, three days later, we got our lucky bounce. My mother recommended we talk to a friend of a friend of hers, Sam Kotzer. Along with his two sons, Sam was the king of closeout toys, meaning he'd buy up all the inventory all the toy companies weren't able to sell. You'd go to Sam with something once you couldn't move it anywhere else. He'd take it for 10 cents on the dollar and liquidate it wherever he could. I brought him a few Earth Buddy samples, and even though it wasn't a closeout toy, he said, "Nice product. We'll try to sell it for you." Two or three weeks went by. We heard nothing. Then, out of the blue, they called and wanted to know if we could deliver an additional twenty-six thousand units—more than five times our original production run. Not long after, Roots, a popular Canadian apparel and leather goods retailer, stepped in and became the first branded store to put our Earth Buddies right on the front counter in all their locations across the country. At that point, I was immensely grateful that we'd brought in my brother-in-law to help us make our manufacturing process as efficient as he did, because we needed to seriously scale up our operation. The Earth Buddy was becoming a big success.

||

Risk is a subject that is woefully misunderstood. It's typically seen as something bad to be avoided. Or, on the flip side, risk is a thrill that adrenaline junkies go chasing. It's neither. Risk is not binary. It's multifaceted. Like the weather, it's ever present. It is inherent in everything we do and it cannot be avoided. Therefore, when making any decision or undertaking any venture, risk is something that must be assessed and evaluated. Then steps should be taken to mitigate or de-lever it. Indeed, when we talk about risk in business, it might be better to use the term "calculated risk," as that more accurately describes what we're dealing with.

So, in launching the Earth Buddy, what were our calculated risks? We had to put up $10,000 of our Campus Faces profits and about a month of our time and our sweat equity. Plus we had to tap into our social capital to call in a few favors, using my mom's car and kitchen table, asking our friend's dad to cut us a deal on office space, and so on. (All of which—as you'll see in the next chapter—were favors people were more than happy to do for us, so cashing them in wasn't much of a cost at all.) On the other side of the ledger, there was the risk of losing out on the opportunity to a potential competitor who was willing and able to move faster, which we determined to be the far bigger gamble. So we chose the calculated risk of action over the calculated risk of inaction. The result was that we sold five thousand Earth Buddies in just a few weeks, and over the next nine months we would sell over a million more.

Even if we hadn't sold a single unit, even if the whole enterprise had gone belly-up, we wouldn't have been out all that much: about $10,000 and a few weeks of our time. For most twentysomethings right out of college, taking $10,000—about $25,000 in today's dollars—and gambling it all on a novelty houseplant might seem like total insanity. But in the grand scheme of life it simply isn't that much to put on the line, and that is the first lesson young people need to learn about risk.

RISK IS DIRECTLY CORRELATED TO what you have to lose, and in your twenties you don't have that much to lose. At that age, you're more likely to be single with limited responsibilities. You can't risk losing a lot of assets because you haven't accumulated a lot of assets. You're not going to lose your house because you don't have a house. You're living with your parents or with a bunch of roommates in a small apartment. You're okay grinding it out in a way that becomes much more difficult when you have gotten older, are earning a higher salary, and have become accustomed to a certain lifestyle.

When I was in my twenties, older people used to tell me about how much it cost to cover their monthly nut, and the number was so insane I didn't believe them. But it's true. Your lifestyle rises with your earning potential and often exceeds it. It is much, much harder to put that lifestyle at risk once it's established. The potential loss from failing becomes overwhelming, and that prevents you from doing what you dreamt of doing in the first place. When you're twenty-two or twenty-three, more than likely none of that is true for you yet.

As far as the capital that you will have to lay out, again, usually, the risks are low. There are many different types of businesses. Some are capital-intensive, requiring large outlays of cash to get started. Others are not; they rely more on ingenuity and effort, needing only a modest financial backing to get off the ground. It may be the case that what you want to do is capital-intensive, and it may be the case that you've got access to family money or angel investors who want to back you. (Compared to when we started, in today's world, the venture capital market is super robust, especially in tech and now in AI. Indeed, there is more capital looking for good ideas than there are good ideas looking for capital, meaning there has never in the past fifty years been a better time to start a business.)

But for the average aspiring entrepreneur, as with Anton and myself, more than likely you won't be putting millions or even hundreds of thousands of dollars at risk. You may be putting up a few thousand, or even tens of thousands, and that may seem like all the money in the world in your early twenties, but in the long run it's not. *It's really not.* Lots of young people are out there running up that much debt buying stuff they don't need on credit cards at 19 percent interest. All you're doing is taking about that same amount of money and investing it in something you passionately believe in. Which, again, is a fairly conservative risk to take. And even if you lose every penny of it, you'll have many years to pay it down.

The one caveat I have to make here is on the issue of student debt, which is something that applies primarily to young people in the United States, where the cost of college and the loans used to pay for it have spiraled out of control. I'm a huge advocate for postsecondary education. If you plan to start a business, it's fertile ground for generating ideas, building contacts, and developing relationships. Practical benefits aside, it's also a wonderful time to indulge in the joy of learning for its own sake; I majored in political science, not because it would help me in business but simply because I found it a fascinating subject. But today, the cost of that four-year experience has risen up to two, three, sometimes four hundred thousand dollars, a huge portion of which students will be saddled with as debt when they graduate. As a result, there are too many young people who aren't bringing new ideas into the world, and society's innovation machine is being severely hampered.

It is both unconscionable and insane that young people should be burdened by that much debt simply as a result of pursuing a post-secondary education. It robs them of the freedom they ought to have in their twenties, effectively fast-forwarding their lives by giving them the financial burdens of someone in their thirties or forties. Which in turn may prevent them from taking the risks they would otherwise desire to take. As much as I enjoyed and valued my college education, if it had cost that much back then, I don't think I would have been able to go.

Unfortunately, the exorbitant price tag of college means that too many kids from working- and middle-class families have to engage in a comprehensive risk analysis simply in the act of choosing a school. If you don't get financial aid, you'll have to ask yourself *Is that degree really worth a hundred grand a year?* You'll need to think about how much debt you can reasonably take on and still have room to maneuver when you go out into the world, especially if you're pre-disposed to starting your own business.

WHEN IT COMES TO RISK, people tend to focus on financial risk, which is understandable given the importance of money and cash flow in any kind of enterprise. But the single biggest risk you'll take isn't with your money. It's with your time. And the good news is that even if society's financial risks and burdens aren't evenly distributed, time is the one asset that all young people have an abundance of. No matter your race, your religion, or your class, you get the same twenty-four-hour day as everybody else. But in your twenties, you have more time than your older, more established colleagues, simply because young people experience time differently.

There are any number of scientific and psychological studies and explanations as to why that is, but I don't need to reference them here because, based on our lived experience, we all know that it's true. We all remember those weekends with friends and those long summer months that seemed to stretch on forever. When I started the Earth Buddy at twenty-three, I felt like had all the time in the world.

Everyone says life is short, but it's longer than you think, especially if you use your time wisely. Now that I'm in my fifties, the days and weeks whip by and I can't believe how fast the time goes compared to my youth. Anyone who's past middle age can tell you how it feels to have fewer days ahead of you than behind you. But that feeling doesn't exist for young people. Not yet. At that age, you've got a seemingly endless supply of weeks and days and hours you can tap into.

And, even with that endless supply, you're not actually committing very much of it. Starting a business doesn't mean planning out a five- or a ten-year commitment. You're not betting your whole life. Odds are, whatever enterprise you have in mind, you're going to start small and take it one step at a time, same as we did with our first run of Earth Buddies. All we risked losing was a month, merely a fraction of the long lives we still had ahead of us.

IN ADDITION TO TIME, there is another asset that young people possess in a seemingly infinite quantity, and that is passion. And one thing you'll never learn in a classroom is that passion de-levers risk.

Passion is what allowed us to go on this journey when others might have counseled us otherwise. Sure, we had no experience with production or sales. We had no distributor relationships. We had next to nothing, really. But I had this article from *Yedioth Ahronoth* that was proof that this thing could be big, and more importantly, Anton and I were deeply passionate about building a business together. Put in a more abstract way, we were deeply passionate about discovering the possibilities and unknowns that come with trying something new and doing for yourself.

Doing something that you're passionate about unlocks a tremendous amount of energy, so much so that it gives you an enormous advantage in whatever you do. If you're passionate about your business, it will never feel like work for you. At a certain point, it's not even accurate to call it work anymore. It's not even following a dream. It's being *propelled* by a dream, being driven by an excitement that wells up from deep inside you. If what you're doing has all the excitement of the unknown, the dynamics of meeting new people, the power of creating something from nothing, then you'll find it's imbued with a completely different type of energy than what we traditionally call "work."

When your business gives you that sense of meaning and fulfillment, you'll find you have reserves of tenacity you've never imagined. You'll find yourself able to tackle problems with a single-minded determination you've never experienced before. What separated Spin Master's biggest successes from our greatest failures was always our attention to detail, the love we brought to the development process. If what you're doing aligns with your sense of purpose and your interests, you're naturally driven to learn and absorb every bit of information you can about that endeavor. The more information and knowledge you have, the greater your ability to connect the dots and navigate the business and make decisions. The more you understand about your chosen endeavor, the less beholden you'll be to feelings of uncertainty and fear.

The antidote to risk is not caution. It's courage. It's having the faith that you are following your North Star and you'll get where you want to go and things will work out, even if you're not 100 percent sure how that is going to happen. Which isn't a call to be reckless. I'm not talking about a blind faith that has you charging into something unprepared. I am actually pretty conservative when it comes to business; you have to plan for things as best you can, and you should work tirelessly every day to de-risk as much as you can. But there's a lot to be said for the power of believing in yourself. Having passion for something lowers your risk, simply because you'll find that you have what it takes to rise to almost any challenge.

Personal conviction can also de-lever your risk through the effect it has on the people around you. Part of the reason I've never used PowerPoint in my life is that I've always let my personal passion make the case for the direction I want to go. Bullet points on a screen can never fully convey the energy you have, and in a sense can mute it. People want to feel something, to be moved to action. Throughout your journey, you'll be compelled to bring people along, both internally and externally, pushing through the resistance and inertia that is common to all endeavors. Which means you'll always need to generate positive energy to move your business mission forward. Your employees, your suppliers, the salespeople taking your product out into the world—they need to feel the energy you're giving off. They *want* to feel it. Nobody wants to plod through life, feeling like they're phoning it in every day. They want to sense that you care, and as a result they'll rise to the occasion as well.

When I look back at how far we've come since standing out on street corners in Toronto selling Earth Buddies to busy commuters, I know that passion is what kept Anton and me going through all the ups and downs. We kept our sense of determination, and we never once thought about giving up.

ONE OF THE MORE COUNTERINTUITIVE aspects of risk is that the supposedly safe path poses plenty of risks of its own. It's often riskier not to do something than to jump in and do it. I am a great believer in doing things when the inspiration strikes, because if you don't there's always a chance that the opportunity will pass you by. If you don't capitalize on those bursts of clarity and insight, they leave and might never return. And since most great ideas are out there buzzing around, waiting to be captured and turned into reality, odds are if you don't move fast on your idea, someone else will. Miss your window, and then you're the person at the party telling people stories about *You know, I should have done it* instead of being the person saying, *Wow, let me tell you about this crazy business I started . . .*

Taking the "less risky" path really usually means that you're taking a risk on someone else instead of taking a risk on yourself. Will your graduate program deliver a great opportunity at the end of two years? Will this person who's hiring you be a great boss, or will that job not turn out to be everything that you'd hoped for? You have no idea what the outcome of those choices will be. More importantly, you'll have little control over what the outcome will be. And whatever that outcome is, you'll be beholden to it one way or another to try to salvage the sunk costs of what you've put into it.

Moreover, with the advent of AI and machine learning, we are witnessing a massive step change in the global economy. We have only just begun to see what types of employment are going to be transformed by this new technology. On the one hand, the future of the job market is more uncertain than ever. On the other, the emergence of a new technology and all the tools that come along with it will provide an incredible opportunity for the creation of new businesses.

And if you don't embark on your own journey when you're young, you risk the worst fate of all: stagnation. You risk getting used to others telling you what to do instead of seeking out opportunities for yourself. You risk finding reasons not to do things and talking yourself out of opportunities. Then one day you'll wake up and realize that you never bet on yourself, that you never followed your passions or went after your dreams, that you aren't living your purpose.

OF COURSE, NAYSAYERS AND CYNICS will often try to get you to question your vision by focusing on the downsides, the worst-case scenarios. *Make a list of the pros and cons,* they'll say. *Lay out all the potential upsides and the possible downsides and make a rational decision based on that.* But that process doesn't actually work, and that is the next lesson you need to learn about risk: Using a list of pros and cons to evaluate risk is inherently biased and flawed because it favors the negative, and there's an asymmetry in weighing the pros and cons that subconsciously pushes us toward inaction rather than action.

That's in part because the downsides of an endeavor are usually plain to see: The product won't sell and you'll lose the time and money you invested and be back where you started, end of story. And while there's a normal human tendency to fret about far-fetched, catastrophic worst-case scenarios, the truth is that most of the worries you put on your cons list will never come to pass. The road to failure tends to be linear and straightforward. There aren't a lot of unexpected twists and turns.

The road to success, however, is something you can't even begin to imagine. There's the short-term upside that you're envisioning and hoping for, namely that you'll sell five thousand Earth Buddies and gross $25,000. But beyond that you have no idea what's in store. The outcome of not doing something is obvious; you remain at the status quo. But the outcome of taking that first step—as later chapters in this book will illustrate—is literally unimaginable. You have no idea what you'll find on the other side of that door or at the end of that yellow brick road. You never know where it will lead you and what interesting people you will meet along the way.

For some of you, knowing what's going to happen when you wake up every morning can get boring, and risk takes you into the world of the unpredictable and the unexpected. Few things in life are more exciting than the anticipation that comes from asking yourself *What happens next?* and then getting to learn the answer. The path that I've taken with Spin Master, from making the Earth Buddy at my mother's kitchen table to making blockbuster feature films, is beyond anything I ever could have imagined at the start. The idea that I would walk into a Toronto homeless shelter and find someone who'd become a valued and trusted colleague for life? No business plan in the world could have predicted or accounted for something so random. No Hollywood screenwriter could have ever written my story; it's a story that could only be written in the doing of it.

So anytime you're making a list of pros and cons, you can't actually list all the pros because you don't have any idea what they're going to be. Which, in the final analysis, should be put down as a big bullet point in your list of cons. The biggest risk of not doing something is spending your whole life not knowing what might have happened if you'd taken the plunge. Not doing something is almost always a bigger risk than doing it, simply because you don't know how much you're giving up through your inaction.

The other problem with trying to evaluate the pros and cons of starting a business ahead of time is that you don't always know which are which. In many cases, what you think are the downsides may turn out to be the upsides, because they turn out to be the challenges that propel you forward, which is something you'll only find out once you face them.

RISK HAS ACQUIRED A BAD RAP. Too often people see it as something bad, something to be avoided, to be hedged to the point of not being a risk at all. Some even seem to regard taking on risk as being somehow irresponsible. And it's true that you have to approach risk with a healthy dose of humility; you don't ever want to bet the farm on some harebrained scheme. But risk is simply a part of life. That twinge we feel in the face of a risk is there for a reason. It's that quiver in your body's fight-or-flight mechanism that's telling you to be cautious about what's up ahead, and you should think of it as a gift. It's not necessarily telling you to charge forward or to run away. It's telling you that you need to look around, assess your surroundings, and be prepared to make an important decision when the time comes.

You should think of risk as its own form of education. When you enroll in Harvard Business School, the main tool they're going to use to teach you is the case method. You're told about a business and a challenge it faced. Then you're asked to come up with a potential solution, after which you're told how that business solved or didn't solve the problem in real life. Classroom learning is certainly valuable, but all of it is theoretical and none of it has any real-world stakes for you other than your grades and however much you put up for the tuition.

When you start a business endeavor, all the theory and philosophy goes out the window. The learning becomes live and interactive and, most of all, *real*. You'll develop the same strategic thinking and high-level analysis you will at Harvard, only you'll learn more in the end because you'll see and live with the actual consequences of your decisions. Again, you learn best not through studying but through doing. It's the doing that unlocks the magic. You can sit there and come up with all the reasons in the world something should work, could work, or maybe won't work, but until you actually go for it, you won't know for sure.

Risk is always there. It's ever present, and it never goes away. Every human endeavor carries the chance of failure, and you need to learn to be comfortable with it. It's a skill you have to learn, a muscle you have to develop. The key is to stop looking at risk as a bad thing to be avoided. Instead, learn to respect it. Look at it as a friend. It's helping you, guiding you, showing you which way to go. The choice you're making might cause you harm, or it might bring you some form of reward, and the more tough choices you face, the better you get at discerning the good risks from the bad. You could even say that the single greatest benefit to confronting risk is developing the ability to confront risk.

The arguments for doing this from an early age are self-evident. We're far more adaptable and resilient in our youth. Our capacity to absorb new lessons and develop new muscles only declines as we age. As I mentioned above, because of my family history I was first exposed to risk practically in utero. Because of my dysgraphia, I was on friendly terms with risk as early as fourth and fifth grade. I developed that skill early, and I'm grateful for that, because it taught me something important not just about risk, but about life, and it is the most important lesson you should take away from this chapter: Following your dreams may feel like a big gamble, but you're taking an even bigger gamble when you fail to believe in yourself.

WE ARE ALL MORE CAPABLE than we think. We are the ones who truly know what drives us and what we want to achieve. When we ignore that inner voice in favor of what others think we should do, we're ignoring our own best counsel. We all have parents, communities, and other pressures telling us what to do, which is why we need to be vigilant about who we surround ourselves with and how much weight we give to their opinions. They may have the best of intentions, they may think they have our best interests at heart, but too often they're telling us to live lives we're not meant to live. When you bet on yourself and succeed, you silence those voices. You eliminate whatever hold those negative forces might have on you, and you give yourself a self-worth and a self-confidence you can't get from anything else.

The day you enter the world as an adult for the first time, it's daunting. The task of finding a job and making enough money can be overwhelming. In that moment it's normal to feel like you ought to avoid risk, to look for the easiest route and the safest place to land. The reality is that those tasks are relatively simple. You can always make more money. You can always find another job. But you only have one life. You only get one turn across the stage, and when it's over, it's over. Time may feel infinite in our youth, but eventually the years start to pass and windows start to close. The riskiest thing we can do with our lives is to fail to live them to their fullest. There is no price you can put on a dream that goes unrealized, and when you reach the end, the single biggest gift you can give yourself is never having to wonder what might have been.

For Anton, Ben, and me, starting Spin Master gave us the ability to calculate, confront, mitigate, and ultimately embrace risk. Because the risk is what brought the growth. Risk is what unlocked the surprise, built the foundation, and generated the capital. Risk is what allowed us to make history and bring joy and magic to millions of kids. Risk taught us to be better developers, better leaders, and, inevitably, better businesspeople. At the end of the day, starting your own business is a choice you alone can make. You don't have to do it in your twenties. You can start later if that makes sense to you, but life has a habit of getting in the way the longer you wait. It's better to jump early.

It's less risky too.

2.

Everyone Is Rooting for You

Because Anton and I are both immigrants who came to Canada when we were quite young, we don't really see borders. During dinner table conversations, our parents always had an international perspective on politics and life. My parents traveled all over—they were Israelis who had their honeymoon in Iran—and it was the same in Anton's family. We loved Canada and were proud to be Canadian, but our focus in starting the business was never centered solely around serving the Canadian market. To us, consumers were consumers, no matter where they lived. So from the moment the Earth Buddy took off, we were already eyeing the much bigger market to our south, in America.

When we decided to go after those consumers, we had no direct connections to American retailers, but as luck would have it, Anton had gone backpacking across Europe the year before and he'd met this guy, Aaron Hermelin, whose uncle David Hermelin was a well-known businessman in Michigan; among his many interests, he owned the Palace of Auburn Hills, the arena where the Detroit Pistons played. We figured that Aaron's family had to have good business contacts and might know someone to whom we could reach out. So Anton called Aaron up, and Aaron said, "Sure. We have connections to Kmart."

Kmart, at the time, was the largest retailer in the world, so we said, "Great!" Aaron offered to set up a meeting in exchange for a 10 percent commission on anything that came out of it. Which was an egregious ask, I now know in hindsight. Five percent, tops, would have been appropriate. But since we were selling an open-market product, breaking into a new retailer was important for us to build the momentum we needed to get the company off the ground. We didn't want to lose any time calling around to see if it was a good deal or not. So, assuming we would make it all work somehow, we went ahead and had Aaron get us a meeting with a buyer at Kmart through a rep that he knew from his family's contacts.

For whatever reason, even though this was Anton's contact and he was the sales and relationship guy in our partnership, we decided that I would be the one to take the meeting. Neither he nor Ben came with me. I did it solo. The morning of the pitch, I had to wake up super early, at around 4:30 A.M., to make the four-and-a-half-hour drive from Toronto to Kmart's corporate headquarters in Troy, Michigan, a suburb of Detroit. Even though I had a 9:00 A.M. appointment, it didn't even occur to me to drive in and stay over the night before so I could show up fresh and well rested. These are the things you don't stop to think about when you're twenty-three. Plus we were trying to save as much money as possible so we could keep putting it into the business. So I just threw on a white button-down shirt and a pair of jeans, loaded a box of twenty-four Earth Buddies into my mom's red Toyota Celica, climbed behind the wheel, and headed out.

The crazy thing is that I did absolutely nothing to prep for the meeting. I didn't do any prep with Anton. There was no PowerPoint.

I had no idea how to make any kind of formal presentation. All I did was rehearse my pitch in my head while I drove down. Which wasn't because I was winging it. PowerPoint just wasn't, and isn't, my style. I was confident in my oral pitch and the enthusiasm I could put behind it with my words and my body language; that's the mode I work in best, given my learning disability. (Doing things your own way—whatever way works for you—brings out your authenticity, and that's what people relate to. That is where the real emotional connection is made.) Plus I knew, first and foremost, that the act of showing up and making the effort is half the battle in trying to achieve anything in life. So I wasn't nervous or anxious at all. I didn't drive down there thinking, *Oh my god, this is America and the biggest retailer in the world and I'd better not screw this up.* That's another great thing about being young. You don't know enough to be intimidated. You don't know enough to not be your authentic self. You don't question anything. You're just like, *Why not go for it?*

Kmart's headquarters were in one of those classic, sprawling 1980s American office complexes, with big, octagonal low-rise buildings made out of red brick. Modern-looking, but nothing fancy. I pulled in, parked, grabbed my box of Earth Buddies, and headed to reception, where Aaron Hermelin was waiting for me with the rep who'd set up the meeting. Then the three of us went into a conference room to meet with the buyer.

A friendly, middle-aged man, the buyer sat patiently for fifteen minutes while I gave him my pitch: a bit of backstory about Anton and me starting together in college, where we got the idea from, that we had a factory manufacturing them in Canada, that we were already selling to Walmart and Zellers and Roots, and that the point of sale and the sell-through were already high. He didn't interrupt me or ask me any questions, but when I was done, he said, "Um, well, thank you for this, but . . . I am not the buyer for this product."

I didn't believe him. I thought it was a dodge to get me out of his office. So I dove right back in and pitched him again. He was very polite, listened to me repeat everything I had already said, and didn't interrupt me. But when I was done he just shook his head again. "I'm really sorry," he said, "but I am not the buyer for this product."

I still didn't believe him. So I pitched him *again,* for another five minutes, this time throwing out all kinds of concessions in an effort to get a deal, telling him that he could have everything on consignment, that he didn't have to buy anything and he could pay us afterward if it sold. He sat through my whole spiel a third time, didn't interrupt me, and then said, again, as politely as possible, "Look, I am not the buyer for this product." At which point I realized, *Oh, he's not lying. He's not making up a story because he doesn't want it. He really isn't the buyer.*

"Well . . . okay," I said. "Then would you mind sharing with me who the right buyer is? Because I just drove four hours from Toronto and it would be great to know who I'm supposed to be talking to."

"Give me a minute," he said.

Then he got up, left the room, and came back a few minutes later. I stood up and he handed me a slip of paper. It had the name "Adrienne Zacks" written on it. She was the buyer for the horticulture department, he said, which was where a product like the Earth Buddy belonged, since it was a living plant. I took the piece of paper, shook his hand, and said, "Thank you very much." Then I grabbed my box of Earth Buddies, and without even saying anything to Aaron or the rep who had gotten me the meeting, I walked out of the boardroom and started stalking around Kmart headquarters, hunting for this woman, reading every nameplate on every door until I found the one that read Adrienne Zacks.

Fortunately, when I finally found the right nameplate on the right door, Adrienne Zacks happened to be at her desk. I knocked politely and gave her a thirty-second pitch on who I was and asked if I could meet with her. She listened, looked through her day planner, and said, "Okay, I'll give you a meeting at three-thirty." I thanked her and found my way back down to reception, where Aaron and the rep were waiting for me.

"Good news," I said. "I found the buyer and got a meeting at three-thirty."

"That's great," they said. "Let's go get lunch."

To which I replied, "Oh, I'm not leaving the building."

I had this crazy idea that if I left, security wouldn't let me back in and I wouldn't get the appointment, or maybe Adrienne would call for me early and I wouldn't be around. "You guys go get lunch," I said. "I'm staying here." So that's what I did. I hunkered down in the lobby with my big box of Earth Buddy samples and I waited. For five hours.

When three-thirty finally came, I walked back up to meet with the woman who would open the door to my future. Adrienne Zacks was a classic Midwesterner, with that demeanor that's pleasant and easygoing but also direct and to the point. She was in her late thirties, maybe, sitting at a big desk in a tiny office, probably not more than 10 feet × 10 feet, with a small credenza behind her and bookshelves off to the side. The room was so cluttered with stuff everywhere that it was impossible to move around—I don't even know how she was able to get behind the desk. There were boxes and boxes, mostly samples of products people had mailed in to try to get her to buy, and the minute I walked in I realized that over on the left side of the room, stacked up against her bookshelf, she had seven other grass heads made by other companies. I hadn't noticed them when I'd stopped in before, because I'd been so focused on her. But those seven boxes were what greeted me when I showed up at three-thirty.

To this day I don't know who made them or where they came

from; I never asked, and I didn't pick any of them up to look at. On the one hand, seeing those other grass heads was great, because it meant I'd been right to jump on the idea right away. It had only been about six weeks since we'd gone out on the streets of Toronto to sell them, and those boxes meant we already had more than a half dozen competitors nipping at our heels. And all those samples had probably been mailed in, meaning I was the first person who'd taken the time to get a face-to-face meeting with her. Since she'd agreed to talk to me even though she already had the samples in her office, it meant she was already familiar with the product and had likely made up her mind to buy it or at least try it, and I'd lucked out by being the first person standing in front of her.

On the other hand, since I wasn't offering her a product she couldn't get anywhere else, I was going to have to do something dramatic to stand out from the competition. So when I launched into the same pitch I'd just given three times in a row to the other buyer, I immediately dropped my price by a dollar, from $2.65 per unit to $1.65 per unit. Because we were manufacturing it in Canada, and because we were able to buy most of our supplies in Canada, with the difference in currency rates we had a lower cost of production; everything was about 30 percent cheaper. I will never know if I could have gotten more money; maybe I could have. However, I was completely focused on getting the sale itself for the momentum it would give us. The price was important, but not as important as the momentum.

The whole time I was talking, she kept nodding and seemed receptive. When I was done, she didn't offer any comments or ask any questions. She leaned back, grabbed this thick book off a shelf, handed it to me, and said, "This is what you need to do to become a vendor at Kmart. Fill it out when you get back home. I'm going to give you an order for forty-eight thousand pieces."

She made her decision that quickly, right there on the spot. The rest of the meeting was spent discussing execution, how and when we'd supply the order. "And if you supply it well," she said as we wrapped things up, "I'm going to back it up with an additional half a million pieces."

Hearing her say those words, "half a million pieces," was a surreal moment. It was almost an out-of-body experience. I stood there, like, "Did that *really* just happen?"

And then I did something a little strange.

I wanted to have something tangible as proof that this moment was real. I also wanted to do something that would give me a bond with this woman above and beyond the transaction of the deal, which is a trick you learn in business. It's a way of establishing a friendship. I looked down and saw that in all the clutter on her shelves, she had this ceramic garden gnome. It was about the size of a house cat. So I asked her if she would give me the gnome. And she did. She gave me the gnome. (I still have it to this day.) We shook hands, then I took the vendor book, said goodbye, and hopped back in my mom's Toyota for the four-and-a-half-hour drive home.

Back in Toronto, the vibe at the office was electric. For a two-month-old company, landing an order for five hundred thousand pieces from the largest retailer in the world was huge. It lit a spark that fueled us for years to come. We were able to move the factory, hire more workers, bolster up supplies, look at securing some form of financing, build out the machines we needed. Suddenly, the biggest TV show in Canada wanted to do an episode on us; we became the country's media darlings.

With hindsight, it's clear that Adrienne Zacks already knew what she wanted before I showed up to the meeting. She was going to order this product from somebody, and the fact that I took the time to show up in person helped persuade her that we were the people she ought to go with. The other big factor, obviously, was price. I came in so low. Looking back now, I probably still would have made the sale even if I'd kept the price a bit higher. I probably sold it too cheap, giving away maybe fifty to seventy cents per Earth Buddy. But when I think about her demeanor and her attitude in that meeting, I honestly believe that something else played a decisive role in her decision to give me the business. When I walked into her office, I was barely four months past my twenty-third birthday, and there I was telling the biggest retailer in the United States that I could deliver on an order of, potentially, more than half a million units of a brand-new product. And she didn't hesitate to say yes. She didn't even blink. She *wanted* to give me the deal. And I believe it wasn't in spite of my youth but because of it.

||

One of the greatest assets you have when you're young is this: Everyone is rooting for you to win. Everyone wants to see young people succeed, even the skeptical, bitter kind of old people who sit around complaining about "kids these days." It's not because they're gleefully hoping that the next generation will fall flat on its face. Even those folks, deep down, are looking for young people who will step up and shine and prove them wrong.

There's a myth that when you're young nobody takes you seriously. Everything I've experienced in my life tells me the opposite is true. If you take yourself seriously, if you pursue your chosen endeavor with passion and conviction and earnest desire, people will absolutely respond in kind. Not only will they accord you the respect and attention you deserve, they'll actively go out of their way to help you however they can. You will experience this wherever you go. Maybe it's someone sharing an idea or a piece of advice. Maybe it's someone introducing you to a contact or opening a door—a door you didn't even know needed to be opened. As long as you're humble, respectful of the other person's time, and grateful for what you're offered, you'll find the help you're looking for. And that kind of help is priceless. It's the wind in your sails. It turns your youth from a seeming disadvantage into an unbeatable advantage, and in order for you to exploit that advantage to its fullest, the first thing you need to understand is how and why you've got it.

WHY ARE OLDER PEOPLE SO keen to help the young? The first and most fundamental reason is because it's human nature. It's instinct. It is at the root of our humanity for us to hope that society will progress and that children will do better than their parents. Indeed, one of the primary engines of civilization as we know it is the old passing on what they know to the young; if certain skills and types of knowledge fail to take root in the next generation, they can be lost forever. So when you're a young person starting out in any endeavor, you've got one of the fundamental drivers of evolution working in your favor from day one.

Another part of it is that every older person can relate to exactly what you're going through. Everyone remembers their twenties, the decade of establishing yourself, of figuring out what path to take— the decade of the unknown. Seeing you in that situation, older people naturally think, *Wow, this young person is just starting out and wouldn't it be great if they succeed in life? How can I lend them a hand? How can I help them avoid the same pitfalls that I encountered?*

It's also true that nobody ever makes it entirely on their own. The myth of the self-made man is just that: a myth. Every successful person, at some point, got a big helping hand from someone else. Maybe it was a mentor who passed on a priceless piece of wisdom. Maybe it was a family friend who offered a vital introduction. And when successful people get to the top of the mountain and look back, they remember who helped them out at those critical junctures. They can't believe how lucky they were, because if that one person hadn't done them that one favor at that one specific point in their journey—as Adrienne Zacks did for me at Kmart that day—nothing that came after that moment would have been the same. Some people are selfish and miserly, sure, but deep down inside, most people are looking for ways to return the favor, to pay it forward. When they see a young person who's motivated and hardworking, they're eager to give something back.

HOWEVER, IF YOU ONLY THINK of this dynamic in terms of the older person giving something of value to you, you're not seeing the whole picture. In truth, a better way to frame this dynamic might be to think of you giving something of value to them.

The fundamental questions we will all face in the end are, "In this life that I've lived, how much have I given and how much have I taken? Have I contributed more to the world than I have taken out of the world?" Ultimately, we all want to come out on the right side of that ledger, so having the opportunity to give back is a gift. It's one of the greatest rewards of a life well lived. But not everyone knows exactly how or where to best give back. Simply writing a check to a charity doesn't offer the same satisfaction as having a direct, tangible impact on another person's life. So when you ask an older person for assistance, whether you intend to or not you're giving them the opportunity to have meaning in their life.

You're also giving them the opportunity to be looked up to and admired, which is no small thing. People often make the mistake of using money as a yardstick for success. It's not. Money is a tool, and having more money simply means having a bigger tool to do more things. The true markers of success are always personal, and one of the most important of those markers is to attain a level of status and genuine respect among your peers and colleagues and in the community at large. Having that status gives someone the platform to share their thoughts and pass on what they've learned. So when you ask someone, "How did you do it?" or "Can you help me out and show me the way?" what you're actually doing is giving them the opportunity to assume that status, to be the expert, and to revel in being the expert. You're giving them the opportunity to look back and take inventory of everything they've learned and take pride in how far they've come.

But the most important gift you'll be giving them, by far, is the chance to feel young again. One of the most bittersweet moments of middle age is realizing that, even as you get to enjoy life's rewards, there are certain doors that have closed for you, certain opportunities that have passed, a lot of "firsts" that you'll never get to experience again. But then along comes this young person, and there's something about their energy and passion that's infectious. Young people offer a sense of wonder and excitement, a positive vibe that's straightforward and unpretentious, untainted by cynicism. They're a bit naïve, perhaps, but all the more charming for being so. They have the tenacity to do something that hasn't been done before, or to do it a bit different—and that's refreshing. It reminds older people of their youth. And while they may never get the chance to be young again, being around that energy gives them the chance to at least *feel* young again, if only for a brief moment. There's a transference that takes place. Part of it is intellectual, but it's really more visceral and emotional. People just love the energy of youth.

It's not only about age per se. People aren't going to rally to your side because your driver's license says you're under the age of twenty-five; it's not that simple. But people are going to root for you if you have youthful energy and passion and a good idea, if you have commitment and determination in what you're doing. It's all those things working in tandem, and I had all those things working for me the day I walked into Adrienne Zacks's office thirty years ago. I kept going on about the sales and how amazing and magical the product was and how the consumers were reacting to it. I was genuinely excited to be there, and that got her excited too, so much so that she had the confidence to bring us on as a vendor.

The same principle was true for me from the first day I went to work. My mother was amazing. From the start, she only gave me words of encouragement, never a doubt or concern, never an obstacle. She opened up her house to be used as a giant nursery, made calls to introduce us to business contacts, loaned me her car. Anything we needed, she was ready and able to help.

I realize, of course, that not everyone has that kind of family support. I know because at the time I didn't have it from my father. At the time we launched the Earth Buddy, he and I had had a falling-out and we weren't speaking to each other; I started the business without his financial or moral support. You may find it necessary to go outside your family circle to get the emotional and financial help you need, but in some ways that can be better, as those people may not bring the same baggage and bias as family. They're able to see a more authentic version of the person you're becoming, as opposed to the still-developing person you were in high school.

One of my earliest cheerleaders was the father of the girl I was dating at the time. Since I was stuck waiting for Anton to graduate, this man gave me a job for three months overseeing a couple of investments that he'd made. Every morning when he would leave for work, I would go to his house and work out of his home office during the day. He even gave me dress clothes to wear since I didn't have any. I was all of twenty-two and I would dress up in dress slacks and a button-down and sit behind his desk all day.

Then when we started Earth Buddies, my girlfriend was off traveling for a month; otherwise she probably would have been a part of the company. Tragically, her father ended up dying of cancer two years later, but he was there in those early days, and he even ended up doing some legal work for us. More than anything, he was a kind, positive person in my life. That was his contribution, which was very valuable.

EMOTIONAL SUPPORT ISN'T THE ONLY kind of help your youthful energy will attract. That energy can bring you the financial kind as well.

In running a business, cash flow is oxygen. It's how you keep the lights on, how you make payroll. It's the number one thing you need more than anything else. If you find yourself in a crunch, you've generally got two options: take a term loan from the bank or bring in outside investors, either of which can put your control of your company at risk. In the early days of Spin Master, however, we were never faced with that decision, and that was in no small part because our youth gave us access to other levers to help grow our business, one of which was that older people in the industry wanted to give us a break.

I still remember the late, great Sam Kotzer, the king of closeout toys who'd bought so many Earth Buddies from us when we were starting out. Our relationship to Sam was unusual because the Earth Buddy wasn't a closeout. It was a brand-new product. But when he decided to buy twenty-six thousand pieces from us, not only did he pay us our full price, he paid cash on delivery. Which he didn't have to do. He could have easily said, "I can only pay you after sixty days." Because he for sure wasn't getting paid COD from Walmart. Walmart was probably paying him net sixty days. Which meant Sam was carrying us on his books for that interval of time. What a mensch. So generous. He didn't even ask us for a discount for paying early.

Several of our suppliers gave us that same flexibility on the other end. They always gave us extra time to pay. David Hertzman from Progress Packaging was a super-nice guy. He met with us and spent time with us and gave us incredible payment terms. He gave us ninety days, and I think his usual term was thirty days. Between all our various suppliers and buyers, I think we were able to push our payables past ninety days on average while we had our receivables paid to us, on average, in fifteen days. That seventy-five-day spread was essentially a perpetually moving free loan. It was the critical oxygen we needed to grow. Without it, we would have been stuck. If we'd had to go to outside investors, we probably would have had to give up a 20 percent equity stake, which is worth exponentially more today than it was then.

Because we were young, people understood that we didn't have much cash. Meanwhile, they had the ability to carry us on their books for extra time because they had more resources than we did. So why not help us out? Not only was it a kind and generous thing to do, but if they helped us grow into a viable partner, they'd actually be helping themselves in the long run. We never played the age card explicitly. We never said, *Hey, cut us some slack because we're young.* But we did ask for time and flexibility when we needed it, and it was simply implied and understood that people would give us a bit of extra leeway.

That flexibility was not limited to a handful of suppliers or vendors. It was all over the show. Kmart paid us net thirty days when they usually paid net sixty. Our landlords cut us some slack too. In our first nine months of operation, we moved three times, trying to find the right-size space as we scaled up our operations so rapidly. They all gave us breaks on the rent and flexible leases as we found our footing.

YOUNG ENTREPRENEURS OFTEN DON'T REALIZE that, at their age, nobody sees them as the competition yet. Indeed, contrary to what you might imagine, in the days when Anton, Ben, and I were still getting on our feet, some of our biggest allies were other Canadian and American toy companies.

In the normal run of business, companies usually make it their goal to best their competitors in the marketplace, but it's not nice to try to crush someone who's so young. And, relatively speaking, we were *very* young. Everywhere we went in the toy industry, we were always the youngest people in the room, usually by a couple of decades. This wasn't Silicon Valley, filled with young techies in hoodies and T-shirts. The toy industry in the 1990s was an older, mature sector run by established players. People didn't necessarily think of it as a place for new blood and innovation. But people who run toy companies are passionate about toys. So when we came along, they didn't see us as a group of canny young sharks looking to eat their market share. They saw us as young people wanting to contribute to and be a part of something that they were passionate about. What could be more exciting for an older person than seeing someone young wanting to follow in your footsteps and emulate you?

At nearly every turn, people from other toy companies welcomed us with open arms and were more than generous in ways we never would have imagined. The single biggest leg up probably came from Irwin Toy Limited, then the largest toy distributor in Canada. At the time, Ben was living with Jenn Irwin, the daughter of the owner, and through her, Irwin Toy shared with us their list of all the major U.S. and European toy inventors, saving us time and giving us direct access to some of the best and brightest minds in the business.

Then there was the late Alan Hassenfeld, chairman and CEO at Hasbro. We called him a bunch of times for help on different issues. He always took the time to speak to us, was very gracious, and gave us great advice. It was shocking to us that the guy running the number two toy company in the world would take the time to speak to us, but he always did. There were countless others across the industry—more than I could mention here—who did the same. They looked at us and thought, *Hey, these young people are bringing new energy and new ideas into the industry. That's really cool.* It was such a blessing, and it had a real compounding effect. Without their trust and confidence, our company would not have gotten off the ground like it did.

That same generosity of spirit extended to the people who came to work for us. People should always be paid what they deserve. That said, money isn't the only form of compensation people are looking for in a job or a career. People want to feel the energy of doing something new and exciting. They want to feel like their work has meaning and purpose. If you can offer people that—with the possibility of deferred compensation or profit sharing or equity down the road—you'll find you can attract highly qualified people at a fraction of what they might normally cost.

As we grew, we were able to bring in a number of older, more experienced professionals from across the toy industry, most of whom would have expected higher salaries had they gone to work for our more established competitors. While those places could offer more money, none of them could offer the dynamism, excitement, and sense of purpose that we could. Our youthful energy made people want to jump on board and put in the sweat to get the company off the ground. Which meant we were able to attract smart, passionate people while keeping our overhead low.

In addition to excellent employees, we were also able to put together a board of advisers. I don't think we paid them, but they met with us every quarter for a couple of years and gave us their time for little in return. It was their way to give back and impart their knowledge to the next generation.

WHEN I LOOK BACK ON my first trip to Kmart, I think about what would have happened if I'd done the exact same thing as a forty-year-old man. If I'd gone in at that age and pitched to the wrong buyer, he might have said, *Wow, you really wasted my time. You came in here and got on my calendar and ate up my morning, all because you didn't even do enough homework to find out that I'm not the right buyer for the thing you're selling.* At that point, would he have taken the extra step to go and find Adrienne Zacks's name for me? Probably not. (I also have to wonder what would have happened if I'd gone wandering around Kmart's offices looking for a random woman's office as a forty-year-old man; I'm almost certain somebody would have called security and gotten me chucked out of there.) But because I was young and enthusiastic, none of that happened. The buyer I met with gave me a pass and even went out of his way to do me a favor. He knew that I'd simply made an understandable mistake for someone my age, and that's yet another key benefit of youth. People will grade you on a curve, and that's okay. It's the same way you'd give a young child a chance to learn from a misstep and correct themselves before holding them fully accountable for it.

That same scenario played out several more times during our early years. People cut us a lot of slack. We never used our age and inexperience as an excuse to screw up or shirk our obligations; we always made good on our missteps and we always paid our bills. Maybe we paid them a bit late, but we always paid, and very quickly we built a reputation as a young company whose energy and enthusiasm more than made up for any problems that stemmed from our inexperience.

OF COURSE, WHEN I SAY everyone is rooting for you and wants to help you, I don't mean literally everyone. There are exceptions and caveats. It's important to delineate between contacts and relationships and connections—the people who'll open up doors and give you free advice and referrals—and the working partners you'll need to actually execute on your plan. When you reach that point, it gets tricky, because you're not just asking people for free advice or favorable terms. You're asking them to make a sizable investment in you, and not everyone will be willing or able to do so. The factories we went with in China to manufacture the Sky Shark, for example. They had to invest in configuring and setting up the production line. They had to hire extra workers, and make sure they had sufficient space in their plants and the tools and dies to make the product. They had to consciously say, "I am going to place my bet on these Spin Master guys instead of going with this other piece of business." When you're asking for that kind of investment, naturally, not every door is going to be open to you, and you'll find that people, as much as they'd like to help you, very often have to protect their own interests first.

And sadly, it must be said, there are unethical, unscrupulous people in the world. For every dozen people who want to help you because of your youth and inexperience, there are at least one or two who are willing to take advantage of you because of your youth and inexperience. When we first started manufacturing our next major product line after the Earth Buddy, Spin Master Devil Sticks, we met with a guy who we thought could sell and distribute the product for us, and he told us, "Unless I own 50 percent of your business, I'm not going to work with you guys." It was really untoward. We ended up not doing business with him, so he didn't take advantage of us, but he certainly tried.

We did get taken advantage of when we went to manufacture the Spin Master Devil Sticks in Mexico. After making them in Canada in the Earth Buddy factory for about a year, we decided to move the production to Mexico to be able to compete on price. We met this guy who had a factory in what was a special industrial zone. You can ship in raw materials with no duties and no taxes, then they add the labor component and ship it back out. So we bought and shipped our raw materials down there, but the guy who owned the factory wasn't honest with us. He wasn't paying his workers, and the workers went on strike, putting up a black flag in the factory. I don't know if that only happens in Mexico or if it takes place in other parts of the world, but raising the black flag is not workers picketing in the streets outside an office, like you'd see in Canada or America. It's more like a mutiny or a coup. The workers literally take over the factory and take possession of everything inside that has any value, and the people who own the factory can't physically get inside. We ended up with a couple hundred thousand dollars of raw materials and finished product that we couldn't get out of the factory or out of the country. So we got burned, and that was the last time we did any form of manufacturing ourselves.

If that was the biggest rip-off we dealt with, the most brazen by far was the guy who walked into our office and sold us some marketing thing to do with sweatshirts. We paid him $50,000, and then a few weeks later we couldn't get him on the phone. He ghosted us. It's hard to imagine being a grown adult who looks at three young kids and thinks, *I bet I can take these guys for fifty grand.* Unfortunately, those people exist. Still, even though not everyone has your best interests in mind, the important thing is to keep moving the ball down the field. Keep trying and keep learning. Every learning is a blessing. Your stumbles are there to teach you and shape you as much as your wins. They sting, meaning you won't soon forget them. It's the yin and the yang of life. And in the end, on balance, there are far more decent people in the world than not. If you reach out, you will always find more help than you will obstacles. As long as you're batting more than .600 in the Everyone Is Rooting for You category, you can get through it.

THERE IS ONE OTHER CAVEAT to add to the word "everyone," and that is that it can mean vastly different things to different people. Not all social networks are created equal, and the "everyone" you know— the people already in your life and the people you can conceivably reach out to—will vary based on your income, your class, and your level of education.

Anton and I were lucky in that regard. Even though we were both from working-class immigrant families, our parents were small business owners who had access to the knowledge of that world. My parents, through their business selling Persian carpets, were able to cultivate a wealthy clientele, which gave us access to a social network outside our own. Anton and I were also able to go to a four-year university, which offers a great leap forward for any working-class kid.

You may not have that. You may come from a low-income community with what feels like limited access to resources. Maybe you can't afford college or can only afford a two-year technical degree. Let me assure you that that is no barrier. You can always start with what you have, with the people you know now. You may be starting from a different position than the upper-middle-class college grad, and you may have a harder road ahead of you, but that doesn't limit where you can go from where you are. Older people and small business owners in lower-income communities are some of the most resourceful people in the world. Because they've had to be. Because nobody opened any doors for them. They had to figure it all out on their own. No matter who you are or where you are, someone around you knows something you can use. And if they don't, they know someone else who does. The key is simply to ask—and that is the final and most important lesson of this chapter.

ONE OF THE MOST COMMON reasons people will use to discourage you from starting a business is that you don't have any experience. And you *don't* have much experience. But that's okay. Because other people do, and more often than not they'll share it with you. For free. There's an MBA's worth of knowledge and wisdom out there waiting for you, and all you have to do to get it is ask for it. So many people are scared of asking for help. They're scared of admitting that they don't know something. They believe that confidence is acting like you know what you're doing even when you don't, when in fact the opposite is true. Confidence is being sure enough of your idea that you're willing to reach out and ask for help because your idea is deserving of that help.

One of the biggest things we did right in our twenties was that we asked for a lot of meetings with people, and in those meetings we asked a lot of questions. We always put ourselves in the position of looking up at these more experienced people and learning everything we could from them. We soaked it all in and started to connect the dots, to make better and more informed decisions. We asked for tangible assistance. We asked for better payment terms. We asked for contacts. We asked for discounts. And every young entrepreneur should do the same.

Because of the experience and wisdom they've accrued, an older person's time is incredibly valuable, and you can get access to their time as a result of your youth, simply because they want to be with you and spend time with you to share in your energy. So don't be shy about it. Lean into it. Ask, ask again, ask again, and then ask some more. The help and advice will be forthcoming as a result of your age. I know it works because it worked for us when we asked Anton's friend to ask his uncle for a contact at Kmart. It worked when I got the wrong buyer and asked him to help us find the right buyer. And it worked when I finally found the right buyer and asked her to hear my pitch—and even when I asked her to give me her garden gnome as a memento.

Indeed, the kind of ask that I'm describing, I wouldn't even put it in the same category as what we normally think of as seeking "help." You're not asking for charity. You're not asking somebody to do something for you that you're capable of doing yourself. It's more that you're providing a catalyst—a spark, if you will. All the wisdom and experience of older people is just sitting there inside them, waiting to be unlocked. And all the energy and passion of youth is just coiled up inside you, waiting to be unleashed. When you ask the right question, you bring those two forces together, creating an explosive chemical reaction and bringing something new into the world that didn't exist before.

||

The first forty-eight thousand Earth Buddies we delivered to Kmart sold so fast they practically evaporated from their shelves. Barely a month later, Adrienne Zacks made good on her promise and called us to order half a million more. Kmart put them in the front of their stores, right at checkout, priced at $4.99. They had a 94 percent sell-through rate, which was amazing. As they continued to sell through leading up to Christmas, she ordered another quarter million for spring, so we made her the Earth Buddy Bunny edition with bunny ears, and then another half a million of a special Christmas edition for the following Christmas. We added a few other themes and variations to keep things interesting to the consumer, but we'd known from the beginning that it was a novelty product that would eventually run its course, and it did.

By the time the Earth Buddy wave subsided, Adrienne Zacks had ordered close to one and a half million units from us in total. Why did she do it? Why did she take a chance on a group of twenty-three-year-olds with no real experience, when she could have gone with any number of better capitalized, more established competitors? I never asked her directly. I never said, "Did you give me this business because of my youth?" But I always felt that was the case, and my hunch was confirmed years later when I found out that she was deeply involved with a local charity focused on helping underprivileged children in Detroit. She asked me to come down to speak with them, which I did, and seeing her lifelong dedication to helping kids gave me a deeper understanding of why she chose to take a chance on the young person who unexpectedly entered her office that day.

Adrienne Zacks changed my life and, in turn, the trajectory of Spin Master's fortunes. What she did was a miracle beyond miracles. It propelled our small enterprise forward like no other. It helped us move to a new factory, hire more workers, build new machines, buy more raw materials. It gave us a great story and landed us in all the newspapers and the morning news shows. The energy was electric. So much was happening that our first nine months felt like five years. It felt like we were bending time, accomplishing more than any one of us could have imagined. Not every older person in your life is going to be an Adrienne Zacks, but there are more people like her out there than you would think. People love to share and help, and they love love love love love to help young people. Which is why starting a business in your twenties offers a huge competitive advantage.

And that advantage won't last.

Once you pass thirty, and especially once you pass thirty-five, you're an adult and people will treat you that way. Not to say that you won't get any help from anyone, but the drop-off is steep. People in your industry will see you as the competition, and people in general will treat you as someone who ought to know what you're doing most of the time. Once you're pushing forty, walking around with a wide-eyed naïveté just isn't the best look. By that point, you're the one who's supposed to be giving advice instead of asking for it. So you have to use the advantage of youth while you still have it, because one day you'll wake up and it'll be gone.

3.

Partnership

n February of 1995, nine months after launching the Earth Buddy, Anton and I went to our first Toy Fair, the largest toy industry trade show in North America. The first one was held in 1903 in a large office building at the intersection of Fifth Avenue and Twenty-third Street in New York City, across from the Flatiron Building and Madison Square Park. With each passing year, the annual Toy Fair continued to grow and expand, and more and more toy companies opened up offices in the building, which eventually became known as the International Toy Center.

The Toy Fair attracts all the major players in the industry from around the world. In recent years some of the exhibitions have shifted over to the Jacob Javits Convention Center, but thirty years ago it all took place inside this one self-contained building, which made it a beehive of activity. Everyone would come and showcase their products, and for ten straight days you would walk from showroom to showroom to see the new products getting pitched for the upcoming year. You literally spent the whole day playing with toys and hanging out with people who loved to make them and sell them—a truly magical experience.

At that point, after our initial success with the Earth Buddy, we were launching our second toy, Spin Master Devil Sticks. If you've ever been to the circus and seen a performer juggling a flaming baton by flipping it between two sticks he holds in his hands, those are devil sticks. Ours weren't meant to be lit on fire, but they were still fun to juggle and twirl in the air. Hoping to find more distribution for this new toy, Anton and I—joined by Melissa, my girlfriend at the time, who came along to help out—packed up our two handmade prototypes, flew down from Toronto to New York City, and got a room. One room. Since we were investing pretty much every dollar we'd made from Earth Buddies back into the business, we were too frugal to splurge on separate rooms.

We didn't even have our own booth. Sam Kotzer, the closeout toy king who'd helped sell the Earth Buddy up in Canada, had kindly introduced us to some guys at a company called Uniworld, Carl Hyman and Bruce Soskin, two old-school New Yorkers who had been in the business for more than thirty years. Carl and Bruce put us in the back corner of their showroom, behind a curtain, and would call us out when the buyers came in. Since I was the best at handling the devil sticks, I was the demo guy. I would go out front and juggle them for the buyers while Anton and Melissa sat back and observed how Uniworld handled the talking and the selling.

Uniworld was not a toy distributor. They were reps. They would take your product, sell it into accounts, and take a commission, which they could do because they had good relationships across the industry. By the end of that Toy Fair, Uniworld would break us into KB Toys and Toys "R" Us, which was monumental for us; Earth Buddies had never gone into those accounts because it was being sold in horticulture, as a plant. Over the course of the next two years, those accounts would sell more than a million of our devil sticks, opening our eyes to the glorious world of the toy business.

Anton and I were the youngest guys at the fair by at least a decade or two, and we had so much to learn. We spent every day networking and looking for distributors and asking questions, and by the end of the week we'd been introduced to two classic toy industry characters, brothers Greg and Rett Hardin. About fifteen years older than us, they'd grown up in the rep business, following in their father's footsteps and joining him at the company he'd started, Diverse Marketing. Based out of Dallas, they represented toymakers to large retailers like Hobby Lobby and Walmart all across the southern United States.

When we met them, Greg and Rett looked like a couple of Texas cowboys. They talked like cowboys, dressed like cowboys—they were the cowboys of the toy industry. The night before the last day of the show, they invited us up to their hotel suite to hear our story and our pitch, and for the first hour or so it seemed like everything was going great. They were going to take the Spin Master Devil Sticks line and rep us in the South, and we were like, "Wow! This is fantastic!"

Then their father walked into the suite. A big, hulking man—also dressed like a Texas cowboy—he was clearly the patriarch of the business. He joined the conversation and we kept on talking and, at some point, Anton said something. To this day I have no idea what it was, but it deeply offended this guy. He started screaming at us in a deep Texas drawl that only got thicker as his voice got louder. It was awkward. We were all of twenty-three, and here was this enraged sixty-year-old guy screaming at us. And then, just as abruptly, he stopped screaming, told us to leave, and kicked us out.

The next thing I knew, Anton and Melissa and I were standing on the corner outside their hotel in the dead of night, utterly bewildered, freezing our asses off in the middle of February with no deal.

We were like, "What just happened? What did we do?" It happened so quick it was like a dream. I turned to Anton and I said, "I don't ever want to do business with these people again. I don't care what they can do for us. Whatever we may have said or done, nothing justifies that response." Melissa and I then turned in for the night to try to get some sleep before the last day of the show.

Anton, meanwhile, had other ideas. .

BY THE TIME YOU'RE DONE reading this book, if you decide that you're someone who wants go on the journey of starting a business, my advice would be not to go on it alone. You certainly *can* do it by yourself, if you like. There's nothing stopping you, and no doubt there have been successful companies founded and run by lone visionary individuals. But that is a small, rare subset of people. For the rest of us, our chances of success are much higher if we find the right people to team up with.

The right partner is someone who will bring out the best in you. They will spark your inspiration and sharpen your best ideas. They will be the sounding board that helps you think through all manner of decisions, big and small. They will be the glue that holds you together and gives you fortitude in challenging times. They will become someone who is more than just a friend, someone with whom you have a unique and special bond forged in a shared commitment to the dream that you've worked tirelessly to achieve together.

My story is one of a friendship that turned into a partnership that, unexpectedly, evolved into a three-man team that I'd never envisioned. The story of your partnership may take a completely different trajectory, and that's because there's no real formula for it. It's an alchemy of who you know, who you like, who you trust, and a dozen other factors, most of them intangible.

I met Anton Rabie at summer camp when we were both twelve years old. We didn't go to the same school, but we lived close to each other, and after that summer, every weekend our group of friends merged into a clique of five guys that hung out together practically all the time. We shared a similar background, growing up as immigrant Jewish kids somewhere between middle and lower-middle class in suburban Toronto. Anton's family had emigrated from South Africa in the 1970s as well. They had come from Lithuania, originally, and his father ran a classic *schmatte* business, importing and exporting clothing.

Anton and I were also similar in that we wanted to go into business but didn't want to go into our families' businesses. For most of my childhood, my dad was a partner in a Persian carpet gallery. After that he ran a small gallery that sold replica antiques and furniture. I used to go in and work for him doing deliveries on Saturdays. One time I was delivering this credenza, and I had it loaded halfway into an elevator when the doors shut and crunched it, and I was like, "Aw shit."

So I wasn't that good at working for my dad. Also, being around the shop and observing things, I knew I didn't want to go into retail. I didn't want to be a middleman, selling things that were made by other people. Anton spent time working for his father's *schmatte* business and came to the same conclusion I had: A family-owned retail operation was too small. There was the instability of it too. The margins were razor-thin, and you were always one bad year away from closing your doors. We'd both known that instability, and we wanted a bigger, stronger foundation from which to grow.

Needing to support ourselves, we both worked all through high school, sometimes at jobs, sometimes with our own entrepreneurial hustles. I had my paper route, shoveled people's driveways in the winter, and sold cable TV subscriptions and other products through different telemarketing jobs. Anton, meanwhile, ran a stand at the local flea market, selling various wares.

From the day I met him, Anton was always excited about something or someone. That passion was constantly morphing and changing, because he was always looking for a new thing to be excited about, but he was always attached to something. He's intense in that way, singular in focus. He's got that classic striving, overachieving type A personality, sitting somewhere on the spectrum. He doesn't like to sit still, and he doesn't really know how to. He marches to his own drum, which is due in no small part to his having ADHD. Having grown up with that condition, Anton, like me, knew what it meant to have to get special accommodations from school, to have to work harder than other kids just to stay at the same level. He was also a late bloomer, physically. Until he hit eighteen and shot up, he was a tiny guy. He loved sports but wasn't that good at sports, so he succeeded by outhustling everyone else. And being an immigrant means you're always one step behind everybody else socially and culturally, so he had to work twice as hard to keep up there as well.

Faced with those disadvantages, Anton was possessed by a drive and a work ethic to do something better with his life. By the time we got to high school, the group of five friends we had was inseparable. We would hang out every weekend doing what many teenage boys like to do: get high and go wherever we could to see if we could meet girls. Then one day, at seventeen, Anton bailed from the group. He was just gone. He told us, "I need to work hard to get into university, and I'm not spending my Saturday nights with you guys getting high anymore." And that was it. From that point on he did nothing but work. He literally became no fun.

As close as we were, Anton and I were also fiercely competitive with each other. We had a shared love of tennis, and we used to play it all the time. Our friendship was formed on the court, playing match after match at summer camp, and then playing in the same tournaments around Toronto. (I would always beat him back then; I can't beat him anymore.) We also competed in work. For a while, I tried to replicate what he was doing at the flea market, and I didn't do as well as he did. Then, after our freshman year of college, when we both ended up selling fertilizer together, Anton was better than me at that too. His energy level is higher than mine, and I got tired of knocking on doors.

In large part because of that competitiveness, one thing was clear: Even though we both wanted to go into business, we swore we'd never go into business together. We were too competitive to think about combining forces. We even said as much to each other on at least one occasion, echoing words that our parents had told us: "The best way to kill a friendship is to go into business together." That's what we believed—right up until we didn't.

When the Campus Faces opportunity presented itself to us, it was such an obvious play that we just went for it. There was no moment where we consciously changed our minds about working together. It just made sense, and in the end our fears proved to be unfounded. In any partnership, egos will inevitably clash in terms of deciding on the right direction or the right strategy, but for the most part our competitiveness never proved to be a problem. If anything, it manifested as a good thing because we were both trying to achieve the same ends with double the power. I don't think Anton or I could have built a business the size of Spin Master had we tried to do it by ourselves. It wouldn't have happened.

Once Anton and I went into business together, despite our initial trepidations, it was clear how well we complemented each other. We were complete opposites as humans, a yin and a yang. He was hard-driving and impetuous. He could sell absolutely anything, and he had an uncanny ability to keep moving forward. Creativity wasn't his strong suit, but his ability to execute and follow through was second to none. He was also a master at building relationships and thinking outside the box, which made him a great salesperson.

I, on the other hand, was always more measured, more detail-oriented and patient. "Cerebral" is maybe the right word. I liked to sit on ideas, mull them over, make decisions at my own pace. I feed off creative energy, and I'm most comfortable thinking about vision and strategy. I was always something of a perfectionist too. I probably could have continued in sales, but someone had to manufacture the product and do product development, and those were not Anton's skill sets, so I gravitated to that side while his relationship skills had him taking the lead on sales. Our differing temperaments caused a bit of friction at times, but for the most part we complemented each other well, a fact that I would come to understand the morning after getting thrown out of a drunken cowboy's hotel room in the middle of the night.

WHEN I WOKE UP ON the last day of the fair, still grousing about what had happened the night before, Anton was already gone. When I finally found him at the conference, he was sitting with Greg and Rett Hardin like they were all old friends, laughing and getting along as if the events of the night before had never even happened. I couldn't believe my eyes. When Anton finally got up from the table, he walked over to me with a big smile on his face.

"Anton," I said, "what's going on?"

"I closed the deal," he said.

"What do you mean?"

"I mean it's done. I just got it done."

Because that's who Anton is. Compared to him, I've always been more sensitive by nature. Today, I've learned to have much thicker skin, but back in my twenties, I was an über-über-über-sensitive person. Getting thrown out of that room, to me, was a personal insult. I couldn't let it go. But for Anton it was water off a duck's back. There was nothing that could faze him. He had a goal, knew it was important for our success, and made it happen. He didn't let his emotions get in the way of the right business decision like I did.

As it turned out, the brothers' father had been drinking that day. His reaction to us was more the alcohol talking than anything else. We hadn't done anything wrong, and it was nothing personal. Greg and Rett still wanted to be in business with us, and the only reason the brothers had the opportunity to explain all that was because Anton was levelheaded enough to go back and reopen the conversation.

I was somewhat dumbfounded that Anton had done what he did. But it was good for the business, so I couldn't even be mad that he'd gone back and made a major deal without giving me the slightest indication that that's what he was doing. Which is classic Anton. That's his nature. He's a good communicator in certain ways, but sometimes he skips steps when he doesn't find it necessary to share something. Or maybe it was that he didn't want to share his plans with me because he knew that I'd already made my very principled decision not to partner with them.

In the end, Greg and Rett Hardin became great partners, representing us for more than a decade—years later, they would break us into Walmart with our mini-BMX Flick Trix bikes, a deal worth tens of millions—and we never would have had that relationship if it hadn't been for "Teflon Anton." And in the near term, thanks to Greg and Rett and to all our other partners in the United States and back in Canada, Spin Master Devil Sticks took off, selling so fast we could barely keep them on the shelves. We were busy as hell, desperately trying to keep up with demand. I was flying back and forth to Mexico, trying to set up our manufacturing process with a factory down there, and we needed help—and that's when Anton stepped up with the idea that changed the course of the company's fate forever.

"Let's bring Ben back," he said.

||

When Anton had first mentioned Ben Varadi's name to me, back in the early weeks of launching the Earth Buddy, I had only the faintest notion of who Ben was. I knew that Anton liked him and that they had spent thousands of hours together over the course of university, studying and doing class projects. Famously, Anton used to trade Ben homemade soup for his notes. But I'd only met the guy once, and I only remembered two things about him. One, that he had this uncomfortable wooden stool that he used at his desk. And two, that he was the type of guy who put a plastic cover over his computer when he wasn't using it so it wouldn't get dusty. That's it. That's all I knew about Ben. But we needed someone reliable to help us manufacture the Earth Buddies, and since Anton thought highly of him, that was enough for me to bring him on.

When Ben came down to our offices at 40 St. Clair, I liked him right away. He was smart, creative, fun, and engaging, and within thirty minutes we had a handshake deal. There was no "Let's sleep on it," no paperwork, no lawyers, only a level of trust that came with Anton knowing the person on a deep level. The decision was also made easier by the fact that we didn't make Ben a full partner. We decided to give him a profit interest in Earth Buddies and take it from there.

Once he was on board, Ben more than proved his value. He got the products made and he filled the orders, successfully scaling the Earth Buddy operation up to more than a million units in an eight-month period. He also worked well with people. The only problem was that even though Ben was great at manufacturing, he didn't enjoy it and wasn't interested in it. Then, when the devil sticks idea came along, he hadn't been a part of the conception and wasn't particularly attached to it. Right about the time Anton and I were going down to the Toy Fair in New York, a friend of Ben's approached him about working on a website, and Ben left to go do that.

Luckily for us, he didn't enjoy tech any more than manufacturing, and he ended up selling that business after only eight months, which was right about the time Anton and I were getting slammed with orders for devil sticks, which is how Anton came to raise the idea of bringing Ben back in to work with us as something more like a full partner.

"Are you sure?" I said, knowing that Ben had no desire to come back and help with manufacturing. "What is he going to do?"

"I don't know," Anton said. "Let's give him a job in marketing."

I was torn. I didn't have any reservations about Ben, personally. I'd enjoyed working with him. Everything about him was familiar. He'd grown up near me, had even gone to a neighboring school, and it turned out I knew lots of his friends. His father was a doctor and his mother was a stockbroker. They'd split up when he was fifteen, and he'd ended up living with his mom. Everything about his background and his experience lined right up with mine, and I found him very relatable.

The thing that made me feel comfortable with Ben was that I could see the underdog in him. He's likable, funny, smart, creative, sharp as a tack—and very eccentric. Ben had always marched to his own drum, and he was surely one of those kids who got made fun of on the playground, the kid who never had an easy time at camp or at school. Which is why the three of us worked so well together—we were all underdogs, outsiders who'd had to work hard to fit in and get ahead.

Ben had also proved to be a good balance to me and Anton. He brought in a third point of view, loosening things up if the two of us were stuck. He was never afraid to share his thoughts—for better or for worse. Some of it was tough and grueling, but the three of us had a good rhythm, and good ideas always surfaced. And Ben never had any ego. He was able to recognize the best idea and run with it, even if it wasn't his idea. I think that, more than anything, was why we were drawn to working with him again.

Still, I had my doubts. The fact was that Anton and I had been best friends for more than a decade at that point. We'd done all the stupid things that teenagers do together, and we shared so much natural understanding, so much implicit trust, that it was hard for me to imagine bringing Ben into that partnership.

I also had some fixed ideas about how a business partnership should work, general principles that had nothing to do with individual personalities. Even though Ben, Anton, and I had worked well together, as a rule, I believed that three is not a good number in a partnership. An odd number means there's always another person for one person to talk to behind another's back, and that creates politics. So I was wary on that count.

My other hesitation stemmed from thinking about our future direction as a company. I knew we were at a crossroads. When we came out of the Toy Fair, thanks to our new reps, all of a sudden we were selling to more than two thousand stores across the United States. Once we had those contacts and relationships—not to mention the $4 million in revenue that the devil sticks were generating—it was clear that we had a good shot to become a successful toy company. All we needed was a steady stream of ideas to sell into those stores.

Deep down, however, I wasn't sure that I *wanted* us to be a toy company. It hadn't ever been my intention to go into toys. The Earth Buddy and devil sticks were just opportunities that presented themselves. As a businessperson in the mid-1990s, I could see that tech was clearly the better direction to go. Thanks to the internet, we were on the cusp of a technological revolution, and that was where all the innovation and capital was going to flow in the next five to twenty-five years.

So part of the reason I was nervous to bring Ben back was because Ben loved toys. More so than Anton or me, he had a strong passion for the toy industry, and because I knew Ben had a strong, influential voice, I knew he would pull us in that direction. Which is clearly what happened. In hindsight, even as tech ended up enabling people to build massive, industry-transforming businesses, going into toys was the right direction for us to take. The trio worked and we've made a lot of kids happy all over the world, which is very gratifying. But I wasn't certain about that at the time, so I was sensitive to bringing Ben in, even as Anton was pushing me to bring him in.

And pushing and pushing and pushing. Because that's what Anton does, which is not the most enjoyable element of our partnership. But what works wonderfully is that Anton, eager as he is, will always be respectful of the amount of time that I need to make my decisions. I like to take a night or two to process things, because I want to make sure I've properly digested all the information. I just take longer to ruminate and come to a decision—and I remember it clear as day the moment I finally did. Anton and I were walking back to our office up Dufferin Street, talking about Ben, and I said, "Okay, let's do it."

John Lennon, George Harrison, and Paul McCartney played a lot of great shows with Pete Best on drums, but the Beatles weren't the Beatles until Ringo joined the band. As successful as Anton and I had been before Ben came on as a partner, it was only by adding him to the team that we finally had the perfect mix of talent and personality. Having Ben on board gave me a creative thought partner, because Anton is not that. Ben also brought a different perspective to the table, one that Anton and I lacked. He had a strong personality and strong point of view, which amplified the diversity of thoughts and ideas in the discussion. Ben also added speed and urgency to the momentum that Anton and I already had. Anton and I had a passion for business, Ben added to that his passion for toys, and that took the intensity of our drive and our mission to a new level. That was when it all came together. That was the moment when our partnership truly became what it needed to be for Spin Master to succeed.

||

Finding the right partner, or partners, is perhaps the most important decision any businessperson will ever make. Your youth not only affords you unique advantages in finding that person—just as importantly, it can help you make sure you find the right person.

Finding a partner is like dating, and your twenties are an unparalleled time in terms of your ability to meet and get to know other people. As with seeking a spouse, your pool of potential candidates is just that much larger. You are constantly hanging out with new people. There is more serendipity, more random encounters, a more eclectic range of personalities. School is one of the best places for it. Whether you're in college, a trade school, a continuing education program, or any other type of postsecondary learning institution, one of the primary benefits is the networks you develop. Just enjoying the ride of youth—traveling, hanging out, going to parties, and seeking adventure—you have tons of opportunities to meet new people.

For us, Toronto back in the '90s was fertile ground. I was out at my favorite bar, Milano's, almost every Friday night, constantly bumping into people I grew up with or went to camp with or went to university with. Since we already knew each other from childhood and from university, Anton and Ben and I didn't tap into that scene to find one another. But the opportunity was there for us had we needed it, and surely it fostered thousands of fruitful connections for other young people as well. Maybe you're a computer engineer with an idea for a new internet retail operation. Maybe you're a young chef with a great idea for a new food truck or a seasonal pop-up restaurant. Whatever your passion, the odds of meeting the right person to get in the trenches and fight alongside you is that much higher.

And like so many advantages of youth, that phase of life only lasts for so long. Once people start getting married and having kids and buckling down into careers, their social circles typically begin to narrow. And when you do meet people later in life, you may well forge a good working relationship with them, but the fact is that by then they'll likely be saddled with commitments other than starting a business with you. You may work well together, but you won't be able to give yourselves over to each other 100 percent, as Anton, Ben, and I did, and the relationship won't have as long a time to grow and intensify.

IN ADDITION TO THE NUMBER of people you're able to meet when you're young, meeting them at that age affords you an especially honest view of who they are. You're seeing them in their natural settings—when they're hanging out with their friends, going to school or work, coming into their own as an adult. You see who they're living with after high school or university, and you see how they treat those people.

Most importantly, you get to see them interact with their families. Once you're in your forties, guys don't randomly invite you over to have dinner with their parents on a Tuesday. That doesn't happen anymore. In college and in your early twenties, it still does. You might even end up crashing with someone's family for a weekend. When moments like that happen, you get to see where people come from, what their values are, and what type of drive they grew up around. Another way partnerships are a bit like a marriage is that you get the whole family, whether you like it or not. A person's family—and the way they relate to and treat their family—tells you something about the type of partner they'll be.

I can't tell you what a difference it made that I knew Anton's grandparents and he knew mine. His late grandmother was a warm, friendly, loving woman, super engaging and super interested. She always wanted to know what you were up to and took the time to listen. His grandfather was also just a kind, gentle man. You could see the influence that both of them had on Anton, and you could see the love and reverence that Anton had for them in return.

Even though I didn't have that same experience with Ben before we started, Anton did. You're not going to get a better read on someone than by sharing two years at business school, staying up late and exchanging study notes week after week. Anton knew Ben inside and out and trusted him implicitly, and since I trusted Anton, once Ben and I had established a good chemistry, that was enough for me. Simply put, when you're young, everything you need to make a decision about a potential partner is right out there on display.

THERE'S ALSO A NAÏVETÉ THAT helps you find and bond with a partner when you're young. While naïveté is typically seen as a disadvantage, I actually think that it's helpful here. When you have fewer lived experiences of what can go wrong in the workplace, when you haven't been burned by trusting people, you're more open, less guarded, less wary. Of all the risks you'll take in business, the biggest is putting your life in someone else's hands, which is essentially what I did with Anton and Ben, and what Anton and Ben did with me. We all made mistakes. No partner is perfect, and it takes a tremendous amount of work and commitment to keep a partnership strong. Not realizing how hard that's going to be makes you more likely to jump in, because if you knew how hard it was going to be, you might never sign up for it in the first place.

Then, once you do commit to each other, it will be both a challenge and a blessing that you're not yet fully formed. You decide to take this journey together and you're experiencing things together, building things together, growing into one another to become a single, larger organism. We hear all the time about the value of mentorship in aiding and nurturing your professional and personal growth, and good mentorship is indeed priceless. But mentorship is largely an intellectual pursuit. It's like seeing your therapist. You go, hear their wonderful advice, and then head back out to use that advice to figure things out in the real world. That is a sharp contrast to how you learn and grow in a partnership. A partnership is more of an organic experiment. It's much less of an intellectual pursuit than a doing pursuit, and through that doing you're building a deep bond with each other. Your partner is shaping you, and you're shaping your partner.

A partnership is a beautiful garden that grows. You don't know how it's going to look and feel, but it's growing right before your eyes year after year. Start a partnership later in life and that probably won't be true. You'll already know who you are, to a large extent. You'll be able to articulate what your talents are, what your shortcomings are, and most of your potential partners will be able to do the same. You may work well together, but the learning and growing experience won't be nearly as profound, and the bonds won't run nearly as deep.

AS MANY UNKNOWNS AS THERE are in forming a partnership, however, there are certain things that you have to know about yourself and about each other before you even begin, five traits or qualities where you have to be in total alignment. If you're not, perhaps you aren't meant to be partners.

First of all, it goes without saying that you've got to have the same work ethic; however much time and sweat you're willing to invest in the partnership, your partner has to be willing to do the same. If not, if one partner ends up paying in well more than their fair share, resentments are sure to fester and cause problems down the road. A strong work ethic was never a problem for Anton, Ben, or myself.

Second, you have to share the same tolerance for risk. When we first started out, Anton and I were good at handling what I call the 80 Percent Rule. In business, it's rare that you ever have 100 percent of the information that you'd like to have when you're making an important decision. You're lucky if you have 80 percent. That's especially true if you want to catch a trend that's right on the cusp of exploding; you won't have the luxury of time or market research. Anton and I were both the type of people that were okay with that. With our first two products, the Earth Buddy and devil sticks, we had even less than 80 percent. Those were educated hunches, but we were both willing to jump in even without knowing, leaving the rest of it up to uncertainty and guesswork. When Ben joined us, luckily, he fell right in with us on his willingness to take those jumps.

Third, you have to share the ability to mind-meld. "Mind-meld" is hard to define exactly, but you know it when you have it. It's when there's a natural alignment, energy, and flow in your conversations. It's when those conversations excite and animate you, when you walk away from them with more insights than when you started, when you can go down winding, sometimes discursive paths of ideas for hours without getting flustered or bored. All of that is evidence of mind-meld. Every week for thirty years, Anton, Ben, and I had partner meetings where we'd mind-meld, and in the creative art of building a business, you need to make sure you have that with your closest partners.

While the three traits I've listed above are critical to a good working partnership, the next two are absolute, iron-clad, nonnegotiable must-haves. The first is shared values. The second is trust. On matters of integrity and principle, Anton and I had so much history together that I knew we were in total alignment. There's a right way to do things and a wrong way to do things, and when we went on this journey together, we'd do things the right way. No questions asked.

The first test of those shared values came early on during the launch of our devil sticks. Ben hadn't come on board yet, and Anton and I were dealing with a buyer, someone who repped one of the largest retailers in America, and this someone took Anton aside and said, "Hey, if you really want to bolster your business with this particular buyer, furnishing him with a whirlpool would be a smart idea for you guys." After hearing the proposition, Anton brought it to me and said, "What do you think?"

That was a watershed moment for us. We were young and hungry, looking for every legitimate leg up and advantage we could get. But how far were we willing to go? Did we want to be a company that pays kickbacks and bribes, or were we going to do things differently? We had a conversation about whether or not we should do it, but it was a very brief one. We turned it down with a flat "No."

Maybe it was "just" a whirlpool, but we knew it would be a slippery slope and we had no desire to go down it, and we've never done anything like it since. Integrity and treating people fairly became our hallmarks.

We were always in alignment on other issues as well. The standard royalty rate for paying an inventor was 5 percent, but historically there were reasons why you might pay them less. You might buy their idea and then end up using the seed of that idea as a jumping-off point to develop something substantially different. In that case, you might go back and try to renegotiate them down to 4 percent, or even 3.5. But Ben, who managed our relationships with the inventors, never wanted to do that. "So what if we overpay by half a point?" he'd say. "If we do, these guys are going to bring us another great prototype and we'll make it back on that one, so it'll be worth it. As long as we're making money, it's fine." And those values became the company's values. We developed a great reputation with inventors, and our integrity in this industry was and remains very high.

When you're a student at university, you don't think about those parts of the business much; I certainly didn't. I could see the strategic and nuts-and-bolts side of running a company, but I had no idea how often running a company was going to force me to grapple with thorny ethical challenges and conundrums. The fact that I was able to stand shoulder to shoulder with Ben and Anton made those difficult situations much easier to navigate. Starting a company together so young, we were able to develop our ethos together. Then, as we grew, we were able to pass that ethos along to other people who were working with us.

Part of the reason we were able to count on those shared values was because of trust. When you're looking for a partner, you need to find someone you trust, wholly and completely. I'm talking about being able to give that person a briefcase with ten million dollars of your own money, in cash, and send them halfway around the world to deliver it—and still sleep soundly at night. I had that with Anton, and not only because we were such close friends but because I knew his family. My faith in Anton was strong enough that I took his recommendation of Ben on good faith. I trusted Ben because Anton trusted him and I trusted Anton.

Today, looking back on thirty years in business, I can point to a million examples of how we made mistakes, stepped on one another's toes, lost our tempers, but not a single instance where one of us betrayed the trust that we shared. In fact, there's not too much to say on the issue of trust, because everybody knows what it is, and you either have it or you don't. We did.

OF COURSE, THE ONE THING we didn't have—and that very few people in their early twenties have—is maturity. Being able to recognize and reckon with your own lack of maturity, being able to see how it's impacting your partnership, that is another important lesson you'll need to learn, and that's certainly how it was for me.

Anton has always been the Teflon man. He doesn't get offended by anything. You can fight and argue with him for hours, and he won't take any of it personally. To him, an argument is never more than an intellectual exercise, and once you fight it out you move on and that's it. Ben doesn't operate in exactly the same way. He's always had the ability to separate his feelings from the rough-and-tumble of hashing out the best idea, but he's also extremely sharp and a great debater. He would push very hard for his point of view, and he insisted on playing the devil's advocate, making you work through every possible counterargument before the conversation could move forward; it could take a long time to get him on board with you if he wasn't on board to begin with. He's also completely unfiltered. You always knew where you stood with him, but at times it could be a little bit harsh to deal with.

I, on the other hand, was the sensitive one. My self-esteem was pretty low at that age, in large part because of the dynamics of my relationship with my parents. I needed to *know* that I was good with people; I needed to get their approval, to hear it. I wasn't the best at controlling my emotions either, and some of my worst traits would come out. My nickname in the office was "the Peacock." A peacock walks around and they're super docile and everything's totally fine, until they get excited and suddenly their feathers are flailing at their sides for two or three minutes, and then they are back down again, like everything's fine. I would peacock on stuff all the time, getting very animated and excited for three or four minutes. I'd throw things around the room or push a chair down the hallway, and then go back in my shell. There was one occasion in the first year or so where I got physical with Ben. We were having an argument, and I grabbed him and shook him.

It took me a long time to learn how to manage those emotions properly, and it took all three of us a long time to grow out of our worst, most counterproductive trait, which was our tendency to micromanage one another. There is nothing more frustrating or soul-crushing than getting micromanaged, and while we all had different personalities and different skill sets, there was enough of an overlap that we often found ourselves walking around with opinions about what the other guys could or should be doing differently. I might have thoughts about how Anton was handling a certain sale or how Ben was negotiating with an inventor, and when that happened it would be hard not to say, "Well, why don't you do this?" Or, "Hey, try it like that." It's the result of a nervous energy that comes with being young, that fear that someone else might be making a mistake when you need to get everything right.

Micromanaging is never worth it. Everyone bakes a cake differently, but as long as you can get the results, why do you care how it gets done? Just embrace the differences. Which, over time, we learned how to do. Part of what worked for us was that we each found our lane. Anton loved dealing with sales, international distribution, and HR, so he took the lead there. Ben loved being creative, developing new toys and the marketing that supported them. I was split, half on product development and manufacturing and half on strategy and vision, thinking about white space and where we could go next. So that's how we divvied things up.

I also realized early on that you need a growing business to create space for people. When a business is stagnant, people tend to crowd one another out. When a business is growing, you create new sandboxes for people to play in without stepping on other people's toes. In the end, it's part of what led us to build such a big company, so that everyone could have their own space to exercise their own competencies. If we'd stayed a small business, there would be way too much fighting, not enough learning, and it would have hurt us.

And rest assured, we did fight. You will too. In business, disagreements will always arise. When they do, it's okay to fight about them. Actually, it's important to fight about them, as long as you do it the right way. Anton, Ben, and I disagreed and argued all the time. By and large, I think we fought about things worth fighting about, things like strategy and whether a given move made sense in the scheme of what we wanted to achieve. Sometimes it got heated, but that's healthy. Friction is healthy because it means that you care, that you still have the passion for whatever it is that you're doing. In fact, the first sign that people have lost their zest for business is when they stop arguing. That means they've stopped caring.

Anton and I have the same fight every year over payroll. He believes that if you just hire more people that you will get the growth, and I don't believe that. I'm always watching the cost. We're now in our thirtieth year, and in thirty years not a single budget cycle has gone by without the two of us having that fight. Ben and I fought about products a ton, about which products to launch and which products not to launch. Then, once we decided which product to launch, we fought about which features to put in the product and which not to put in the product. Looking back now, I get tired even thinking about it. It was like going into the dragon's den. It was too much, and I don't know what fueled it other than ego and a passion to win, or a fear of not putting out the best. It took us years to learn that our most successful products were the ones that we didn't fight over in the first place.

After any fight or disagreement, I was also the one who couldn't move forward unless I got an apology. I was the one who needed the apology most, and Ben second, and Anton third. So that initiated this need for clearing the air. My mother was a big clear-the-air type of person, and that ultimately became a vital and important part of our dynamic. We never waited more than a day to get resolution on anything. Whenever one of us crossed a line, either that same day or by the next morning, one of us had apologized, the others had accepted it, and all of us had moved on. You knew that you were clean with the other person, that the argument wasn't taking up any headspace, and you were able to focus on the business,

And, most importantly, even if we fought, we never pointed fingers. We'd fight on the front end of an issue, over whether or not to move forward or how to execute if we did, but once we made a decision, we made a decision. If it didn't turn out to be the right one, we always owned it collectively. Whether it was a product that failed or deal that went south, like the marketing guy who ripped us off for $50,000, we never singled out anyone for blame. Never assigning blame is critical, because momentum is the key to building a business and blame slows you down. We were all aligned on that. A business is like a river in that it needs to be moving all the time. Even if you make a mistake, the water must be flowing; in our partnership, we had a rule that no still water was allowed.

Fortunately, we never fought about the little stuff. We never counted who worked more hours, because we knew that all three of us were committed to building this company. We never questioned if one of us wanted to donate toys somewhere, or how much they chose to donate. We learned to keep our emotions and egos in check in order to stay focused on our larger, more important goals. The truth is that you cannot build a business while fighting on multiple fronts. If you have to fight internal drama, which is something that's entirely within your control, it will sap the precious energy you need to deal with the external challenges that you can't control.

In the end, the upside of going into business with that shared lack of maturity is that you'll develop it together. There are few greater challenges than building a successful relationship with another human being, and your efforts to create a successful partnership will humble you. Dealing with those growing pains will create a deep, lifelong bond. Getting through all those fights and arguments will be like a living workshop where you learn how to tame and control your own ego. You'll learn how to not throw up all your personal defense mechanisms the moment you feel threatened, learning how to put your own needs in perspective in order to put other people's needs and the greater good of the company before yourself.

FINALLY, AFTER YOU'VE ACCOUNTED FOR everything that needs to go into a successful partnership, you need to remember what you want to get out of a successful partnership. You can't ever forget that you're not just building an organization to sell stuff and make money. You're doing it to create an entity that is worthwhile and good *in and of itself*. You're doing it because you want to achieve success in your life's chosen endeavor, because you want to grow and refine yourself as a person, and that will only come through other people, primarily your partners, reflecting back to you the things you need to improve on.

In my case, as we were all quite verbal and not afraid to give feedback, I lived in a constant feedback machine with Anton and Ben. They held me accountable to being my best self, and I did the same for them. Early on, our egos ran high. Luckily, they gradually shrank over the years as we gained the self-knowledge to understand who we are and how to work well together. That's where we are now. We try to be more self-aware, to celebrate one another's successes and strengths, and to not harp on one another's weaknesses. Which is the only way to be, because as the business has grown and our responsibilities have expanded, we've had to evolve as people or else we wouldn't have been able to keep up.

A business partnership is not the same as a marriage, but it's just as difficult in its own way. Learning how to do it well takes, above all else, time. It takes time to learn how to have a partner, and it takes time to learn how be a good partner yourself. You have to learn to listen, and to wait for your turn to talk. You have to learn each other's quirks and pet peeves. You have to figure out each other's strengths and weaknesses and how to balance them. You have to learn how to get along, and you have to learn how to *not* get along as well.

So how long did it take Anton, Ben, and me to reach a point where we'd moved past micromanaging one another? To where we could argue without getting personalities involved? To where the business ran as smoothly as any business reasonably can?

I'd say it took about twenty years.

Which is another good reason to start when you're young.

PART II

Build

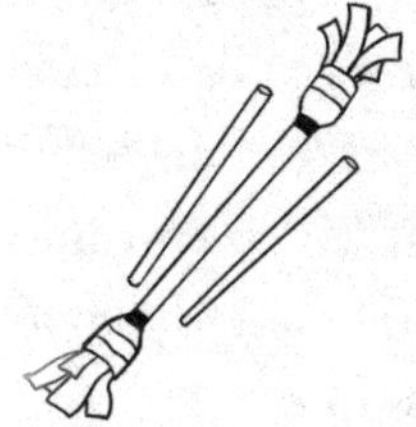

4.

The Zeitgeist

Sometime in the fall of 1994, about four or five months after we launched the Earth Buddy, I was walking around Toronto and I saw a group of elementary and junior high kids playing with devil sticks, which were a toy I remembered from when I was a teenager. A couple of weeks later, I came across another group of kids playing with them in the park. Then, a few days after that, I saw another bunch playing with them outside their school. By that point, I was intrigued enough to stop and chat with them.

What struck me as curious was that these kids were only ten or eleven years old, and to me devil sticks were something that adult hippies played with at Grateful Dead shows, because that's where I'd first seen them. I was never a Deadhead. I wasn't addicted to traveling with them from city to city to city all the time. But you could say that in high school I was Deadhead-lite. By the time I was twenty, I had probably been to about fifteen of their shows, mostly in the 1974 Volkswagen Westfalia that I'd bought with two of my friends when I was seventeen. It was the kind with the pop-open roof. We called it the Brown Bull. My dad had told me not to buy it, so of course I totally bought it. Driving home in it was one of the happiest days of my life, but when I pulled into the driveway with it my dad was so pissed. "You can't park that thing here or on this street or anywhere near this house!" He was upset because he knew it would cost me a ton of money, and he wasn't wrong. My friends and I paid $1,500 for it, and we ended up pouring five grand into it just to make it road-worthy. But to me it was worth every penny.

That summer we spent two months driving the Brown Bull around the United States to six different Dead shows, which was where I saw all these hippies playing with devil sticks, tossing and twirling them and doing tricks, the way you would with a hacky sack or a yo-yo. One of my buddies even made a bunch of them, and we sold them at the shows. Fast-forward to 1994, and here were all these young, clean-cut suburban kids playing with them around Toronto. So how did that come to pass? How does the universe work so that these kids, in this generation, suddenly wanted to play with this thing that had been around for twenty, thirty years? The answer is that, at that particular moment, those toys were part of what's called the zeitgeist.

The zeitgeist is the cultural climate of the times, the defining spirit or mood. It's the pulse running through society at any given moment, shaping what's "in" and what's up-and-coming. You see it in fashion, in art, in music. You see it in the consumer products people buy, the celebrities they adore, the politicians they vote for. And it's always shifting. New generations come along with new ideas, new technologies, new social and cultural norms, and they upend every-thing that came before.

The zeitgeist is all around us all the time, so much so that we typically experience it without even stopping to think about it. We can't always see the concrete cause and effect that's driving it. It's just happening. And that's how it was with these kids. How did they first hear about devil sticks? I have no idea, and they probably didn't know for sure either. Word of mouth? Older siblings, maybe? The only real answer is that the idea was percolating in the atmosphere around them.

When I stopped and asked the kids where they'd gotten them, they told me that they'd made them themselves. They'd even customized them, decorating them with tassels and making designs of their own. That's what got me excited, seeing that kids were making these old products feel new with their own designs. They were breathing life into something that had been around for decades. That combination of timeless appeal coupled with a modern twist meant there was a market—and, more importantly, a moment. I knew it was a thread worth pulling on.

The Earth Buddy had always been a novelty product; we knew it had an expiration date the moment we launched it. As we headed into that Christmas season, we knew that we were getting close to the end. At that point, a more mature company would have turned to its product development pipeline. We didn't have one of those. In fact, we didn't even have a business plan. We were too busy running around trying to figure out how to source, manufacture, and deliver product. None of us had time to put together a strategy document or think too far into the future.

What we did have, however, was our finger on the pulse of what was starting to trend around us. Sometimes the best ideas aren't forced. They just appear when you're doing your thing and open to the universe around you. In the same way that a simple newspaper article led us to launch the Earth Buddy, we were always on the lookout for other signs in our day-to-day life that might present business opportunities, and that's how I felt about these kids I was seeing around town. I think most people would have looked at devil sticks and thought very little of the fact that kids were playing with them in

1994. In fact, the first time I saw them, I didn't think too much of it. But once I kept on seeing it, I felt there could be a larger market for what was once a niche product for hippies. I went to Ben and Anton and said, "I think this is it."

Ben wasn't feeling it and wasn't necessarily sold on the idea of working with Anton and me permanently, so that's when he peeled off to work with his other friend. Anton and I, meanwhile, jumped on the devil sticks idea and started prototyping right away. We bought a few of the models that were already on the market and started taking them apart to reverse-engineer the design. With what we learned, we made a crude version of our own, taking wooden dowels and wrapping them with black rubber strips and hockey tape for decoration. Then we added colorful felt tassels on the tips so that when you twirled the sticks there was a sensation of blurring colors. They were fun to twirl, and—if we were right about the wave that was coming— middle schoolers across North America were going to love them.

We were prototyping with the intention to manufacture, so we were already finding suppliers, sourcing inputs, looking at raw material prices, all that stuff. Once we had something that worked well, looked good, and was a reasonable cost to manufacture, we were ready to go. As he had with the Earth Buddy, my brother-in-law helped us set up the manufacturing line in exchange for a modest profit share. Then, once we designed and prototyped the packaging, we took some of the proceeds from Earth Buddies and invested in our first commercial. At that point, because "devil sticks" is a generic term, we knew we needed to give these things a name, something we could trademark. We settled on Spin Master Devil Sticks, because that was the catchphrase we used in the commercial: "Become the spin master of the sticks!" And then, because these were the kinds of toys you had to see in motion, we hit the road.

Our first stop, in February of 1995, was the Toy Fair in New York, where Anton sealed the deal for us with the cowboys of the American toy industry. After that, we took them on tour. We bought two big purple vans and put huge decals on the side that said "SPIN MASTER DEVIL STICKS!" alongside a picture of a model juggling the sticks. Since I was the best at devil sticking, I was the model on the side of the van. We hired some college kids and they drove the vans from town to town, stopping at carnivals and concerts and festivals, where they'd demo the product. We were also lucky that, as with the Earth Buddy, our youth made our success a good story. The Canadian media gave us plenty of coverage, all of it positive. But our marketing and PR efforts, effective as they may have been, were hardly the main driver for what happened next. The fact is that the insatiable appetite for devil sticks was already out there, and once we put our brand on the shelves it just . . . exploded.

The next year of our lives was pure magic. The experience of devil sticks was even more fun than the Earth Buddy because it was something I had nostalgia for from my teenage years, and it was a product we were making specifically for kids, which was very cool. We sold about a million and a half pieces that year, and we were back-ordered the whole time, sometimes for months. We could never produce enough to supply the demand. It was like we were getting pulled by a speedboat that kept tugging at us and tugging at us. Toys "R" Us and KB Toys were our two biggest outlets, and together with all the specialty shops that our reps sold us into, we were in more than two thousand stores across North America, which was unbelievable. There were days when I'd sit back and watch the sales numbers come in, hearing from retailers that they'd sold eight thousand that week or twelve thousand the next week. It was staggering. And where the Earth Buddy retailed for $4.99, Spin Master Devil Sticks retailed for $14.99, so the value of what we were generating per sale was three times as high.

Since we didn't actually own the idea of devil sticks, we ended up splitting the market with a competitor out of Montreal, Harvey Freeman Devil Sticks. Retailers sold us side by side, and we more than held our own from a price, quality, marketing, and supply perspective. It was cool that two Canadian firms were the driving force behind the product, and fortunately the space was large enough to share.

Once Ben came back on board, our three-man partnership began to take shape. We even got a new name. After starting out as Seiger Marketing, we'd changed our name to Earth Buddy, since that was the only product we had. Now that we were growing and expanding beyond that, we needed something else. Because the Spin Master Devil Sticks had been such a runaway success, we decided to name the company Spin Master Toys. Then, a few years later, we dropped the "Toys" when we decided we didn't want to be just a toy company moving forward.

By nearly every measure, the success of Spin Master Devil Sticks marked a major milestone for us as a company, and when I look back on the reasons for that, I can confidently say that we did a great job with them. We executed well. We designed well. We manufactured well. We marketed well. However, what carried the day and made the product such a success was that we caught a specific moment in time. We rode the zeitgeist, and that made all the difference.

||

Tapping into the zeitgeist is a powerful way to move your business forward. The collective society is talking about something, doing something, obsessing over something, and you get to benefit from the energy they're already generating. Those cultural currents are a magical factor that give you a multiplier effect over and above what you yourself are doing directly. It's a force so powerful that, if you catch it just right, it can put tremendous wind in your sails. And if you try to go against it, it almost doesn't matter how good your product or idea is, because you're swimming against a tide with a superhuman force. In fact, when it comes to evaluating potential products to launch or ideas to pursue, being in touch with the zeitgeist may be the single most important factor to your success.

So, first things first, how do you do it? It's an ability that comes from having a sense of what is about to come or what is already happening in society. It's not an intellectual pursuit. You can't market research it or focus test it. It's a visceral feeling. It's knowing which way the winds are blowing, or where the tide is going to flow. Indeed, catching a wave of the zeitgeist is not unlike catching an actual wave in surfing. You paddle out to what's called the green water, where you wait patiently, sensing the movement of the ocean and the wave coming toward you. Timing and positioning are everything.

When you watch good surfers, you see that they're always moving; they'll paddle up and back, constantly adjusting their position to be ready for what's coming. The best surfers are the ones who are able to anticipate where the swell is going to go; they're *always* in the right place, and they make it look effortless. More than their athleticism, it's their ability to read the environment around them. They just know, *This is my wave, and I'm going to ride it.* When you have that, you can get a long, clean ride, the immense power of the wave moving you along with unimaginable speed.

Bad surfers, on the other hand, are stuck inside their heads, overthinking it. They're nervous, anxious, always looking for the wave because they can't feel it. If that's your approach, you're not going to catch too much. If you go too early on a wave, you'll miss it and it will pass you by. And if you go too late, it'll crash on you and maybe even break your board, which has happened to me a couple of times.

Surfing cultural waves requires that same sense of timing and patience, and the same lack of fear. Those waves are bigger than any of us and almost impossible to predict. But that doesn't mean they're impossible to spot. You can get a sense of them by observing, by developing the ability to pick up on social cues and conversations, on the newest fashions and the latest music. You see how people are spending their time, what their interests are, what their needs are, and you learn how to connect the dots. And while you can still spot those trends out in bars or in the streets, these days you're more likely to see them online, in social media posts, in Reddit threads, and elsewhere. If you follow what people are posting, how they're expressing themselves, how other people are commenting on what they've posted, there's a wealth of information available to you right at your fingertips.

I DIDN'T START SURFING UNTIL I was forty-five, which may have something to do with why I wound up with those broken boards. I had to learn to read the waves. I didn't feel them as naturally and intuitively as someone who grew up on the water—and therein lies the first key advantage for young people when it comes to tapping into the zeitgeist: You were born into it. Everything you've grown up with, all the cultural forces that had an influence on your generation, they've shaped your thinking and your outlook. Which is why young people intuitively understand cultural changes. They feel them, viscerally, in a way that's harder to ascertain as you get older. Theoretically, people can be hip at any age, but in your twenties you are that much closer to the trends. You're not only in the zeitgeist, in many ways you are the zeitgeist. To be clued into whatever's new, it helps if you're already immersed in the space where it's happening, and wherever young people are gathered, by definition, that's where the future is taking shape.

When I first stumbled across kids playing with devil sticks, I obviously wasn't a middle schooler anymore, but I was young enough that I was still out and about on the streets of Toronto where young people hung around. When I approached those young kids, I was close enough in age that I could see the world through their eyes. I could stop and chat with them and, from their point of view, I was old enough to be cool and not yet old enough to be . . . well, old. Which allowed me to connect with them and see that their pastime offered a moment of opportunity. As a young person starting a business, you are uniquely positioned to sense cultural changes in a way that older competitors simply can't.

As we were getting Spin Master off the ground, there were many times when we looked around at the way older people in our industry were operating, and it felt so out-of-date. They were smart and capable people, but they were stuck doing what had worked well for them in their time, which obviously wasn't going to serve them well in the future. At the time, none of the established toy companies in Canada were designing or manufacturing their own products. They were satisfied with acting as distributors for the toy manufacturers in the United States. For us, that never made sense. It seemed like an artifact from a bygone era. (Indeed, seven years after Spin Master launched, what was then the largest toy company in Canada would file for bankruptcy.)

Anton, Ben, and I had grown up in a rapidly globalizing world, where communication was getting faster and the world was getting smaller. We could hop on a plane one day and be in a Chinese factory the next. We'd grown up in an age where entrepreneurship was celebrated, not to the extent it is today, mind you, but more than it had been in the past. So unlike previous generations, we were absolutely certain that the right approach was to design our own products and bring them to life. That one decision was transformative for us. We said we would be open to ideas wherever they came from, that we would design them ourselves, owning our own IP, and sell it around the world. Which may not have been a revolutionary insight, but it reflected the way the economy was headed: Manufacturing and trade continued to open up for the next twenty-five years, and we rode the wave right along with it. Meanwhile, our older, more established competitors couldn't adapt fast enough to make the switch. They weren't able to grow and scale.

In a sense, different generations almost live in parallel universes. As every new cohort comes of age, they bring about a changing of the guard. They reset the clock. They're bursting with new ideas—ideas that the previous generation may not understand. When you start your business, you may find that some older people second-guess your approach, and you may be tempted to think that those people are smarter, wiser, and more experienced—and they are, in certain areas. But not necessarily when it comes to the zeitgeist. Some of them may still be hip, but odds are most of them won't be able to see it as clearly as you can, because they aren't close to it anymore.

OF COURSE, AS IMPORTANT AS it is to be able to spot the coming waves and shifting winds, that's not enough. You also have to be open to the change, and that's where youth gives you a tremendous advantage as well. When you're young, in your teens and early twenties, you spend so much time watching and observing the world. Everything is new and filled with wonder. Your mind is less cluttered. It's more open, less jaded, which affords you clarity, heightened senses, and more intuitive insights.

The reason time slows down and the days seem so rich and full when you're young is because you're seeing and experiencing things for the first time. The freshness of everything means you're able to process all that information without a filter or any preconceptions. All of which makes picking up on the cultural and technological currents easier to do.

You're also more open to the changes in society because you yourself are actively searching for who you're going to be in this life. You have a deep, inherent desire to actualize on some talent or idea and reach your full potential. It's a natural wellspring inside you, and it wants to come out. It's been there, really, since you were five years old, but as long as you were living under your parents' roof you were mostly stuck, observing and dreaming and waiting for the day when you'd get to leave home and live your own life instead of your parents' lives. As soon as you leave home, you're able to dial your radar in to the open frequencies of the universe. You're searching for the right signals because you're searching for opportunities for yourself. You're simply more tuned-in to everything going on around you.

ONCE YOU SPOT A WAVE, the key is to act fast because other people will invariably see it coming too. But it's important to remember that tapping into the zeitgeist isn't about being first. You don't need to discover entirely new things. In fact, you need to be able to point to some form of early adoption; for something to be in the zeitgeist, by definition it has to already exist in the world. Oftentimes, the most successful innovator isn't the first or even the second person to give it a try. In the mid-2000s, the idea of what we now know as social media was out there floating in the ether. At least a half dozen contenders—including Six Degrees, Friendster, and MySpace—all came and went before Mark Zuckerberg and Jack Dorsey hit on the right formula with Facebook and Twitter.

At Spin Master, especially in the early days, we didn't create markets. We tapped into existing ones. If you think about the opportunity as a curve, you want to launch your product at something like in the 15–20 percent mark. Early enough that you can ride the wave, but not so early that it's impossible to get traction. Take the smartphone. Today, the idea of a portable, handheld computing device has become so ubiquitous that most people can't even imagine life without one. Steve Jobs saw that wave coming, and he rode it perfectly with the iPhone. Apple had tried to predict and ride that wave fifteen years earlier with its first personal digital assistant, the Apple Newton. On a $100 million investment, the Newton bombed in the marketplace. The Newton may or may not have been a good product, but it wouldn't have mattered either way, because it was just too early.

Here it's also important to point out that surfing the zeitgeist is rarely a matter of catching a single wave. It often requires a confluence of seemingly disparate things coming together. That's especially true when you talk about tech. Improvements in hardware, software, processing power, battery life, Wi-Fi, Bluetooth—all of those innovations and transformations had to come to fruition for a portable, handheld digital device to be truly viable. When Apple first brought the Newton to market, none of those developments were there to support it.

When the confluence of those innovations came about, along came the BlackBerry, the once-ubiquitous handheld device that captured the first real wave of demand for that category. But the crosscurrents of digital technology move so fast that even the inventors of that revolutionary product failed to predict where the next wave would come from. Then Steve Jobs swooped in with the iPhone and its touchscreen and all its apps and features, taking BlackBerry's entire market share and leaving it for dead. One of the greatest cultural surfers in history, Jobs managed to stay in the water long enough to catch the right wave when it finally came along. And, of course, the flip side of being too early is being too late. If you're too late, the trend has become obvious to everyone else. The wave has crested and someone other than you is already riding it.

Some companies don't just catch a wave. They catch a tsunami. They keep growing and growing until their brand practically becomes synonymous with their category. Nike and basketball shoes, Google and search, we all know these iconic brands. A more recent and very instructive example would be Lululemon and yoga/athleisure gear. Yes, Lululemon has great products made with great material, and they've created a brand that's captivated millions of consumers. They've also had fresh, brilliant marketing ideas, like hosting yoga classes in their stores. But the larger truth is that, as with Nike and running, if Lululemon hadn't launched at just the right moment of yoga's rise into our cultural consciousness, there is no way they would have built a $50 billion company. Are there other brands of yoga pants and athleisure out there? Sure, but none of them are Lululemon, and if you're not Lululemon, then you've missed the first wave. All you can do is paddle back out to the green water to try to see—and, more importantly, feel—where the next wave is coming from.

Because the zeitgeist is always changing, and there's always another wave.

Here it's important to note that, yes, Lululemon's Chip Wilson was forty-three when he started the company, but that was only after founding his first athletic apparel company, Westbeach Snowboard, when he was twenty-four. And he'd started his first hustle with his mom, importing and selling swimwear, when he was only *twelve*. Today Wilson is seventy-three. He's a legend in his industry, which means that his younger competitors just might be more attuned to the future than he is, and that's precisely what's happened with Alo Yoga.

Alo Yoga has caught that next wave, and they're using it to eat into Lululemon's market share, becoming the next big thing in athleisure clothing. Where Lululemon focused on comfort and durability and positioned itself to the broadest possible audience, Alo has focused more on wellness meets fashion, taking advantage of social media influencers like Kendall Jenner and Hailey Bieber to reach a younger demographic and position themselves as the buzziest brand in the space. In 2023, Alo's TikTok followers grew from 340,000 to 1.2 million, and 65 percent of its revenue came from e-commerce. They've also radically rethought their retail strategy, turning their stores into immersive brand experiences with yoga studios, cafés, and wellness events. Alo even opened most of its stores in direct proximity to Lululemon locations; more than 80 percent of its stores are within half a mile of the competition, making it simple for consumers to just shop somewhere else.

Because the world is always changing, there will always be new opportunities for younger entrants, new ways of manufacturing products and reaching customers. Which is why younger entrepreneurs should never be afraid to take on the incumbents. There is no business so big and powerful that it's immune to the shifting tides of history, and youth will always be an advantage in sensing which way those tides are going. Just look at the $3 billion eyewear giant Warby Parker, founded by Neil Blumenthal, twenty-nine, and Dave Gilboa, twenty-eight, who saw a way to slash prices and costs by selling direct to consumers online. You've got Dropbox, the cloud storage giant founded by Drew Houston, twenty-four, and Arash Ferdowsi, twenty-two, which is now worth around $9 billion. You've got Stripe, the online payment processing firm started by two brothers, Patrick and John Collison, twenty-two and twenty years old, respectively, and now sitting on a net worth of tens of billions of dollars.

Spotify, Casper, Airbnb, Reddit, Sweetgreen—the list goes on, and it also includes dozens of non-consumer-facing businesses that have achieved massive success without becoming household names. The founders of these companies shared the ability to gauge and feel the zeitgeist. They were also deeply passionate about their chosen fields, which helped them succeed in launching their new ventures. The more deeply you are immersed in a space, the more you are able to spot the changes in society that will open up new opportunities. You know what's been done and what's innovative. You have a sense for what has worked in the past, and whether something new might in the future. Simply put, you have a sense of the way the waves have broken and, with enough focus, you should be able to take the many inputs coming your way and predict where the waves might be forming next.

IT'S ALSO IMPORTANT TO REMEMBER that the zeitgeist isn't always what everybody thinks it is. It's not necessarily the latest trend on Instagram or the latest technology on the cover of *Wired* magazine. The waves come in all shapes and sizes. There can be huge ones and tiny ones. There might be sets of five quick waves in a row. Then there might be a long doldrum with no waves at all.

When Spin Master was forming in the mid- to late nineties, the prevailing wind in business was to go into tech. The internet was the future of everything. That was the monster swell, with sets that kept coming and coming—and still keep coming to this day. There was no indication at the time that the toy industry was the sexy new place to be. If anything, it was the opposite. It was old, staid, and low growth. But if you were attuned to what was happening, you could see the big wave of change that was coming. Opening up markets and trade with China was going to completely change the way manufacturing was done, not just for toys but for nearly every consumer good.

All of which is to say you don't necessarily have to go into the newest or most popular industries. You can use what's happening in the zeitgeist to reinvent and redefine older-growth industries, whether it's toys or fashion. Even a field as old and established as home construction is always going to be changing with new developments in materials and concerns for environmentally sound practices. Reinvention and innovation can be done in any sector of business, because every sector of business is subject to the uncertainty of shifting tides.

AND THAT IS THE FINAL thing you need to remember about the zeitgeist: It is always moving. The only constant is change, as they say, and the business world is littered with the bodies of giants—titans of industry who failed to see the future coming. When we started, Kmart and Toys "R" Us were the biggest retailers we could possibly land. Thirty years later, they've been wiped off the map, first by Walmart and then by Amazon. Fifteen years ago, online retail was a tiny part of our business. Now it's 40 percent of our business.

The funny thing is that as we're getting older and our business keeps getting bigger, I see younger companies catching the big waves in our industry while we miss them. We are now like Lululemon, at risk of being outmaneuvered by some enterprising young upstart like Alo. That's the new challenge to our potential to grow and stay relevant, and we're looking to buy younger companies to manage this issue. But the true value at the best cost is to have an awareness of the changing times hardwired in your company, which means actively listening to your younger employees, the people of the next generation, to find out where they see the zeitgeist going.

Because the zeitgeist is always going *somewhere*. Not only does it keep moving, but some would say the pace is even accelerating. The decisive advantage for you is that all that movement creates opportunity. Technology, tastes, desires, thoughts, feelings, ways of living, ways of thinking, cultural norms—all of it is changing all the time, enabling new people to sprout up and start new businesses.

Catching the right wave at the right time is the ultimate growth driver. It's a start-up elixir, more powerful than advertising and a lot cheaper too. And by "cheaper" I mean it's literally free. The ability to observe, absorb, and think about ways to capitalize on the ever-changing zeitgeist is available to anyone who wants to use it. Walking around Toronto watching kids play with devil sticks cost me nothing. Understanding that it represented a cultural shift from what I'd seen at Grateful Dead shows five years earlier, that cost me nothing. And that simple, zero-cost moment of insight yielded millions of dollars in revenue, all because I was at the perfect age to make something out of it, young enough to talk to middle-school kids on the street, yet old enough to be setting up a manufacturing operation in Mexico.

Those kids I saw playing with devil sticks around Toronto, that was happening with or without us. There was a wave coming in the youth culture, and that wave would have come and gone with or without us. Luckily, we caught the wave at the right moment. If we'd come out too early, maybe a year or two years before, there would have been no demand. If we'd come out too late, we probably would have missed it and been stuck with tons of excess inventory. In fact, my guess is that we could have made and sold the exact same quality product, but if we hadn't caught that wave, we would have sold 80 percent less. That is the power of the zeitgeist, and the ability to harness that power belongs disproportionately to one group of people—yours.

5.

The Power of Not Knowing

On a beautiful summer day in June of 1996, at the height of the devil sticks craze, Ben and I found ourselves in Toronto's Wenderly Park with two guys named Peter Manning and John Dixon. They had something to show us. Something big and exciting and new.

Peter and John belonged to a unique part of the toy industry that was and still is largely invisible to the public: toy inventors. From its earliest days, our business has always relied on these unsung heroes. Fueled only by their passionate love of toys, and a desire to make new and exciting ones for the next generation, these eccentric, self-employed Thomas Edisons toil away in their workshops and basements and garages, coming up with fresh ideas for games, puzzles, dolls, action figures, and everything in between. They design and build their own prototypes by hand, and then bring those prototypes to companies like ours to be manufactured and brought out into the world. Typically, they don't get a ton of credit or accolades, but they're responsible for some of the most iconic toys the world knows and loves: G.I. Joe, Furby, the Super Soaker—the list goes on. Today, the big toy conglomerates like Hasbro and Mattel all have their own internal research and development teams, but good ideas can come from anywhere, and they still rely on inventors for many of each year's new toys. They're the lifeblood of the industry.

There were probably about a couple hundred toy inventors working around the world at that time, and we were first introduced to them through Ben when he came back to join us. At the time Ben was living in downtown Toronto, sharing an apartment with three women, one of whom was Jenn Irwin. Jenn's father, Bryan, ran Irwin Toy, which was then the largest manufacturer and distributor of toys in Canada. Bryan Irwin was one of those older, more established industry figures who was rooting for us and eager to help us out. He took a liking to Ben and went out of his way to share any information he could with us about the business, including his complete list of American and European toy inventors, an incredibly generous gesture that gave us direct access to some of the best and brightest minds in the business.

Which we needed.

By that point, firmly established as a toy company in our third year, we'd enjoyed an amazing run of success, but the Earth Buddy had almost completely tapered off, as we always knew it would, and even though devil sticks were still doing okay, we could see the end of their natural lifespan coming as well. We had a couple of low-end, low-priced novelty products that we'd put out to pay the bills and keep the payroll going. One was Grow Things, these little dinosaurs made of an expanding plastic material encased in eggs. You'd dump the egg in water and it would break and this dinosaur would grow out of it. The other was called the Radical Reptile, made from cut pieces of foam attached to the end of a metal stick. You'd wiggle the stick and the Radical Reptile would wriggle on the floor through the vibration.

In other words, we weren't exactly breaking new ground. Even the Earth Buddy and the devil sticks, as much fun as we'd had with them, hadn't been new, original ideas. We had a real desire to do something groundbreaking. We needed a signature product that people had never seen before. We wanted to bring something into the world that was creative, unique, and innovative—something with pixie dust. "Pixie dust" is the term we've used over the years to describe that magical quality in a toy that makes you connect with your inner seven-year-old self and get excited. Anytime we tested out a new prototype, that's what we were looking for.

Because Ben had a such a strong passion for toys, he made it his job to go out and meet with all these inventors so he could listen to their pitches and then bring them back for us to sift through in search of that magical pixie-dust moment. By the summer of 1996, Ben had met with about fifteen or twenty different inventors and had started developing good relationships with them. Which is how we found ourselves in Wenderly Park with Peter Manning and John Dixon and this new thing they were dying to show us.

Peter and John were both classic toy industry characters. Peter Manning has since passed away, but at the time they were both in their mid-fifties, sort of gruff, old-school British gentlemen. Peter was the inspired, fun-loving inventor type with a zest for life. He had the mechanical mind and the dexterous hands for building and putting things together. John was more of the business guy. But they were both incredibly passionate about the toy they had to show us that day: a toy airplane that flew with the power of compressed air.

Not knowing what to expect, we watched with curiosity as John and Peter pumped it up, flicked the propeller, launched it, and it just . . . took off. It worked on the first try, soaring fifty to sixty feet in the air. We stood there, our necks craned back, big smiles on our faces, watching it circle and circle and circle above. Ben and I were both like, "Wow! That is *so* cool! I had no idea it could get so high!"

The way the plane worked was ingenious. It had a plastic bottle that you filled with compressed air using a pump. Attached to that was a single-cylinder piston engine that moved up and down as the air was released. The piston drove the propeller, which gave you the flight. The key to a good flying toy is the weight-to-power ratio, and because this model was nothing more than a plastic bottle with a foam fuselage, foam wings, and a plastic propeller, they'd been able to get that ratio of power to weight just right, giving you about forty-five amazing seconds in the air. It was a marvel of engineering, which is another way of saying it was like magic.

As the plane came down, my visceral response was to go and run and chase it so that I could pick it up the second it landed and bring it back and take my turn pumping it up and launching it. Then Ben wanted to take a turn. I think we flew it about four or five times, which was all John and Peter wanted us to do; it was a one-of-a-kind prototype, after all. But we were so excited we wanted to do it over and over again.

This plane hit a core note inside us. It was pixie dust with wings. Watching it fly was one of those moments where it felt like time stopped a bit. We became a couple of ten-year-old kids who don't want to come home for dinner because they're having so much fun. We'd been looking for something magical that we'd never seen before, and now we'd seen it. It captured our imaginations.

We were so inspired that we came up with a name for it right on the spot. The little single-piston engine was so loud that it sounded like a Harley Davidson motorcycle, a hog, only a hog that you filled with air. And it was so much fun that you wanted to hog it for yourself, hog the next turn, hog the sky, not let the other guy have a go so that you could do it again.

"Maybe we should call it Air Pig?" one of us said.

"No, that's not gonna work."

So we went with Air Hogs, which we already envisioned not as the name of the plane itself but as the umbrella brand for a whole fleet of different flying toys. We didn't have any data on flying toys. We didn't have a single piece of market research on their viability. We just had a feeling that said, *Let's go with this. Let's bring it to market.*

In the toy industry, when you work with an inventor, you typically pay them an option, which is what we did. Since Anton stayed out of product discussions, the decision was mine and Ben's to make, and we gave John and Peter a $25,000 option fee right there on the spot, which bought us three months to do our research and come to a final decision to actually move forward, which we ultimately did, paying them an additional $25,000 advance to secure the rights. The rest of their compensation would come from a 5 percent royalty paid in perpetuity.

Part of the magic for Ben and me with this plane was that we'd never seen anything like it before. Flight is the ultimate fantasy. There isn't any kid alive—or any adult, for that matter—who hasn't dreamed of being able to fly. Yet the market for flying toys was terrible. You had a couple of crappy options at the low end, those cheap balsa-wood planes with propellers that ran on wind-up rubber bands that would inevitably break after four or five short, wobbly flights. Then at the high end you had expensive remote-control airplanes that ran on gasoline and were actually somewhat dangerous; their propellers can literally take off your finger because they're spinning so fast. Those were more for adult hobbyists than for kids, and even then you usually got one flight before the thing broke because the fuselage was made out of plastic. There was nothing in the middle. Nothing safe, reliable, durable, and affordable. Nothing for the ten-year-old kid who just wanted to experience the joy and fun that we felt in the park that day.

Of course, because Ben and I were so young and so new to the industry, we didn't think to stop and ask *why* we'd never seen anything like this before, and the reason why we'd never seen it before, the reason why the perfect flying toy didn't exist, was because a good flying toy is an absurdly difficult thing to try to pull off. The potential problems are enormous. What goes up must come down, and when it does there's a good chance it'll crash and possibly break, which means you've got a big problem with customer returns. Anything that flies can career off course and hit a child in the face, or the propeller could slice a kid's finger open, so you've got safety issues you've got to address. We weren't completely blind to those possibilities, but the truth is we were so naïve that we didn't see them as impediments to getting the product to market. We were so green that we genuinely didn't know any better. All we did know was that flying this plane had been so much fun that it made us feel like kids again, and that was enough for us to go on.

It was only years later, long after Air Hogs had become hugely successful, that John and Peter admitted the one fact about their prototype they'd left out of their pitch. Namely, that they'd already pitched it to everyone else. We thought it was a new idea that we were just lucky to snag before anyone else. The reality was that they'd already shown it to every toy company in the world, and they'd all turned it down—several times. Hasbro, Mattel, and all the others had passed because they had the experience to see all the risks and setbacks and headaches that lay in wait. Never mind all the problems you were looking at once the planes got into kids' hands, any experienced toymaker could tell you that just getting a product like this to market was going to be a nightmare. From a manufacturing point of view, the Earth Buddy was simple, just pantyhose filled with seed and sawdust. Same with the devil sticks, which were wooden dowels wrapped with tape. Air Hogs, on the other hand, were going to require serious engineering development at a scale and complexity unlike anything we could possibly imagine. We had no idea how long, how hard, and how expensive it was going to be.

All the more experienced people at Hasbro and Mattel knew better than to take this thing on. Since we didn't have that experience, we came at it with the classic entrepreneurial "Anything is possible" attitude. "*Of course* there's a way to make it safe and durable," we thought. "*Of course* we can figure out how to mass manufacture it." It simply didn't cross our minds that the facts would prove otherwise. We just shrugged and said, "Okay, we'll figure it out."

And we did.

ONCE WE DECIDED TO LICENSE the idea for Air Hogs, we set ourselves to the task of figuring out how to take this prototype and engineer it for mass production. What followed was a two-year process that consumed almost all my time and virtually all the money we'd made in the business to date, hundreds and hundreds of thousands of dollars.

Step one was getting a workable design. The prototype we'd bought was a one-of-a-kind proof of concept, assembled by hand; it needed to be redesigned from the ground up to transform it into something that could be manufactured on an assembly line. For that purpose, John Dixon and Peter Manning referred us to a guy named Chuck Kownacki at K Development in Erie, Pennsylvania. His job would be to take John and Peter's initial proof of concept and engineer it, producing the drawings necessary to take the idea from the theoretical to the practical.

For the prototyping, we turned to Rehkemper Innovation & Design in Chicago, which was run by Jeff Rehkemper and his brother,

Steve. They actually had the facilities to make the motors, the wings, and the fuselage, and put it all together. We were already working with Jeff on our Grow Things dinosaurs. We liked him, and Ben wanted to work with him again. More importantly, when we had dinner with Jeff at the next Toy Fair, in February of 1997, as soon as we told him about the concept, he got excited. In what would prove to be another example of Everyone Rooting for You When You're Young, when we showed Jeff the drawings K Development had put together, he was instantly caught up in the excitement of what we were doing. "This is amazing," he said. "This is unbelievable. I really want to work on this project." So we made the decision right there at dinner to go down the road with them.

Chuck Kownacki and all the engineers at K Development were excited and rooting for us too. So much so that they were willing to forgo a cash payment and do all the design work for a piece of the back end, which allowed us to keep more of our cash on hand and reduce our downside risk. We ended up giving them a 1.5 percent royalty on the sale of the product, in perpetuity.

While Ben worked on the packaging and marketing and Anton took the lead on sales, the task of product development fell to me. I started traveling to Chicago every month to test the new prototypes for the first-generation Air Hog, a model we would dub the Sky Shark. I would fly in and meet up with Jeff, and he and I would take the latest iteration and head out to Washington Park to see it fly. Or not fly. It was always a two-steps-forward, one-step-back type of process. Sometimes it would go up and soar. Other times it would go up and come right back down, crashing and breaking parts. There was always a new debug or detail to work out. Then we'd take the results of our test and send that information back to K Development so they could tweak the design. Then Jeff would use those new blueprints to make another prototype, and I'd fly down and we'd test it again.

It went back and forth and back and forth like that for almost a year and a half, and I loved it. I loved flying in to Chicago and going to their office, filled with anticipation about what I was going to see. To this day those trips still rank as some of the most magical moments of my career. It's exciting to develop something new, and this was a real, bona fide invention. We patented it. It had never existed before, and we were birthing it into the world. It was the first time that we willed something out of nothing into the universe. Even when we hit setbacks, I never got discouraged because I was so eager and keen to watch it come alive.

Just as the Sky Shark was being born out of those trips, it felt like I was doing the same. I was taking a big step up. Chicago is a rich place for the toy industry, home to lots of inventors and development houses. In the 1970s, '80s, and '90s, they were the powerhouses of the industry. Working with Jeff and Steve, going to dinner with them and getting to know them, I was getting deeper into the business. I'd go to their office and see all the products they were developing for other toy companies. I'd see pictures of their past successes lining the walls and we'd talk about them and I'd learn about their rich history. It felt like being in the big leagues.

Every month the Sky Shark prototype would get a bit better. Then, once we finally had something we thought would work, we were off to China to mass manufacture it. Two years before, knowing we were never going back to Mexico after getting burned there so badly, Ben and I had taken a trip to Asia to scout potential factories and get a sense of who the major players were; we were thinking of making a light-up devil stick, and we felt China was the place to make it happen. As we would soon learn, companies in Hong Kong have an amazing openness to explore any inquiry for new business; they believe that every inquiry comes from karma, and no potential opportunity should ever be overlooked. From the first day you meet with their people, even though they might ultimately decide not to partner with you, they give you the same level of respect they would give to a trusted, long-term business partner. Which is how Ben and I found ourselves, at the age of twenty-five, being taken to lunch in a Rolls-Royce with one of the most famous and wealthiest factory owners in all of Hong Kong.

Despite touring several different factories on that trip, we didn't find the partner we were looking for. Fortunately, the Rehkempers introduced us to William Babbs. Babbs, the son of an English father and a Chinese mother, ran a manufacturing company called Kin Seng. He was very British in his mannerisms, soft-spoken, even-keeled, equanimous. About twelve years older than me, he was still a young guy, and extremely hardworking, and as soon as we told him about the Sky Shark he was eager to get that piece of business as well.

Kin Seng's factory was located not in Hong Kong but in the city of Chaoyang, some six hours north in mainland China. When the tooling from K Development's Pro E drawings was completed, we were ready to start making physical parts in mass quantities, which required us to be on the assembly line to debug the pieces as they came out of the injection molding machines. We did one big kickoff trip with the whole team: myself, Steve and Jeff Rehkemper, Chuck from K Development, and Alex Perez, a new engineer we'd hired from Mattel. They all came to work on it for three to four days to make sure that our manufacturing process got up and running properly. Making that trip was above and beyond what Chuck and the Rehkempers were obligated to do, but they made the time for it because this product was that important to them.

The same was true for our new factory partner as well. At the time William Babbs's factory was not a large operation. He would go on to have incredible success not only with the Air Hogs but also with the SpinBrush, John Osher's first cheap, battery-powered electronic toothbrush. But up to that point I don't think he had ever attempted to manufacture something as complex as this, and his attitude was "I want to get something like this under my belt." The fact he had the same ethos we did was a large part of why we went with him, and it meant we had yet another highly motivated person on the team.

After that great initial kickoff, there was still a ton of work to do, so I stayed behind for a few more weeks. Compared with today, there was not a whole lot going on in China in the mid-1990s. Chaoyang was a poor, remote city, just dusty streets lined with three-story concrete buildings that all had retail storefronts at the base floor. As far as I could tell, I was only the white person for miles in every direction. I used to go to the only McDonald's in town because it was the one place that reminded me of home.

My hotel was a trip. Before I went to check in, the people at the factory all told me, "Be prepared. You may not get the best night's sleep."

"What do you mean?"

"People might knock on your door at night."

"Really? People are going to knock on my door?"

"Yes."

"Why?"

I would soon find out, because twelve o'clock came and someone knocked on my door. *I'm not opening that door,* I thought. One o'clock, another knock. *I'm not opening that door.* Two o'clock. *I am not opening that door.*

Finally, at around four in the morning, I heard another knock and in my woozy dream state I said to myself, *All right, let me at least go see what's happening.* I got up, looked through the peephole, and there, standing in the hallway, was a beautiful young woman.

I won't lie and say I didn't think about opening the door.

I thought about opening the door.

Then I went back to bed.

By the fourth or fifth night the knocking finally tapered off. I guess they got the message that the man in that room wasn't interested in their services, and I was finally able to get a good night's sleep, which is all I did at the hotel anyway, because for my whole time there I basically lived at the factory.

Since I wanted to feel like I was really inhabiting the customs and traditions of this foreign place, instead of taking a car I rode to work in a rickshaw every day. There was a stand where I'd stop and pick up fresh oranges every morning to bring in for the team I was working with. I didn't speak a word of Mandarin, though. In the hotel and in restaurants I did my best to get by, but because the factory was run out of Hong Kong, which the British had controlled for the last hundred years, all the engineers I worked with spoke English, and there was always someone on hand to translate for any workers who didn't.

The reason I had to stay in China was to do what's called a debug. When you mass manufacture something, making parts with an injection mold machine as we were, even the tiniest problem can throw everything else off, so everything has to be 100 percent perfect. The upside of that is that once it's perfect, you can scale production up as high and as fast as you might need to. The downside is that it takes a long time to get everything right. With the Sky Shark, we had a lot to work out with the wings, which had to be stiff enough to keep their shape but flexible enough to handle the impact of a crash landing without snapping apart. Debugging the motor was an enormous challenge as well, because the tolerances there had to be exact, and with so many tiny, intricate parts to get just right, it took a long time to make the necessary changes. Every time we ran into a problem, it would take a day or two to revise the CAD work and another two days to take the mold down and change the engraving inside it. Then we'd shoot the parts and put it back together again and see if it worked. That's when we'd usually find another bug and have to make another change, and then we'd have to hurry up and wait again.

When we first bought the Sky Shark after a single test flight in Toronto, I'd had no idea that any of these headaches would be waiting for me down the road. Zero. My mother was always fascinated by how I figured them out. "How did you learn to do all that stuff?" she asked. Invariably, the answer was "Because I had to." Especially since we'd already sold the product. The traditional sales cycle with toys is front-loaded. You go to the Toy Fair in February with your prototypes and you sell for the upcoming year with the hope that you'll have the exciting new toy for the following Christmas. The buyers who pick you up do so on the implicit promise that you're going to deliver, and most people do deliver at the end of the day. If we had waited until we'd completely debugged the product to start selling it, we would have lost a year—a year of carrying all those costs and overhead. We couldn't afford to do that. We needed to start recouping on the product as quickly as possible.

About a year out from the target on-sale date we'd set for ourselves, we still didn't have a fully workable product, but we did have the prototype from Jeff Rehkemper that looked and worked better than the model that the inventors had pitched us; it had the right design and the right feel. So with that we put together a nice package and a video sizzle reel and went to the Toy Fair to start talking to buyers. For a full year, Anton was out selling the product while we were still executing the development in Chicago and the debugging in China.

In January of 1998 we started getting confirmed purchase orders for delivery that May. We had commitments we needed to fill, which meant I had the pressure of delivery sitting on top of my head the whole time. We hadn't taken anyone's money yet, but retailers had already allocated space for us on their shelves and started to arrange all the ads and promotions for the product, and in the toy industry, if a retailer had an empty shelf set aside for you, that was sacrosanct. Plus, if we didn't deliver the product we couldn't start invoicing for the product, and if we couldn't start invoicing for the product we would be in serious trouble.

At that point, with 100 percent of the profits from our other products going to pay our R&D bills, which had run in the hundreds and hundreds of thousands of dollars, pretty much everything we had was riding on the Sky Shark. If it failed, it probably wouldn't have been the death of Spin Master; we were young enough, resilient enough, and resourceful enough that we would have pivoted and taken a different course, but it definitely would have set us back significantly, and I'm not even sure we would have stayed in the toy industry.

Even when the debug was finished and I was ready to fly home, I didn't leave with any definite sense of "We've made it." I left cautiously optimistic that everything was going to be okay, but still slightly paranoid. Because it's always a leap of faith when you leave the assembly line, praying that all the parts are going to continue to come out right, that they'll assemble it correctly, and that the quality control will continue to be at the standard that you left it in.

At that point, amazingly, after two years of endless toil, we'd only made our way to the starting line. Now we actually had to take the Sky Shark out into the world, and with that the learning curve only continued to climb. We had to learn how to ship products from China, how to load up forty-foot containers and get them on container ships.

Then there was the marketing. Even though our PR and word of mouth were good, the Sky Shark represented an entirely different level of effort to get the awareness we needed to drive the consumer to the store to get the product. We had to learn how to do proper TV commercials. We had to learn about end caps, ad support for retailers, promotions at trade. We had to build in-store display units, so that right there in the toy aisle we could have an Air Hog in a plastic dome for kids who wanted to pump it up and flip the propeller and see and hear it work. All of which came out of the $2 million marketing budget we had to spend, which was how much it cost to launch any major new toy at that time.

Then came the learning curve with customer service, because after two years and hundreds of thousands of dollars of development, from the moment the Sky Shark started to sell we were getting complaints. The main wing kept breaking, and consumers were upset. That was a real "Oh, shit" moment. The wings breaking off had always been one of our biggest fears. We thought we'd addressed it sufficiently, but either we'd rushed the debug or we hadn't looked at a large enough sample size to appreciate the scope of the problem. So we scrambled and within two weeks we had a solution. We reinforced the underside of the foam wing with tape so it would flex and not snap. We also adjusted the fastener that held the foam wing in place. That way, instead of breaking on hard contact it would pop out and you could just pop it back in. Luckily, that seemed to work, and the Sky Shark took off, quite literally.

From the moment we hit stores, the demand was insane. We went from $7 million in sales to $35 million in the first nine months alone. The following year, led by the Sky Shark, our total annual revenue shot up to $100 million. It was our first truly global success. It sold in literally every country around the world, breaking down all kinds of barriers. We even ended up on the cover of *Popular Science* with one of the top innovative products of the year.

The magic was that we'd built a new category, flying toys, from the ground up. We owned the category and were able to dominate it. We kept producing more planes and more line extensions: the V-Wing Avenger, the Storm Launcher, the Stinger. It wasn't a trend, and it wasn't a novelty. It was a signature product. From that day forward, toy inventors started pitching us more ideas, and we were able to build the business as a result of that. We had carved out and anchored our position in the industry.

The Sky Shark was the defining moment where we felt, "Wow, we have something real here," meaning the business as a whole, not just the product. We had built a good operation before, but this gave it a heft and weight and substance. Between the revenues and the global distribution and the accolades and the consumer satisfaction, our whole gestalt was "This can be a real business." And from that moment on, everybody in the toy industry was taking notice of us and saying, "Wow, look what these guys can do."

||

Strange as it may sound, there is a great deal of power in not knowing what you're doing. In business, as in many other endeavors, a healthy bit of ignorance can be one of your greatest assets. Because it means you don't know what's not possible. It means you don't know your own limitations. It means your confidence hasn't been slashed by the sting of failure. All of which means you're not starting out with any self-imposed limits on how far you can go, so there's a good chance you'll go further than you ever could have imagined.

It's also true that knowledge, experience, and evidence can

often lead you wrong, as it did for the far more experienced and qualified decision-makers at Hasbro and Mattel who passed on the multimillion-dollar opportunity of the Sky Shark because they "knew" that it couldn't be done. The history of the world is full of things that "couldn't be done." But then, inevitably, somebody came along and did them, and that somebody was typically someone who started out not knowing that the thing they were trying was supposed to be impossible. And while young people certainly don't have a monopoly on ignorance, you could say they have a distinct competitive advantage.

WHEN WE STARTED SPIN MASTER, we didn't know what we didn't know, and it served us well. It meant our minds were open to any possibility. Having that open mind is critical to one fundamental aspect of entrepreneurship, what I call "seeing the white space." The ability to see the white space is the first thing you need to understand about the power of not knowing. It's the ability to identify an opportunity in the marketplace that's not being filled and then fill it. Earth Buddies and devil sticks did not exist in the white space. Those were trends that were already happening that we were able to grab onto. The Sky Shark wasn't a part of a trend at all; nobody else was out there making anything similar. You wouldn't say it was a part of the zeitgeist, either, because the joy of flying is timeless, eternal. The Sky Shark existed in a white space. There was a massive void in the market, because people love flying toys, and there weren't any good flying toys that were safe and enjoyable for kids. Because we were able to see that white space and fill it, we reaped the reward for it. There's white space all around you, it's simply a matter of you being able to see it, identify it, and come up with something innovative and different to fill it with.

Oftentimes, the obstacle that's preventing you from seeing the white space is something that in other circumstances can have considerable value: knowledge and experience. Sometimes, knowing too much is actually a hindrance. It can make you overthink things, which then impedes you from taking action and taking risks. When we were offered the idea for the Sky Shark, if we had known all the risks and complexities and problems and expenses involved, we would have passed on it like Hasbro and Mattel did, because the whole process would have seemed too daunting. "We'll never be able to develop something this complex. How are we even going to afford it?" When you can visualize all the potential downsides of something, it's easy to talk yourself into saying "No."

Which is why, somewhat counterintuitively, sometimes it's better to know less. If you can't see a roadblock or a dead end up ahead, your possibilities are endless. As discussed in the earlier chapter on risk, there are always naysayers who can map out the downside for you, always. But you can't map out the upside. It's impossible. The upside is the most magical thing in life because whatever it turns out to be is probably something beyond your wildest dreams. When I started out making Earth Buddies at my mother's kitchen table, did I ever imagine myself ending up on the cover of *Popular Science* with one of the top innovative products of the year? Never. Not in a million years. But that's exactly what happened.

RECOGNIZING THE ENDLESS POSSIBILITY OF the white space, however, is only the first step. Once you see it, you still have to execute. You still have to get started and see the endeavor through to completion, and if you don't have a road map of knowledge and experience, what is it that guides your choices and actions along the way?

When I talk about the power of not knowing, another way of

saying the same thing would be to say that there are different ways of knowing. There is the rational, analytical part of your mind that knows things. It takes facts and information and processes them to reach logical conclusions. But there is another "knowing" part of the self, and that is intuition, following your gut. It's that nonrational, visceral feeling that tells you "This makes sense." You're not sure why it feels right. It just does. You don't know how you're going to do something. You just know that it needs to get done. You know something has to be true because you get so excited when you think about it.

In the early years of Spin Master, all through our twenties, intuition was our only guide. We never did anything for any reason other than "This would be really magical to create for the market, and if we make it the sales will follow." We focused on the idea of the product first and foremost. That was the driving force telling us "Let's go for it."

When we launched the Earth Buddy, literally all we knew was that the product was selling well in Israel. Our intuition told us, "Why would it not sell well here in North America? People are people, after all." That same gut instinct soon had us jumping feetfirst into the devil sticks business. We saw the kids playing with them around Toronto, we had a feeling in our bones, and we went for it. With the Sky Shark, we had that same sensation again, only magnified a thousand times over. The magic of watching it fly, feeling like kids, that was all we needed. We thought for half a second about the obvious issues we would face with safety and manufacturing. Then we shrugged and said we'd figure it out somehow. The one thing we didn't do was wait till we had all the answers.

Our naïveté gave us the power to start doing, and by being in the doing mode we unlocked a world of potential. We started to figure things out. One door opened and then another door opened and then new ideas came and those ideas opened even more doors down the road. It all built on itself. Very quickly we started getting feedback to our actions, and it was that accelerated feedback loop that gave us the critical information we needed on what to do next and how to do it.

You do have to be practical. You do have to balance your head and your heart. You need to research what's already out there in the marketplace, see who you're competing against. But don't overthink it. Don't spend your energy and time fretting over how it won't happen. Spend your energy and time on how you're going to make it happen. And above all else, at the end of the day, trust your passion and intuition to carry you through.

OF COURSE, WHEN YOU'RE YOUNG, the marketplace isn't the only thing you don't know about. You don't know a lot about a lot of things, including yourself. When you're in your twenties, you don't truly know who you are. You *think* you do, but when you reach middle age you'll likely look back and see that, really, you didn't. You didn't yet know what you were capable of. You didn't know your limitations, nor did you understand your real potential, and that is because you hadn't been tested yet.

None of us wants to endure hardship. Nobody wants to go through bad times, but as countless movies have shown us over and over, conflict and struggle are what reveal character. Life knocks you down, it humbles you and challenges you, and it's only in those moments that you're forced to dig deep and find the strength or the smarts to rise to the task in front of you. It's only then that you'll discover you have the qualities necessary to succeed.

For me, having a learning disability forced me to develop the ability to grind my way through school. I also learned a great deal about myself from having parents who were emotionally—and often physically—absent. Finding myself stranded when no one came to pick me up after hockey practice and Hebrew lessons, I learned how to take care of my own needs, how to find creative solutions to my own problems.

Still, even though the particular hardships of my childhood taught me a few valuable things about myself, when we started Spin Master I still had a lot to learn. At that point, I knew that I liked business and wanted to run a business, but I didn't yet have a handle on where and how my personality would best serve the business I wanted to build. It was with the development of the Sky Shark, however, that I threw myself into the deep end of the pool without knowing how to swim, and it was only by surviving that two-year crucible that I found out what my real strengths and talents were. The realization came to me one day deep into the process of working on the debug in China. Alex Perez, the engineer we'd hired from Mattel, had joined me at the factory to help oversee the debug. We were about a week into the process, stuck waiting for three days for certain parts to come out of the molds. Then, when they came out they didn't work. That set us back another five days and my temper flared and I lost it with Alex. I was mean to him. We're talking about a twenty-six-year-old kid dressing down a forty-year-old man, someone who was an experienced, highly qualified professional and a kind, decent person as well. Thank god it didn't happen in front of other people; it was only me and him. But it was still totally uncalled for, and it upset him a great deal. Most people would have quit on the spot and flown back home, but he stayed. I think our age difference and his maturity are part of what allowed him to get past it; he could see that I was young and I'd never been in this situation before. When I look back I'm always upset with myself for blowing up the way I did. I didn't mean anything personally, but the pressure got so high and Alex, unfortunately, happened to be standing there when I needed to vent.

Still, as much as I regret it, it served as a valuable lesson. I realized that we were nearly two years and several hundred thousand dollars into an extremely grueling and difficult process that was still having major problems, and this was the first time the stress got to be too much for me. Which is pretty remarkable. There are some who would have started getting frustrated and blowing their stack back in the design and prototyping phase in Chicago, and they would have kept on yelling and screaming at people, thinking that that was the proper way to motivate a team. The fact that I had kept my cool for that long, only blowing up at Alex that one time—and knowing it was a mistake almost as soon as I did it—taught me that I have a naturally high threshold for being patient with people, for staying calm and using positive energy as the means to motivate and inspire them, even under incredible levels of stress. Even with Alex, I'd built up enough goodwill working together that he was willing to take my outburst as the isolated incident that it was and not let it define our relationship for good.

During the whole two-year process of developing the Sky Shark, we encountered countless logistical and technical difficulties. But on the human side of the equation, in terms of managing egos and office politics and keeping everyone engaged and enthusiastic and working together, we didn't hit a single snag—and that was because of me. That was my superpower. Both of my parents were real characters with strong personalities, and being the peacemaker in the family was a skill I had to learn early on, so maybe it's something in my DNA. But whatever the reason, I was able to keep everyone happy and humming along while working in a quiet, humble fashion. That trait was probably in evidence during the early days of the Earth

Buddy and devil sticks, but neither of those endeavors had presented me with anything near the complexity or the pressure of manufacturing the Sky Shark. That was the real crucible that showed me I possessed a skill and a strength that I never knew about myself before.

It was only in setting myself an impossible task that I learned it was possible after all. I learned that I loved bringing new things into the world; I thrived on the creative process of willing things into being and all the magic that comes with it. If I'd stuck with what I knew how to do and what I had experience doing, Spin Master never would have grown into what it is today.

There are many reasons why we work—to support a family, to provide a service or a good for society—but one of the primary reasons to do anything in life is to learn more about yourself. That's why we're here, after all, to constantly work toward becoming the best possible version of ourselves. Which is why there's so much magic in not knowing how to do something, throwing yourself into it, and learning how. Traditional education certainly has its place. But traditional education is prescriptive. It's fed to you. When you learn through doing, you gain the experience. Then you need to extract the learning out of it, which you get by being curious and asking the right questions to the right people. Once you start to learn, the process becomes exciting and fills you with energy.

The magic of any undertaking comes from whatever feeling of discovery and growth you take away from it, which means that you have to start out in a place of not knowing, of being unsure, of taking a leap into the unknown. Of course, you won't stay young and inexperienced forever. If you're working hard and challenging yourself, you will begin to amass knowledge and, hopefully, even wisdom, which I would say takes at least twenty years or so. And experience and knowledge have myriad benefits as well; there is a joy that comes at the other end of the spectrum from not knowing, and that is in the total mastery of a subject or a craft. That is a rewarding place to get to in any endeavor. The trick in amassing that mastery is to never let the process become rote, and you achieve that by always balancing what you know with what you don't know, by staying out at the frontier where you're always exploring and learning and growing.

When I look back at the biggest failures in the history of our company, most of them have come from knowing too much, from intellectualizing our way to a product based on our ability to reason with the facts and evidence in front of us. "Why would this product *not* work?" we say. "There aren't any strong competitors in this category. The category itself hasn't been innovated in a while. This makes sense." When we've thought that way in the past, we haven't put 100 percent of our efforts into the details that make a project great, because we weren't as engaged in the process of challenging ourselves and learning something new.

Once you have the knowledge and experience to balance out your naïveté and intuition, the question you have to ask yourself is, *Should I let my mind make this decision, or should it come from my soul?* For me, the answer is that your mind can always help you figure out how to execute, but it's the soul that is best left to make the decision. Deferring to the mind takes the power of not knowing out of the equation and will always limit the realm of the possible.

Looking back to the beautiful summer day when we first flew the prototype of the Sky Shark in Wemberly Park nearly thirty years ago, it's staggering to compare how much I know about this business now versus what I didn't know then. But the not knowing was what made the magic happen. Without the slightest clue what we were getting ourselves into, like we did with the plane itself, we took our company, pumped it up, and flicked the propeller—and the damn thing took off. And suddenly, amazingly, we were flying at a totally different altitude than we'd ever experienced before.

6.

Luck

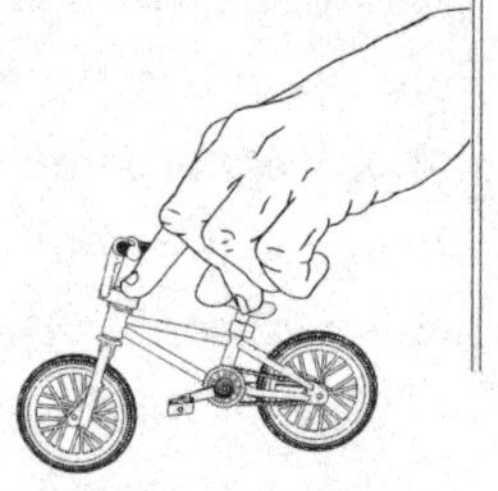

Jeff Rehkemper, in addition to running a company that de-signed and engineered toys, was a toy inventor himself. One morning during one of my many trips to Chicago to work on the Sky Shark, Jeff grabbed me in the hallway outside his office and said, "Hey, let me show you this cool new thing that I've been work-ing on."

At that point, I wasn't meeting with toy inventors. It had become Ben's responsibility to go and sit with them to hunt and gather new products. My role was to join Ben in reviewing the prototypes he brought in, so that we could make the final decision on which prod-ucts we would develop and bring to market. So I wasn't in Chicago that day looking for anything new. I was just there to check in on the next iteration of our plane. But toy inventors are a bit like kids them-selves. When they come up with an idea, they get excited and can't wait to show it to you. Plus, by that point, Jeff and I had developed a good relationship. We were friends, and he knew that I loved a good product, so he pulled me into his boardroom and showed me a prototype of a new toy he had made: a miniature BMX bike. It was made of white plastic, and he'd designed it so that if you put one finger through the handlebars and another finger on the seat, you could emulate the tricks that BMX bikers do in real life.

Putting the bike down on the table, Jeff used his fingers to start spinning the bike around, doing 360s and other cool moves. "It's got a real brake on the front," he said, using it to pop a front wheelie. "And if you press your finger down on the back seat, then you can push down on the back wheel and lift up the front wheel. And look, it has a real chain on it. You can move the pedals too. You put your finger in the handlebars and you can ride this thing around and do all these tricks."

I'd never owned a BMX bike growing up, but I'd seen people riding them around my neighborhood doing tricks all the time. The kids who could do it well, like the kids who could skateboard, were very cool. Part of me had always wanted a bike like they had; I'd just never gotten one. So as soon as I saw Jeff playing with his prototype, I said, "Cool, let me try." I slipped my finger through the handlebar and right away I could tell that it had a great fiddle factor. I instinctively wanted to play around with it. I started doing 360s and other tricks, and they felt real, like the moves that professional riders did on their bikes. It gave me great feedback, and that's the thing you're always looking for in toys, that magical feedback. Jeff had nailed that. The bike just *worked*, which meant my imagination was free to run wild with cool things to do with it.

I knew right away that the prototype I had in my hand had the pixie dust that Ben, Anton, and I needed a toy to have. I also had a feeling in my gut that this was another moment where the zeitgeist was waiting for a toy like this to come along. In the late 1990s, alternative sports were having a moment. The X Games had started a few years prior, Tony Hawk was becoming a household name in skateboarding, and snowboarding was named an Olympic sport at the

1998 Winter Olympics in Japan. BMX racing was a huge part of that rapidly growing subculture, with the American rider Dave Mirra becoming a sensation, winning four consecutive X Games medals. Kids followed the biggest stars and tricked out their bikes to be like the bikes that their idols had. In that moment, an older person might have said, "Who wants to play with a miniature bike that fits between your fingers?" But my intuition told me that Jeff was onto something. He watched me as I kept on fiddling and playing with it, and he could tell I was having fun. He knew he had me hooked.

"Why don't I option it right now?" I said. "How much?"

He thought about it for a second and said, "Five grand."

Five thousand was a small option; the fee for the Sky Shark had been fifty. But Jeff's attitude was not "This is the greatest toy ever and I need to shop it around to get the highest offer from the biggest company I can." It was more that he loved it and saw how much fun I was having and so a reasonable option made sense. Plus the size of the option doesn't matter much since the royalties are pretty much standard on all inventor products. So we signed the deal right there on the spot. It was all done in twenty minutes.

Because the prototype was so small—and because I loved playing with it so much—I said to Jeff, "Let me take it back to the office," and I took it home with me to Toronto and showed it to Ben and the team. Their immediate response was, "Yeah, that's really cool. Let's go." Everything fell into place.

Over the next few months we took Jeff's design and improved on it by producing real, die-cast replica bikes that had miniature rubber tires, working brakes and pedals, everything a kid could want. Knowing how much BMX fans idolized their favorite riders and the bikes they rode, we went out and got licensing deals with some of the major bike manufacturers, companies like Redline, Mongoose, and Hoffman, so that our bikes would be scaled-down versions of the same ones the most popular BMX riders were using. The whole idea was that the bikes would be collectible, like Hot Wheels, so that kids would want to collect all their favorites. We even hired a guy from a bike shop, Connor, to come in and help us get the designs right. He ended up having a hand in helping us think up the name, which in the end was pretty simple and obvious. It was a bike, and you did tricks by flicking it. So: Flick Trix.

Proof that we were riding a good wave of the zeitgeist came when we learned that another company, Jakks Pacific, was coming out with a similar product called Road Champs. They were out chasing licenses from the major BMX brands as well, and we ended up splitting the market; we got half the licenses and sales, and they got the other half. Luckily, the market turned out to be more than big enough for both of us.

When Flick Trix hit stores in 1999, they took off. It seemed like everywhere you went, young boys were playing with them. Soon we were selling ramps and bowls to do tricks in, and those accessories became some of our biggest items. Same as with devil sticks and Air Hogs, we were working overtime from day one to keep up with the demand, selling tens of millions of dollars a year of inventory to the biggest retailers in the world. I can still remember sitting in the Walmart offices with Frank Craven. Frank was the buyer for Hot Wheels, and if you wanted a spot in the aisle for the die-cast toys at Walmart, he was the guy. I always felt like Frank had a special spot in his heart for us. He looked at Anton, Ben, and me and felt like something of a father figure to us. He was the one who chose to stock Flick Trix over Road Champs, which he did in part because we had a better product at a better price, but also because he just liked us. He liked that we were young and passionate. Every time we'd go meet with him, the four of us would sit there, eating M&Ms and smoking cigarettes and talking about life. He'd give us advice, teach us about the business, and then sign another purchase order for the next big shipment of Flick Trix.

And the only reason those sales happened—the only reason Flick Trix even came into existence—was because I happened to be in Jeff Rehkemper's office the day he felt like grabbing someone and saying, "Hey, I've got something cool to show you." In other words, it was luck. You can't run a business without luck. Fortunately, when it comes to luck, the popular cliché is actually true: You can make your own.

||

Luck is when you create an opportunity for yourself, have the ability to see it, and have the confidence to actualize it. Some people believe that luck is something that comes from the universe, and that is true, in part. But the secret is that the universe is willing to meet you halfway. When you're putting forth a real effort to make your own luck, the universe will reward you in ways your mind can't even begin to fathom.

To start, it's important to differentiate luck from what might more accurately be referred to as dumb luck, or chance. Chance is what comes from a random spin of the wheel of fortune. Good or ill, it's a fluke that manifests in your life through no meaningful effort of your own. Chance is winning the lottery. It's pulling the lever on a slot machine and—with the odds at a thousand to one—actually hitting the jackpot. Or, on the negative side of the ledger, it's getting rear-ended at a stop sign on your way to work, or watching as a terrible winter storm puts a tree through your roof. Luck is something else entirely. When you get lucky, it can have that same feeling of randomness that comes with bad weather or a good roll of the dice. But true luck isn't random at all.

||

Luck comes from doing. Luck is what manifests in your life because of the hard work and effort you're putting out into the world. With Flick Trix, at the time, the whole thing felt like it fell in my lap. It just so happened that Jeff had finished his prototype and was eager to show it off the day I dropped by his office. It just so happened that I'd chosen that exact day to visit; if I'd come down the following week, someone from Hasbro or Mattel might have wandered through and snapped it up before I did. It just so happened that alternative sports like BMX racing and skateboarding and snowboarding were having their moment in the zeitgeist, and it just so happened that I was enough of a fan of that stuff to feel the magic in what Jeff had built.

So I got lucky. But my being in Jeff's office on that day wasn't random at all. I was in that office as frequently as I was because I was dedicated to making the best product we possibly could with the Sky Shark, and that dedication and perseverance had put me in the mix of everything that was happening in the toy industry. Whenever you hear stories about someone being "in the right place at the right time," it might be attributable to pure chance, but it's far more likely that there's a reason that person was in that particular place at that particular time. It's because they did something to put themselves there.

The fact that I was someone whom Jeff was eager to show his invention to, that wasn't random either. Through the Sky Shark, we had committed ourselves to a serious, intensive working relationship with his company. I'd made something like ten trips to Chicago by that point, and I think he was able to see the seriousness and earnestness in my approach to business. He saw the effort I was putting in. From that he had a sense of my character and our company's work ethic, and that is likely what made him feel comfortable showing me the prototype and signing an option with me right there on the spot. If I hadn't been putting in that kind of time and effort, I don't think he would have felt comfortable striking up a deal with me as casually as he did.

The same thing was true in all our early successes as a company. There were always elements that felt random and serendipitous as they were happening, but when I look back and reverse-engineer the process, from the very beginning our lucky breaks were almost always the fruit of efforts we'd been putting out into the universe, inviting the universe to meet us halfway. We were young kids with an openness to engage with the world, asking people to help us and get involved, eager to listen to what they had to say. And because we were putting ourselves out there in such an open way, launching the Earth Buddy went from lucky to luckier to even luckier all the way through: We get set up with a buyer at the then-largest retailer in America, only it turns out that he's the wrong buyer, but I'm lucky that he takes the time to find out who the right buyer is. Then I go roaming around Kmart's corporate headquarters—with zero permission from anyone—looking for this lady and I'm super lucky again that she's sitting at her desk at that exact moment in time. She's not in a meeting. She's not out sick or downstairs having a smoke or a coffee. And then, just like that, barely two months after my mom picked up her newspaper, we've got an order for half a million pieces from Kmart—all of which grew out of a relationship that Anton had with a guy he met backpacking in Europe the year before.

How lucky is that?

OF COURSE, IT SHOULD BE clear by now the way in which luck typically manifests itself: through other people. We've all heard the cliché about nepotism in business, that "It's who you know." We're all well-versed in the need to be "networking" all the time. But that's not what I'm talking about here, not exactly. Indeed, if you approach life as nothing more than networking, if you treat your relationships with other people in a purely transactional way, they'll know it, and they won't regard you as a genuine partner or friend.

Luck is not a quid pro quo. It's not doing a favor just to get a favor in return. The luck—as I've said before and will say again—is in the doing. Meaningful bonds, whether personal or professional, are built on experiences, time spent together engaged in whatever gives you a shared sense of purpose. And, paradoxically, the more you focus on the happiness and fulfillment of the other person, the happier and more fulfilled you will feel yourself. When you approach life that way, by being a good friend or family member, by being a good colleague or classmate, what you're doing is seeding ground that will eventually bear fruit, bringing you the luck that you need. Then, to bring that luck out into the open, typically all you have to do is ask for it. Whenever you ask for help or advice, like Anton asking his Michigan friend for help getting into Kmart, the opportunity that you set in motion years before will suddenly manifest itself.

The entire history of Spin Master is a history of relationships generating some form of luck, starting with my mom. My mom wanted to read me the article about the Earth Buddy, translating it from Hebrew, which I could never have read on my own, because she wanted to share ideas that might help me start a business. My grandmother wanted to bring me an Earth Buddy, which I never could have ordered for myself in that pre-internet era, because our family always put in the effort to stay in touch, even across the ocean.

My sister and brother-in-law wanted to help us as well, and it was an incredible stroke of luck not only that he was an autodidact genius who was able to engineer a mass-manufacturing process for us completely from scratch, but that he was willing to do the whole thing for a back-end profit share in lieu of an up-front fee. I can't even begin to give my brother-in-law enough credit for our success. Maybe someone else could have figured out the same process, but not at the speed, scale, and precision that he did. I wouldn't even have known where to go to find someone like him if he hadn't been in my family.

The same serendipity repeated itself again and again through the people we encountered in every subsequent endeavor. Jenn Irwin wanted to introduce Ben to the toy inventors her family knew, because he'd always been such a good roommate and friend, which led us to the Sky Shark. Jeff Rehkemper wanted to show me his BMX bike prototype, because he'd seen what a diligent and dedicated partner I'd been. Frank Craven wanted to put Flick Trix in Walmart, because he found joy in being a mentor to young guys in the business.

None of those relationships were purely transactional. They were built on genuine affection, mutual respect, and a shared feeling of purpose. You put good work and good energy and a positive attitude out into the world, and then someday, somehow, via some means you never could have imagined, an opportunity will come back your way. It will feel random and serendipitous in the moment. It won't appear to have any direct, concrete correlation to any of your actions in the past. But once you sit down and analyze it in hindsight, you'll see how that moment could only have been generated by the dense web of interpersonal connections that you yourself created, and as noted in the partnership chapter, your early twenties are an unparalleled time for being out in the world, meeting people, and forging lifelong relationships.

Given that people are the primary vectors of luck, it's also true that you can exponentially increase your own luck by surrounding yourself with other lucky people, and by "lucky people" I simply mean good people, people who carry around good karma because they've been building their own powerful web of meaningful interpersonal connections. If you've surrounded yourself with lucky people, people who have the same values and the same drive that you do, then their luck will inevitably rub off on you.

And, needless to say, you can't outsource your luck. When I wanted to sell the Earth Buddy to Kmart, I could have mailed the product to the rep and had him do the pitch instead of waking up before dawn and driving to Detroit to pitch it myself. But then most likely nothing would have come of it. Nothing counts for more than in-person, personal relationships. Or, as I'm fond of saying, "If you don't go, you don't get."

OF COURSE, IT'S ONE THING to surround yourself with opportunities to get lucky. It's something else to convert those lucky opportunities into tangible results. The funny thing is, some of the smartest, most well-connected people in business, the people who get into Wharton and Harvard Business School because they come from established families with powerful social networks, often end up taking the conventional route of working for other people. They're sitting on all this potential to get lucky, and they can't see it, so they don't ever tap into it, perhaps because they've never needed to.

Networking alone is never enough. You have to have the ability to see an opportunity as soon as it pops up in front of you, and you have to have the confidence to jump on it and actualize it. There are plenty of people who work hard their whole life but don't feel like they ever get lucky. I would contend that hard work always generates its own luck, but the people we consider to be lucky are the ones who are able to capitalize on an opportunity when it's there to be seized.

Luck exists. Your actions are generating more of it all the time, and it's there whether you actualize it or not. I've always found the term "überluck" to be helpful. "Luck" is the word I use to describe the good fortune that's waiting out there in the universe, while "überluck" is what comes when you understand the opportunity life is giving you and you have the confidence to move forward and capitalize on it rather than let it pass you by. It's having the faith that on the other side of that opportunity there's something interesting and magical.

There is luck to be found in anything, even failure. If you fail so badly that it destroys your business and that's the end of the road, well, that is what it is. Life happens. But any failure that doesn't kill you is, ultimately, another form of luck. Because you have to learn how to run a business, and—as we'll see in a subsequent chapter—failure is the lucky break that gives you the opportunity to learn something. I call it learning luck. You may lose a couple hundred thousand dollars and have to liquidate a season's worth of inventory, but odds are you'll take something away from that experience that will give you an even bigger win in the future. I always tell people that if you're batting .600 in the toy industry, you're doing well. That 60 percent success rate is where you find the luck. And the 40 percent where you've failed? That's where the learning luck is. So, at the end of the day, whether you're succeeding or failing, as long as you're doing, you're still getting lucky.

In fact, I would go so far as to say that the universe *wants* you to be lucky. Just look around you. From the Big Bang straight through to today, creation and evolution and transformation are the driving forces of life as we know it. (Destruction, too, but that is simply part and parcel of the process of creation.) The universe is one humongous engine that takes energy and transforms it into new and different kinds of energy. The universe wants things to happen. The universe is dynamic. The choice for you is simply to decide to be a part of that dynamic creation and transformation that's happening all around you all the time.

||

Or you can decide not to be a part of it. Because that's the other option. You can let yourself be held back by the voices of doubt and fear in your mind—and that, in my experience, is the only thing that can stop you from being lucky. Doubt is the antiluck, and that is because doubt is a momentum killer. Once you lose your momentum, your luck evaporates. If you pass on an opportunity out of fear, then all of a sudden you're not in the hallway outside Jeff Rehkemper's office when the next opportunity comes along—you're out of the mix.

Which is not to say that you should barrel ahead in life saying yes to everything. If there's a sound reason to pass on a project, then pass on the project. But don't let doubt and fear cripple you and hold you back from something that excites you. Do your due diligence, but learn to go with your gut. Go back and check your facts and figures, but don't check too much. When something feels right, when your intuition says go and the inspiration hits and the opportunities present themselves, don't take too long to walk through that door. Commit when the feeling is fresh, because there's magic in that feeling that may not be there a week or even a day from now. Luck exists only in the moment; it doesn't wait for anyone.

The more we trust in ourselves and don't second-guess our intuition, the luckier our life becomes. I remember having the conversation with my mom and my late grandmother about buying the Earth Buddies from people in Israel. They thought it would be less risky to source the product there, but for me it was clear that we needed to manufacture them ourselves so we wouldn't put our fate in someone else's hands and get stuck waiting for fulfillment. I just knew it. I had zero doubt.

Doubt is the momentum killer. The more you let it creep into your life, the less lucky you're going to be. I know this for a fact because, as confident and as lucky as I've been in business, I've let doubt and fear govern my personal life for . . . well, for my whole life. Which is not to say that personal relationships are the same as business. They're not. But as I write this, I'm fifty-four and single with no kids. All through my twenties and thirties, with every serious girl-friend, instead of opening my heart and going with what felt right to me at the time, I was crippled with doubt. I always overanalyzed and second-guessed everything about every relationship I was in.

For me, committing myself to the business meant throwing my-self into something that was always dynamic. It's called the shiny penny syndrome. When you're developing products, there is always something new and different and original that you're bringing out into the world. A growing business is like an ever-expanding uni-verse. I believed, wrongly, that the commitment of a marriage would feel like a contracting universe. Deep down I think I had a fear of being trapped in a space that was confined and static. I wasn't mature enough to have an understanding of the shiny penny potential of having a family and kids and a home and a wife. Having made that mistake, what I'm trying to do now is to take my own advice, to get back to a state of openness and wonder and possibility, to put myself out there so that, hopefully, the universe will meet me halfway.

But it's hard. At fifty-four, it's hard. Which is why, as with everything I've set out in the book, it is so critical to start when you're young.

Luck is all about momentum. The energy you have when you're young, the stamina to travel the world, to go to every trade show—all that creates a flywheel effect, generating the energy and the opportu-nities that will keep you moving. Like bank interest, it compounds over time. Slowly at first, but with remarkable returns over the long haul. You start out with a bit of chutzpah and you get out there in the universe, pushing it and driving it, and the universe starts feeding you back, creating a constant feedback loop. One thing builds on another thing, which leads to another thing—which is exactly what happened with Flick Trix.

Right around the time we went out with Flick Trix, another company in San Diego launched Tech Deck, which was a finger skateboard to fiddle and do tricks with as opposed to a finger BMX bike. Tech Deck became a direct competitor of Flick Trix, and they had such an incredible brand there was no way we could make a skateboard to compete with theirs. Five years later we ended up buying them, paying the founder about $7 million for the business with a 7 percent royalty over ten years.

Today, Flick Trix has come and gone. We rode its $100 million a year for three or four years, and then it petered out. But Tech Deck is still going strong. It's been around for twenty-plus years now, and it still generates around $70 million a year for us. And none of that happens if I'm not in the hallway outside Jeff Rehkemper's office on the day he decides to share his new BMX bike prototype. And that doesn't happen if we don't buy the Sky Shark. And we don't ever buy the Sky Shark if Ben isn't out cultivating relationships with inventors he met through his roommate's dad's toy business. And Ben isn't even a part of our company if Anton doesn't make him homemade soup in exchange for his notes in college. And on and on and on— you get the idea, the fundamental premise of which is this: If you put yourself out there, if you put in the work, you will create opportunities for yourself that you can't even fathom today. One day down the line they'll appear seemingly out of nowhere and you'll think, *Hey, isn't that lucky?* And it *is* lucky, because unbeknownst to you, you've created your own luck.

In the moment, you won't see exactly how everything fits together; I certainly didn't. It's only in looking back that I understand how lucky we got along the way. In fact, for a long time, at least the first ten years we were in business, I thought eventually we'd run out of ideas. Certainly we'd reach a point where we were tapped out and couldn't come up with anything new. And it's never happened. We've never run out of ideas. There's always something new and exciting ahead of us, and that's because we keep creating it ourselves, feeding the universe—and it always, always feeds us back.

7.
Failure

did a lot of dumb things as a kid. As a result, my high school years were colorful, and not always in a good way. Since I was always entrepreneurial, and because I always needed spending money, I got myself into trouble more than once. I didn't take any major risks; I made most of my money the old-fashioned way—delivering newspapers, shoveling driveways, selling cable subscriptions. But at the same time I was always trying to work an angle, and whenever I did that I usually fell flat on my face.

One time I bought sixteen tickets for a Pink Floyd concert. I had to camp out for three days to get them. Then I went around and put up posters saying I had Pink Floyd tickets, cutting those little tabs on the bottom for people to tear off my number. My phone started ringing and I scalped them for $300 a pop, netting about $3,000 in profit, which would be about ten grand today. Then I took all that money and bought a penny stock that a guy in my high school recommended to me. My dad cautioned against it. "If you want to buy this stock," he said, "take $1,500 and invest that. Save the rest." But I was stubborn, and the guy who'd told me about the stock was one of the smooth kids in my class, the kind of guy who seemed like he knew what was up. So I sank the whole $3,000 into this one penny stock. Naturally, it went to zero, and I lost everything.

Not long after, I bought a bunch of tickets for The Who, put up my posters, and started to scalp those. One evening I got a call and told the guy he could come to my house to pick them up. The doorbell rang that night while we were eating dinner. I went to the front door, and there was this couple.

"How many tickets do you have?" they asked.

"A lot," I said.

"Can we see them all?"

"Give me a second."

I ran down to the basement where my bedroom was. I had sixteen tickets, but as I was counting them out I started to get this weird feeling about the couple, so I only took six tickets up to show them. They looked at the six tickets, and the next thing I knew they pulled out their badges.

"This is not legal," they said. "We need to write you up a summons."

"Ma!" I called to the dining room, not knowing what else to do.

Soon I was sitting at the dinner table with my parents and two cops as they wrote me up a summons and confiscated the six tickets. Then they left and we sat down and finished dinner. My mom and dad didn't skip a beat, didn't care in the least. There wasn't even any conversation about it. I think they probably thought, *Our son is being commercial and entrepreneurial, and that's a good thing. So what if he had to break some silly rule. Don't the cops have better things to do with their time? Don't they have real criminals to catch?*

In fact, I think it was my mom who encouraged me to go to the police station the next day and ask for my tickets back. Which I did. I went down and said, "Those are my tickets. How can they take my tickets?" Luckily, there was some gray area in the law. Yes, I'd tried to scalp them, but legally they were still mine. So I got my tickets back from the cops and I unloaded them quickly and quietly, pocketing far less than I'd made on the tickets for Pink Floyd.

My abject failure as a ticket scalper and penny-stock speculator offered me an important entrepreneurial learning moment. I'd been trying to do things quickly to make money, only to lose that money just as quickly, even getting busted for skirting the law in the process. What I learned was that get-rich-quick schemes never work. Even if they seem to work, they always collapse. You can't cut corners to make money in life. Luckily for me, even after the ticket-scalping fiasco, the universe kept teaching me lessons on how to take the long road. "The short cuts are long cuts," as my father liked to say. You have to be methodical, dedicated, and diligent. So with the universe telling me to stay in the middle lane of life, I stuck to shoveling driveways and selling cable subscriptions.

Given that learning experience, as Campus Faces grew into Spin Master Toys, Anton and I both knew we weren't in this to build some fly-by-night operation. We moved fast and took risks and challenged ourselves, but we were actually fairly conservative and calculated in the endeavors we took on. We took some big swings, but we weren't out there chasing wild pitches. To this day, I think our company could have been even bigger if we'd been looser in our approach. Still, as a result of how measured we were, for the first several years we were in business, we didn't have any big, spectacular failures. We had missteps and misjudgments, products that didn't meet expectations, things we might have done differently with hindsight, but nothing in the way of a total, complete, and absolute face-plant.

Then came Key Charm Cuties.

||

Key Charm Cuties were Spin Master's inauspicious debut in the category of dolls. One of the biggest complaints kids have about dolls is how difficult it can be to dress and undress them, stretching the tiny blouses and skirts around the stiff plastic arms and legs, and one of our big innovations with Key Charm Cuties was that they each came with a wardrobe made out of this plastic material that you could easily take on and off. They were small dolls, about three inches in height, and the other unique thing about them was that they each came inside their own purse. You could open up the purse and there was a play set inside, so you could travel with your doll and have your own play set wherever you were. The big feature item of the line was this rolling suitcase. You opened it up, and inside was a whole world for kids to play with. Then there were a bunch of charms and other accessories that came along with it.

When the pitch for Key Charm Cuties first came in from an inventor, my gut feeling was that I didn't love it. I didn't have that Air Hogs moment where I said, "Wow, this is incredible." At the time, as eager as I was to move into new categories, I didn't have a feel for what were known as "girls' toys." That type of play pattern—what we called the "donkey donk" play pattern, moving a doll around in a play set—wasn't my thing. I was and still am much more connected to the action of flying toys and radio control cars and such.

Ben, however, was very excited about the pitch, and because we were a company started and run by three young guys, we had a fairly large gender gap in the kids we were reaching. Air Hogs, Flick Trix, devil sticks—they all appealed mostly to boys, which meant we were failing to fully tap into half of our potential customers. Girls' toys are a huge market. The doll business alone is a billion-dollar category. And since Ben was excited, I wanted to be a good partner and back him. Plus I had that classic entrepreneurial spirit in me that was thrilled by the fun of taking on a new challenge simply because it was a new challenge. So I said, "Cool. Let's try it. If you have the vision for it, I'll back it up." But I was definitely reasoning more from an intellectual place instead of feeling it in my gut.

Development on Key Charm Cuties took about a year and a half, and in all that time none of us foresaw doom on the horizon. Whenever you're working on something that takes that much effort, you want to keep a confident, positive attitude about it. That's absolutely necessary to keep up the creativity and dedication that it takes to bring something to market. But that positivity has a downside in that it might prevent you from having the healthy skepticism you might need. That was our first mistake. We were working in a bit of a bubble and were quite naïve about what we were getting into in terms of girls' toys and dolls. We didn't understand the category, and we didn't do the research that we should have.

The fact is that when it comes to dolls, Mattel owns the category. They've got Barbie, Polly Pocket—they're the single biggest player in that space, doing about a billion-plus dollars a year. Challenging Mattel in dolls is like going up against Google in search. You can do it, but you'd better give people a compelling reason to try your product, and that was our second mistake. The fact that Key Charm Cuties had unique clothing that you could put on the doll, coupled with the fact that each purse transformed into its own play set, was innovative, but not innovative enough. It didn't have a wow factor. There wasn't enough magic in the toy to give us the differentiator to break into the category. Our execution, in terms of the style and fashion of the dolls, wasn't where it needed to be to compete against a company like Mattel. Our third mistake came with the marketing. If you're going to compete against Mattel in the category of girls' toys, your marketing had better be top-notch, and ours was nowhere near where it needed to be.

On top of that came the normal challenges that accompany the launch of any new product, chief of which is that you never know what big new toys you're going to be in competition with. In any given year, you might get excited to jump into a new category. You pour your heart and soul into a new idea, develop it over a year and a half, bring it to market, advertise it, and give it the biggest push you can. But there's always going to be something else on the shelf that's vying for the same dollars in the same category. And that was true here as well. I don't recall specifically what was happening in the doll category that year, but whatever it was, it was better than Key Charm Cuties. We were only three weeks into the launch when we started reading the point-of-sale (POS) data and realized, "This is not going to fly." The numbers were awful. Retailers were stacked with merchandise, we had tons of it sitting in our warehouse, and even more on the water from Asia. We were still in a full-court press with marketing and advertising, but the product wasn't gaining the momentum that it needed to gain.

Then, in rapid succession, came two more disasters. The first was Don't Free Freddy. Don't Free Freddy was a big stuffed animal with two arms locked together. Anytime you unlocked his arms he had these sensors that would go off and he'd start to roar and freak out. Which is a *terrible* idea for a toy. Why would you make a product like that? Just writing that description of it now, twenty-five years later, makes me wonder what the hell we were thinking.

The truth, for me at least, was that I wasn't thinking. Don't Free Freddy was another toy that came from an inventor. At that point, we were still trying to develop relationships with established inventors, and the only way to do that was to produce some products with them. Plus, at that point we were all a bit enamored with the inventors because they were older and more experienced than we were, which put us in the position of thinking they knew something we didn't. They would be pitching us, selling us their dreams, and it was hard not to get caught up in their enthusiasm, so what happened was that I ended up outsourcing a bit of the decision-making to them.

Don't Free Freddy was also another instance of us being excited to do something new and different because it was new and different. We had never done a plush toy, which is a big category we were eager to break into because it offered a lot of upside. We had also never done anything mechanical, like these sensors that popped his arms open, so that was an interesting challenge as well. It would have been better to be more judicious and wait for another pitch, but we didn't, and we struck out again. Don't Free Freddy was an even bigger flop than Key Charm Cuties. Key Charm Cuties was, in and of itself, a good product. It just wasn't innovative enough to stand out in a crowded marketplace. With plush toys, kids have to buy into that character, which is why it's actually a higher-risk category than dolls. A plush toy is either a hero or a zero, and Freddy was a zero. No one liked him. That was a stiff, a total bomb.

Then came the real stinker, Tickle Secrets Baby. Tickle Secrets Baby was a disaster. The idea was that you'd tickle the baby in various places and it would emote in different ways. The desire was for it to be a must-have doll for girls, for it to be engaging and lovable and interactive. But baby dolls, as we would soon learn, are an even riskier bet than plush toys. It's one of the hardest categories to get right, and we were out of our depth. Despite the fact that our execution was good, we failed because it was a weak idea from the start.

The simple fact is that the more established a category is, the higher the threshold for innovation needs to be to break through. We got lucky with Air Hogs and Flick Trix. Those products weren't just the fruit of our hard work and dedication. They were both highly innovative compared to the competition, were backed up by an ongoing trend that captured the zeitgeist, and in many ways blazed trails into new categories of their own. With Key Charm Cuties and

Don't Free Freddy and Tickle Secrets Baby, we had none of that going for us. We had no wind at our backs. If we'd been smarter, we would have said to ourselves, "Okay, because we're going into an established category, this has to be the most magical toy ever." But we didn't have that knowledge, and Tickle Secrets Baby failed as a result.

Those three failures—Key Charm Cuties, Don't Free Freddy, and Tickle Secrets Baby—all came back-to-back-to-back over the course of two years, two disastrous Christmas shopping seasons. Luckily, we were well diversified. Flick Trix and Air Hogs were still going strong at the time, so we were able to take the hit, and, as with my brief and lackluster career in ticket-scalping, the upside of our failure came in the form of a real world-class education on toys—and the best time to get an education, obviously, is when you're young.

||

Too many people believe that failure is a bad thing, a mark of shame, something to be embarrassed about. The fact is that, in business, there are two types of failure. The first is systemic. It's failing to run a competent organization. It's buying too much inventory and sitting on it as it eats up your cash flow. It's hiring too many people and getting out over your skis. It's letting your ego get in the way of good judgment, creating an unhealthy work environment that can't recruit or retain good employees. That kind of failure *is* a bad thing. It's completely unacceptable.

The second kind of failure comes with the products and services you're putting out into the world. You have an idea, invest yourself in it, work hard on it, and give it all the love you can, only to turn around and watch it crash and burn in the marketplace. Those failures are nothing to be ashamed of. Those failures are necessary. They're *good*. As Anton is fond of saying, "Failure is a gift."

||

The first reason it's good to fail when you're young is that, at that age, it's not such a big deal. Any setback can seem catastrophic while it's happening. You might *feel* like everything is on the line. But the truth is that when you're young you don't have very far to fall. You probably don't have a family to support. You don't have a massive portfolio to lose. You can take your licks, crash on someone's couch for a few weeks, put yourself back together, and move on. Failing when you're young also means you've got lots of runway left, not to mention the energy to start over and keep going. When the dust settles from your spectacular face-plant, you'll find you've got plenty of time to recover and figure out the next path. You might pick yourself up and say, "I loved the experience, and I want to try again." Or, "That was grueling and horrible and this life is not for me." Either way you will have lots of time to either push forward in business or to find a different road and take your learnings with you. You will also give yourself the gift of taking a potential regret off your bucket list. You won't ever need to wonder, *Should I have pursued that dream?* Because you did, whether you succeeded at it or not.

It's also good to fail when you're young because the world is more forgiving of your mistakes. You're not supposed to have everything figured out, and everyone around you knows that. It's not like you're forty-five years old and you ought to know better, so you don't need to feel like an idiot for screwing something up. As long as you own your mistakes and take responsibility for cleaning up whatever mess you made, people are inclined to cut you a little slack. More than that, they'll likely be impressed that you took a potential catastrophe and managed it as well as you could. Instead of being written off as someone who failed, you'll gain the reputation of someone who can cope successfully with failure.

YOUR EARLY TWENTIES ARE ALSO the time when you *need* to experience failure in order to learn the lessons that it can teach you. People tend to respond to failure in one of two ways. The first is that they don't take it seriously. They're shortsighted, wide-eyed, and naïve. They don't see disaster looming on the horizon, don't take responsibility for averting it, and even when it happens they don't fully appreciate what's happened to them because they don't want to stare their own shortcomings in the face. Other people obsess over failure. They take it personally. Every stumble, every mishap, they let it eat away at their sense of self-confidence and self-worth. Neither of these is the correct response. The fact is that you have to take failure seriously, but you can't take it personally. You've got to tackle it and grapple with it head-on, but you can't let it get to you.

When it comes to failure in business, the old cliché is true: Anything that doesn't kill you makes you stronger. The more you fail, the less catastrophic each failure seems, and you learn how to not feel crushed, how to get back up, dust yourself off, and start again. You develop resilience, grit. You learn to see failure not as disaster, but simply as a natural part of the ebb and flow of running a business. Some products work, some don't, and no one setback is the end of the world. You begin to learn that success and failure are not two separate things but more a progression of experiences, each one providing more data and clarity on where and how to go next. You can't learn that in a classroom, or from reading this book, because even if you grasp the concepts of grit and resilience intellectually, you only begin to develop those traits once life has knocked you around and forced you to develop the right coping skills.

The need to develop qualities like grit and resilience is universal. We all have our own weaknesses and personality quirks that we have to learn to cope with and compensate for, and we all have to go through our own crucibles to test ourselves and find out what they are. For me, one of the most important lessons was learning not to get emotionally attached to things that don't work. In our business, when a toy doesn't do well, very rarely can you revive it and bring it back. It's possible, but the odds are against you. Ninety-nine percent of the time, a failure is a failure. Anton and Ben never had a problem letting go when something didn't work out. It's actually scary how emotionally detached they are. They can let go and move on in a heartbeat. Anton's passion has always been for forging relationships and making deals, not for products. Ben, meanwhile, loves toys, but what he's really excited about is the creative process itself, the craft of finding and developing something new and innovative, something with that magic spark. When a product flops, by definition it doesn't meet his standard for being new and innovative and fun, at which point Ben is more than happy to move on.

I was different. I used to get very wrapped up in whatever we were making. I was a walking sunk-cost fallacy. I'd be like, "Well, we've invested all this time and we've got the tooling and these molds and these raw materials. There's got to be more that we can make out of all the effort we've put in here." But while I was agonizing, Ben and Anton would already be ready to move on, and their approach was 100 percent the right one. Being able to make decisions quickly and cut your losses early is something Ben and Anton were always able to do exceptionally well from the start. In my case, it was something I had to learn.

||

Your failures will offer you practical nuts-and-bolts lessons as well. For us, the biggest of these was learning how to clean up a major product that blew up on the launchpad.

The cycle in the toy business is that you do a ton of work for a year and a half to get a new product ready to launch. Then you sell it in and get your retail space and your marketing campaign up and running. Then, once you're in stores you start reading the POS, and from there you can game out what's going to happen. It's incredibly scientific and weirdly accurate. As you head into the fall holiday season, by September 1, you can look at the amount of shelf space you have and say, "I'm selling three pieces per week per store." From there you can extrapolate the rest of the year and know your quantities and know whether or not that product is going to make it. That's when you make the call, well in advance of the actual Christmas season. If you know you're not going to make it, you do some price cuts for the retailers so they can bring the $29.99 item down to $19.99 and the $19.99 item down to $9.99 and so on. You can't be in love with any of it, even with a year and a half of your life invested in it. You clean it up and clear it out and move on.

Key Charm Cuties was the first major closeout we had to do, and luckily, having been in the industry for six years at that point, we had a sense of what needed to be done and we pulled it off. It wasn't one of those things where you're a deer in headlights going "What do we do?!" We knew from the Irwin family that the thing that will kill you in the toy business is having product sitting on the shelf at the retailer or in your warehouse. Piled-up inventory is the kiss of death, because it's sucking up the cash that's the oxygen you need to breathe. From the start we had always been judicious about how much inventory we kept on hand. We would actually err on the side of caution and sometimes lose sales as the result of not having enough units ready to ship. So, fortunately, when Key Charm Cuties failed to take off, while we had a fair amount of inventory to move, our exposure wasn't as bad as it might have been and we were able to close out the product at the right time, before it could do enough damage to sink us. In fact, I don't think we lost money in the end. We probably broke even, so the damage was more about the opportunity cost and missing our chance to make profits and apply them against overheads.

ON TOP OF THOSE PRACTICAL lessons, probably the single most important thing failure will give you is a better understanding of what failure is and the role it plays in business—and the younger you are when you learn that lesson, the better off you'll be down the road.

In any business, you have to keep moving. Momentum, the quantity of a body's motion, measured as a product of its mass and velocity, is the foundation of any successful enterprise. That's because momentum begets momentum. And the truth about failure—counterintuitive as it may seem—is that failure creates its own momentum. Even as you're falling and flailing and fumbling about, you're still *moving*. You're still generating energy, and you can use it to push yourself forward instead of being pushed backward—and that's what we did throughout the whole two-year debacle of Key Charm Cuties and Don't Free Freddy and Tickle Secrets Baby. Even as we failed, we were getting to learn how to design and develop in those categories. We were making commercials, buying media, and seeing the effects of the media on sales. We were reading the POS in those categories and learning what constituted a good POS in those categories. We were going deeper with the competition, allowing us to compare ourselves to them directly in a way that we hadn't been able to before.

We took the lessons and changed our whole approach to product development. We never did a baby doll again, never did a promotional plush again, and never did a small doll again. We became more innovative in the categories that we had strength in, and we didn't go up against the big competitors in other categories unless we had something super innovative to challenge them with. We also learned how to improve our product vetting. We developed a much better, more judicious process, creating an inventor group that goes out and looks at prototypes for us to option and review, and we're much better at using our intuition to judge which ideas have real pixie dust and which ones do not. A toy as terrible as Don't Free Freddy wouldn't even make it in the door today.

Failure also gave us more and better relationships across the industry. We were shipping more goods than we'd ever shipped before, working with new suppliers and a new factory. We ended up hiring several new people, some of whom parlayed their experience into better products down the road. We got to meet new buyers among multiple retailers across the country and have deep conversations that yielded valuable insights, helping us sell them other products in the same category in the future. We even picked up some new international distributors. All those different touchpoints of action and movement provided opportunities to learn and gain valuable information.

Looking back now, the single biggest upside of those failures was that they helped cement our reputation with inventors and with retailers as guys who were willing to innovate, willing to take a risk, willing to try. In the early days, back when it was just me and Anton and Ben, people in the industry used to call us "the Boys." There was a bit of mystique around us. People's attitude was "The Boys are doing something different. Even though they failed, it's so nice that young people are pushing the envelope and taking unconventional risks, because that's great for the industry." As much as our successes, it was our failures that solidified our reputation as the young guys on the block who were doing new and exciting things.

Contrary to what people might think, our failures also improved our relationships with the toy inventors. Yes, the products failed, but we got them sold into stores, which meant the inventors got their day in court. They got their toy into the marketplace, which at the end of the day is all that you can ask for. In a way, our failures were almost like an initiation in the inventor community. It showed people that we would take their ideas and go the distance, trying the best we possibly could to make them successful. Indeed, after those flops, we had more inventors knocking on our door, and they started showing us more and better prototypes.

Failure is not the opposite of success. Failure and success are merely two different forces you have to learn to contend with. That rushing river you're trying to navigate as a business, it's not all flowing in one direction. There are eddies and crosscurrents, even massive Niagara-size cataracts that can send you plunging hundreds of feet into the rapids below. Ultimately, being able to navigate those different currents will give you the momentum that takes you where you want to go. The key is to keep going. Keep the new products flowing, keep the inventory moving, keep generating cash, don't get married to one product or idea, know when to stop and pivot—and at all costs, whatever you do, don't stagnate.

At Spin Master, we've developed a rule that no still water is allowed. We don't waste time blaming anyone in the company for a failed product. The truth is that in any endeavor there are usually too many people involved to put all the blame on one person. It's not nice, nor is it productive. To this day, if we're faced with a systemic problem in the way we're running the business, we take the time to overhaul our operations to ensure the problem doesn't recur. But if a product fails in the marketplace, we don't hesitate even for a moment. We mark down the price, sell off any excess or slow-moving inventory, and then move on. In the last thirty years, we've repeated that process many times. Our ability to fail properly has become one of our greatest strengths as a company. Because we don't see that failure as a setback to our progress. We see failure as an essential element of our progress. We see it as a natural by-product of the risk-taking that is necessary for progress. As long as you've got more hits than misses, and as long as you diversify and never bet the farm on something that could bankrupt you, failure isn't something you should ever fear. It's something you should embrace.

AT THE END OF THE DAY, no matter what endeavor you undertake in life, a good test of whether or not it's the right path for you is to ask yourself, *Do I enjoy failing at this?*

"Enjoy" is maybe too strong a word. Perhaps the question might be better phrased as *Do I find failure in this as compelling and rewarding as success?* Because you can't be in it for success alone. Building a business of any size from scratch is stressful, unpredictable, and risky. It has many moving parts. It involves sacrifice, long hours, working weekends, travel, and near-constant blows to your ego. It burdens you with responsibilities for other people's lives and livelihoods, which is no small thing. Even the greatest businesses in the world didn't get off the ground with the first idea or concept. It takes time, and there will be lots of stumbles and setbacks along the way. If those stumbles and setbacks make you miserable, get out. Do something else. But if running that business is indeed your true calling, an unsuccessful product will be every bit as interesting to you as a successful one, because the failure is what gives you the opportunity to grow and learn and improve at doing the thing that you love.

For me, in my business career, whether I fail or succeed, the act and the process of doing has been my best teacher. I've enjoyed my successes, but it's the failures that have forced me to grow the most as a person, that have pushed me into a better understanding of who I am. Twenty-five years ago, looking on as Key Charm Cuties and Don't Free Freddy and Tickle Secrets Baby all collapsed in the marketplace, one after the other, the biggest sense of failure for me wasn't in the fact that we didn't make money or the fear that we might look bad in the eyes of our industry peers. The single most disappointing moment for me came on the day when I caught a commercial for Don't Free Freddy on TV. I looked at the kids' faces in the commercial and I thought, *Wow, they don't look happy.* And these were professional kid actors that we *paid* to look happy, and even they weren't having fun. "Something's not right here," I said. "What did we do wrong?"

It stung that the product didn't sell, but the fact that it didn't sell was merely the evidence of the real problem: The toy didn't sell because it failed to connect with kids—because *we* failed to connect with kids. We'd created something that didn't fill them with joy. We hadn't given them the same fun and energy and excitement that they'd had with Air Hogs and Flick Trix. For me, that was the real failure, far more than the financial one, because it meant we'd failed to fulfill the primary purpose of a toy company, which is to fuel the imaginations of children.

That particular failure was an invaluable experience for me, because it gave me a much clearer sense of my purpose in running this company. It was a crystal-clear message telling me why I was doing what I was doing, and what I needed to do better if I wanted to succeed. And that's a lesson I'm glad I was able to learn when I was young.

PART III
Reward

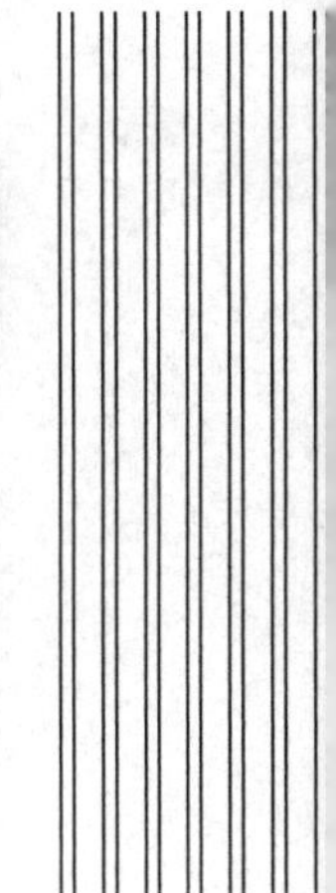

8.

Equity

was an unusual kid. Growing up, whenever we drove through downtown Toronto, I would look up at the tall glass towers of the big banks and dream about having an office up there one day. At the breakfast table, whenever I opened the newspaper, I always went to the business section first, then the front page, then entertainment. I wouldn't even look at the sports section. I never dreamed about growing up to be a famous baseball player or hockey player or even a rock star. My idols were always the entrepreneurs who started and ran big businesses. And there was one thing I understood about these people on an intuitive, fundamental level: What made these people important, what made them worthy of admiration, was that whatever business they ran, they owned it. It was *their* business. Long before I'd ever heard of things like IPOs and stock splits and dual-class share structures, I understood the idea that if you don't have controlling equity in something, it's not yours.

Part of the reason I understood this so well was because I witnessed firsthand what can happen if you don't have it. After we moved from South Africa to Toronto, for ten years my father built a small retail business selling Persian carpets. He did reasonably well. At a quick glance, you might look at him and think he embodied the life of the striving, bootstrapping immigrant business owner. But the truth is that he always had a senior partner. So while my dad always had a share in the profits, he never had a controlling equity stake to make the real decisions. He was always working for someone else.

Given that my mother worked with my father for many years, business was talked about around the dinner table all the time. Their partners and associates were in and out of the house constantly, and the conversation was always flowing. It was an incredible education. One thing I learned from my dad was the art of conversation itself. He had so much charm in the room and had a great ability to get people excited. At the same time, I also saw just how much stress and instability came from my dad not having real equity, or controlling equity, in what he did.

In 1985, when I was fourteen years old, my father and his partner in the Persian carpet business split up, and because my dad was the junior partner, he had no say when the other guy decided to shut it down. After being unemployed for about a year, my dad was hired as VP of sales for Sun Ripe, a large juice-box company. I can still remember how proud I was that he was now a VP working for this big company. I can also remember the wonderful feeling of stability that came with him having what I thought was the security of a salaried, corporate job. However, that was an illusion. He got let go after six months. After that, he opened up another business, a gallery selling reproduction antique furniture. That one never really got off the ground. It did okay for about two years, then he closed it and was unemployed again for another couple of years.

From the day the Persian carpet business closed down, even when my dad was working, his income was never stable, and the burden of supporting the family shifted in part to my mom. She took a job in retail, working as a salesperson at a lingerie store called La Vie en Rose. Fortunately, through the Persian carpet business, my parents had become friendly with their clientele, which included several high-net-worth individuals. One of them was a plastic surgeon, and when he decided to open his own clinic, he asked my mother to help him run the business side of the operation. He even gave her a profit-sharing stake, and together they grew it into the number one plastic-surgery clinic in Canada. Suddenly, my mother was the breadwinner while my dad was unemployed.

Then, on top of the business problems, my parents separated.

Looking back now, I have a great deal of admiration and respect for so much of what my father achieved against the odds. He took bold, courageous chances in his life, moving to South Africa on his own at twenty-one, starting over in Canada in his thirties with a family, having to build up a network of contacts all over again. But he was never afforded the same opportunities I was, and despite taking big risks in his personal life, his attitude toward risk in business was significantly more conservative, which limited his upside and his growth. He never wanted to put up his own capital, so he was always the minority partner in his businesses, hedging his exposure instead of investing everything in himself and having full control of his own destiny. And when he started having personality differences with his partners, he was powerless to stop those businesses from falling apart. So when I started my own company I knew, deep down inside, that I never wanted what happened to my father to happen to me.

||

Not long after Anton and I delivered half a million Earth Buddies to Kmart, we found ourselves sitting on a windfall. What had started as an idea at my mom's kitchen table had netted us each a couple hundred grand, which seemed like a small fortune to a couple of young guys in the early 1990s. There was a moment—a very brief moment—when I asked Anton if we should take the profits and call it quits. Or, if not quits, at least pause, take the money, and travel somewhere exotic before we sat down to figure out what came next. It was a moment of fear, actually. Nothing was wrong. Everything was going great. But when you look at that much cash you say, "Wow, that's a lot of money. Should we take the money, or should we keep on betting the money on the next thing?"

The moment I gave voice to that thought, Anton looked at me, like, *What are you talking about?*, and we quickly decided that we'd do nothing of the sort. He and I weren't in this to get rich quick; we were in this to build a business, which meant reinvesting our money back into the company instead of taking it off the table.

From the start we'd been on the same page about how we'd split the equity, fifty-fifty down the middle. Even though we had enough trust in each other that we could have done it on a handshake, we didn't. We sat down and wrote up a shareholder's agreement—and that is the first and most fundamental rule of how to handle your equity. People change over time. Their memories and their feelings about their perceived contributions to the business, all of that shifts, and you can end up in a dangerous place, arguing over who deserves what. And, if you ever want to change or get out of the partnership, it's important to have a mechanism that speaks to that. If not, you could be locked into years of trying to move on, waiting for the courts to figure it out for you. So Anton and I drew up the agreement and stuck it in a drawer, where it has gathered dust ever since; we've never had to pull it out again because from that moment we've been in total alignment, not just on how we split the equity but also on how we handle it.

Anton and I both knew that we wanted to hold on to as much equity as possible for as long as possible, only taking out what we needed to live. In terms of our own personal salaries, once we were established, we started paying ourselves about $100,000 a year. So we were doing okay. It was enough to live comfortably, and I was able to put down a deposit on a house when I was twenty-six. But whenever the big windfalls came—as they did with the Sky Shark and with Flick Trix and other toys that followed—we could have taken more money off the table and allowed ourselves to live much larger. We didn't. For years and years and years, we never paid ourselves a dividend. Not a nickel. We left it all in the business in order to grow the business.

Beyond the general principle of wanting to retain as much equity, ownership, and control as we could, I have also always felt that if you believe in your business and the fundamentals are sound, then you should reinvest in yourself so you can take in as little outside investment as you can for as long as you can. You don't want to have another large voice around the table determining the direction of how your company is going to be built. You don't want to have to run the business with someone else's needs in mind. Oftentimes, when you take outside money, the investor will want an exit at some point, and that can impact your direction as well.

When we turned thirty there was a moment when a company approached us and said they'd like to buy a 10 percent stake in the company. They wined and dined us and took us to hockey games and all that, and we considered it, but in the end we turned it down. I didn't think the people were a good fit. I also didn't want another voice in the mix, especially someone we didn't know very well. In the end, the decision came back to my sense of needing control—and also from learning more about private equity. As one mentor told me, "Finding a private equity partner that matches with your ethos and long-term goals is harder than finding a wife."

The moral of the story is don't raise money if you don't have to, and we didn't. Whenever we faced a cash-flow issue, we always preferred taking money from the bank. It was a cleaner arrangement in our minds, as a bank has no influence over the direction of your business. But we were so debt averse that we were reluctant even to take on a term loan because we didn't want to worry about interest payments. We did get a line of credit against our receivables and our inventory, and we stretched that as far as we could during some crunch times, but we tried to rely on that only when it was absolutely necessary. Anytime you need more working capital, your options are to find an outside partner, go to the bank, or use your own profits to reinvest in yourself. We always said, "If it's our money keeping the lights on, no one's ever going to show up and close our doors." So that's what we did.

I am also a big believer in the idea that if you're going to share the fruits of your labor, better to do it with your own people inside the company rather than with outside investors. When we launched the Earth Buddy, we knew we were missing some much-needed expertise, but we didn't have the money to hire many people, and we were up against the clock to get the product to market. Anton and I didn't want to bring in other long-term equity partners that early on.

I firmly believe that everyone should profit from their contributions, and that society would be better off if equity in the marketplace were distributed more broadly—more shared risk and more shared reward. But human nature makes that difficult. Many if not most people are risk averse; they want and need a guaranteed salary up front. And if you're the one putting your chips on the table and taking the bigger risk, the natural instinct is to not share the reward. Giving away money to charity is one thing. Giving up equity in something you own is something else entirely. Maybe in the future we will live in a more evolved society where everyone shoulders risk and reward together, but that's not the world we live in now. And Anton and I felt strongly that since we started the business, taking the big risk and continuing to shoulder that risk, we deserved to maintain as big an equity position as possible.

The philosophy we developed was to be conservative, maybe even a bit stingy, with sharing equity, but generous with sharing profits. What we decided to do was bring on partners for specific products and share profits on a transactional basis without diluting our equity stake in the overall company. Micropartners, we called them, and the first two we brought on were my sister Michelle and her husband, Austin. When Michelle jumped in and designed the Earth Buddy packaging and Austin helped us scale up and build out the Earth Buddy production line, we gave each of them 5 percent of the Earth Buddy's profits, and they did well enough that they were able to keep cashing profit-sharing checks for the next few years, enough for Michelle to fund and start her food company, Wildly Delicious.

That micropartner model, giving people profit interests for specific work, became something of a framework for us in the early days. We used it over and over. We sought out people with different skill sets but similar values, and then we incentivized them with a portion of the eventual profits of their own work. I loved the power of sharing profits for "extra sweat" rather than raising money through private equity. I loved using it because it gave people a sense of ownership. It spurred them to bring their energy, drive, new ideas, creativity, and sense of purpose to the table, and I don't believe you get that taking straight cash from an investor. The enthusiasm of human beings working together becomes something of a self-renewing resource, as opposed to cash. Because cash is finite; once you spend it, it's gone.

Along the way, a few of our micropartners proved themselves to be truly indispensable to the company, and Anton and I gave each of them small amounts of phantom equity, a stake that would convert to actual shares at one of two events, if the company went public or if the company got sold. The problem with micropartners, however, is that sometimes a point or two of profit sharing alone is not enough. Sometimes you work with someone who you want to be all in with you, 100 percent of the time. Ben Varadi was one of those people. From the moment Anton invited Ben into the fold, we called him a partner and treated him like a partner. He had a seat at the table and a say in all our critical decisions, everything from choosing which products to launch to picking our company name. But even though we treated Ben as an equal partner, he was not an equal partner from a monetary perspective. He had an equal vote, but he didn't have an equal stake. Anton and I had the exact same salary and the exact same equity share, and we were both continually reinvesting our dividends back into the company. But instead of cutting that arrangement into thirds, we gave Ben a 10 percent profit share, which he could convert to equity in the case of a sale or an IPO.

We came up with that structure with the short term in mind; it was a substantial share but not a permanent stake. But by the time we hit the ten-year mark, that arrangement was well out of date. Ben wanted to have, and had earned, a long-term commitment. Plus, economically, it wasn't that good for the business to have him taking 10 percent of the profits out every year while Anton and I were still rolling our profits into the business to grow it, and we knew that Ben having some real skin in the game would bring a lot of value to the relationship. So we started to negotiate.

It didn't go as smoothly as it should have. What followed was a torturous process that went back and forth and back and forth and back and forth. Ben wanted 20 percent. Anton and I went back to him with 14 percent. Eventually, we ended up at 16.5 percent real equity and no more profit sharing. It took years and was far more difficult than it should have been since all we were doing was consummating a relationship that already existed. In the end, Ben was happier with the new deal, but we didn't land in a place where he was super happy; he didn't get his fair share at that percentage, and the way we went through it didn't make him feel as valued as he truly is.

Looking back, I would have done it differently, because it was much too hard on all of us, but especially on Ben. We should have given him the 20 percent and not slogged through the endless negotiation. But we were nervous. Giving up that big a stake was hard. Still, we moved forward, and once we did the deal we never revisited it and everything worked out in the end because we were all aligned on the same goal: building something for the long term. There was never any talk of selling or cashing out, only building. We all knew we were sharing a wild, creative adventure, and we wanted to see how far that road would take us.

For the first ten years, we stuck to our guns, not taking a single dime out of the company beyond our base salaries. At the ten-year mark, in our early thirties, before cutting Ben in, Anton and I paid ourselves a small dividend, but no large sum. It was only five years later, after the success of Bakugan, that the three of us sat down and said, "Okay, the company is making some large returns. Let's take some money out." We took four dividends of sizable amounts. So, really, we let it ride for fifteen years before we saw any substantial outside returns. Then, right after the Bakugan peak, the company took a downturn, and we didn't take any money out for another six years.

I was rounding forty when we hit that bump in the road, losing money for two years straight for the first time in the company's history. Turning everything around was a momentous endeavor, and as a result of that I went through a bit of a midlife crisis about what I wanted to do with my life and my career. Ben and Anton were doing the same. I think for a time each of us entertained the thought of selling the business and moving on. The money was tempting, and the change was tempting. Ultimately, we decided to reengage and build a company that would not only live beyond us but continue to thrive and grow on its own, with each of us making the commitment to remain involved to the extent that we desired, and we felt that the best long-term structure to allow us to do that would be to become a public company. When we started, our driving philosophy had been to forgo the short-term money and hold on to as much equity as possible, and at a certain point we flipped. We decided it was time to sell off some of that equity both for the company's future and for our own individual futures, and we started thinking about succession planning and setting up the company to make that happen.

Once we decided to go public, I was adamant that I would only do it with a dual-class share structure, meaning that our shares would maintain a ten-to-one voting ratio compared to the shares that we sold. So that's what we did. At that point, Anton and I each had a little under 42 percent, and Ben had 16.5 percent. With the IPO, the employees who had phantom equity were able to convert, and then over the years we tendered in about 12 percent of our shares into the market, got paid for those shares, and took that money out ourselves. Today, Anton and I each have 30 percent and Ben held on to 10 percent, so 70 percent overall, with 30 percent sold to the public and to investors. Because of the dual-class structure, however, even though our share is 70 percent, our voting power is still at 98 percent. Even if the three of us were somehow diluted to 25 percent, we would still control the decision-making of the business in terms of who sits on the board.

As a result of those moves, in 2018, Anton and I were both named to *Forbes*'s 32nd annual billionaires list. The whole experience wasn't really believable, and in some ways still isn't. It was never a conscious thought of mine that the business would be worth that much, or that I would be worth that much. I never thought we'd get there. As much as I'd been driven by a need for financial security, I didn't ever think it would go that high.

The irony about money is that the way you feel about money isn't really related to how much money you have. It is, but it isn't. It's really about whether or not you see the world through a lens of scarcity or a lens of abundance. I'd always seen the world through the lens of scarcity, and I still do. A million, a hundred million, a billion—it doesn't really change who you are, and that's who I am. Intellectually, I know the money and the equity are there, but I don't necessarily *feel* that I'm any more secure. It's just very hard to reframe your mind to look at the world through a lens of abundance.

There's a saying in Judaism: "The person who is truly rich is the person who's happy with what they have." That's the real definition of wealth, and it's what we should all strive for, but it's difficult to get there, and it's partly why I choose to focus on equity over money, because having equity gives you something that money in a bank account never will.

||

So, what is equity? Equity is ownership, and all the benefits and perks and responsibilities that come with ownership. You can get equity from making a financial investment in a company. You can get it from putting time and effort into a business—"sweat equity," as we commonly refer to it. But most equity comes as a result of creating something. How do you get that kind of equity? Well, you just give it to yourself. You start something out of nothing, and that very same day you own 100 percent of it, lock, stock, and barrel. At that point your equity might not have any monetary value, but that doesn't mean you own 100 percent of nothing. While we typically think of equity as being related to money, and it is, the deeper truth is that there is equity in your ideas and your execution as well. Just having an idea or finding an opening, that creates equity, and from there it's the doing that will open up the opportunity to build something.

There is a crazy amount of equity value in just starting something; in a way, it's not proportional or fair. You don't have to be given anything by anyone to create equity. It's magical in a way. You take a spark of a thought from your mother's newspaper, work hard, and turn that spark into something you never dreamed possible. In the end, the ability to own something is your gift to yourself for taking a risk and for continuing to take that risk, forgoing benefits in the now for even bigger payoffs in the future.

I would go so far as to say that any business started from nothing is a miracle. How was it possible? How did it happen? It's something we can only know looking backward, and what I can say with great certainty looking back, as I have in every other chapter of this book, is that there is no better time to start building equity than when you're young.

||

For starters, equity gives you motivation, a sense of purpose, a clear direction. For many young people, your twenties are a decade of indecision, of stops and starts, of aimless shifting from one short-term goal to the next. Which isn't necessarily a criticism; the energy inside you at that age is so full and abundant that it flows in many directions. Owning equity in something gives you a place to channel that energy. Owning equity in something means that you're more motivated to care for it and be thoughtful in how you handle it. You hold more space for it. When you own equity, work becomes more than just showing up for an eight-hour day with a lunch and two breaks. It's now about the ideas you generate, the relationships and contacts you develop, your ability to inspire people, your ability to make the right decision at the right moment, and your ability to move with momentum. When you own equity, these intangibles seem to kick in more often than not. It's because having a stake in something draws out the best in you.

Also, when you're building equity, you don't need to agonize over questions like "Why am I pursuing this?" or "What am I working for?" Because you know the answers. You're working for yourself. You're shaping your own destiny, investing in your own future. Having that clarity is an intangible form of compensation that will spur you on over and above whatever your take-home pay might be.

And in terms of that take-home pay, you'll decide what that should be, and it's simply a fact that in your twenties you need less to get by on. Many twenty-year-olds have no kids, no spouse, the cheapest apartment they can find, roommates to split the rent, maybe a down payment on a house if circumstance allows. Barring some personal or family emergency, that's all you need. Which allows you to do as Anton and I did, plow everything you can back into the business, giving you a longer runway to grow and greater deferred value in your later years.

AS I'VE NOTED, IN YOUR twenties you have access to seemingly boundless levels of energy. Physically and mentally, you're in the best shape you will ever be in your life. The power of that fuel is magical, almost like a force of nature. It helps you get the plane down the runway and into the air. And the thing about the power of youth, again, is that it will get spent. Whether through partying, working, or just wasting time, you will burn it off. It will diminish with age. So the question isn't whether or not that energy is going to be used up. The question is, How do you want to use it and who are you using it for? When you burn off that fuel and release all that energy, do you want the benefits to accrue to yourself or to someone you work for?

Yes, there are numerous advantages to having a full-time job. You don't have to shoulder the risk of running a company, meeting payroll, and paying suppliers. You have the freedom, in theory, to clock out when you leave the office and spend that time on family and other pursuits. But that's only in theory. In reality, most high-paying, high-status jobs in business—hedge funds, investment banks, sales jobs—will demand nearly the same amount of time and effort as running a business. You might find yourself on call fifty, sixty, sometimes eighty hours a week, spending all that time building equity for someone else instead of yourself. Entrepreneurship is really a path that starts with asking yourself a few simple questions: *How much do I value my time? How much do I believe in my ideas? And, at the end of the day, do I want to take a risk and have faith in myself and my ability to execute? Do I want a larger return on my efforts, or do I want that return to accrue to someone else?*

||

The next benefit to building equity from a young age is one that anybody with a savings account can understand. We've all heard Warren Buffett give the example of a $5 cup of coffee. A $5 cup of coffee doesn't actually cost $5. It costs $5 plus whatever interest you might have earned if you'd left that $5 to compound over time. We always talk to young people about the importance of saving for retirement early. But we never talk to young people about entrepreneurship and equity in the same way, even though the same principles apply. The magic of equity is that it compounds over time. The longer you have to let it compound, the greater the value it accrues. The younger you start and the less you take out, the more you'll have as the years go by. All your effort gets accrued to you through your equity, which becomes a repository for your time spent, available for you to tap into when you reach your later years.

The beauty of getting old is that even as the energy of youth begins to dissipate, you have, hopefully, accumulated a little more wisdom. And because you took all the energy and power of your twenties and socked it away in equity, now you've got the best of everything, an enormous reserve of rocket fuel at your disposal, plus the experience and acumen to put it to good use. Now that the plane is flying and stable, you can pull back on the throttle a bit, diversify your focus, find other priorities. Whatever you choose to do, it's the extra time you put in during your twenties that affords you greater options later on.

SO WHAT SHOULD YOU DO with your equity? Some entrepreneurs reach that point and they choose to cash in and walk away to start a whole new life, and that may be the correct choice for them; how one chooses to use the equity they've built with their own sweat and blood is a very personal decision, and there is no right or wrong answer. That being said, when we went public, we never considered selling. Just in our observational research, looking around at people our age who'd sold their business and moved on, we noticed that most of them carried some form of regret. Those people had a big pile of money, but their platform, the thing they'd worked so long and hard to create, was gone. Most of them went straight back out and started investing their money with the goal of finding something new to have a piece of.

I've often compared starting a company to birthing a child. It's wonderful and difficult and exhausting all at the same time. But if you stay with it and do a good job, eventually you get to the proud parent stage, watching the kid go off and stand and succeed on their own. Then you get to be the grandparent, coming to visit, sharing your stories and your wisdom, enjoying everything the grandkids have to offer without any of the day-to-day responsibilities. Why would you abandon your business entirely when you can have all the joy that comes with staying involved?

Because, at the end of the day, why do we do any of this? You work and work for years, sometimes even decades, and at the end you have to ask yourself, *What was it for? Where did the time go, and what did I accomplish?* I have always believed that the true measure of success would be to build a business that continued to grow and thrive without me, Anton, and Ben steering the ship. I wanted Spin Master to become a living, breathing organism that could potentially live on for generations, with our culture and a methodology embedded in the DNA of the company, still contributing to the conversation long after we've passed on. If we could accomplish that, like a parent raising a successful kid, we would have done the best job we could.

Going public was the first step toward sending our child off to live and thrive on its own, but we knew we needed to continue playing our parental role, at least for a while. The ugly truth is that when a lot of businesses are sold, the founders' culture and the institutional knowledge don't survive the transition. The soul of the company is deeply wounded, or lost completely. Maintaining our majority equity stake gave us the ability to continue to guide and shape the culture and the direction of the company.

I am a huge proponent of having older people stay in companies for longer periods of time to impart their wisdom and knowledge, creating a perpetual flywheel of learning. They do this well in Japan, where they mix together workers of different ages, in case you were wondering why companies like Nintendo and Sony have been around for so long. Similarly, in Judaism, when you turn fifty, according to *Pirkei Avot*, a compilation of ethical teachings, you are imparted with wisdom and have the ability to teach and mentor. Older people in companies should be coveted and put in positions to teach and pass on everything they know, allowing the institutional knowledge to be passed on. Both Anton and Ben have stayed very involved in the company, stepping up into mentoring and teaching roles in order to pass Spin Master's values on to the next generation.

Maintaining your equity stake also gives you a platform, the ability to be part of an industry, to meet interesting people, to be involved with government, policy, philanthropy, and so on. It lets you be an expert in your field and share that knowledge with others. Owning a business means you're engaged and taking risks, and keeping your platform ensures your opportunity to stay in the conversation, engage with interesting people, help shape legislation, and continue to provide jobs, even if you're not running the day-to-day of the business. You have a place to hang your hat, even as you pursue other goals in life.

In addition to giving you that platform, maintaining your equity also gives you something deeper. It gives you an identity. When you're an entrepreneur, people's perception of you is inextricably linked to what your company is and what your company does, like Steve Jobs and Apple or Phil Knight and Nike. That doesn't happen when you become an employee of an established company, like Google or Facebook. You may be successful there, but you'll always have that brand attached to you, not an identity you've built for yourself.

If had written this book five years ago, I would have said that rooting your identity in the success of your business was 100 percent a healthy thing. But writing here today—having stepped up from my day-to-day role at Spin Master to serve as board member and founder, and to work on special projects—I have to add a caveat. In truth, it's not healthy to vest your *entire* identity in your business, to let your feelings of self-worth move up and down with the markets or what the public says about you. You should feel healthy and secure in who you are as a person. You are enough, just being yourself, and you should get that feeling internally, not from other people's judgments.

That said, when you own a company, people are going to form their perception of you based on what they know about your business. It's going to happen, and it happened to us almost right away. Because we were so young when we started, our success made us an interesting story for the press. We were famous in our hometown three months after being in business; everybody in Toronto knew about the Earth Buddy. Pretty soon it was the whole country. We were "the Earth Buddy guys" for a number of years. Then we became "the Bakugan guys," and now, no matter what we do, we'll forever be known as "the PAW Patrol guys."

For Ben, Anton, and me, having an identity thrust upon us so young made us conscious of the fact that people were watching. I don't think we would have run our company any differently if we'd been more anonymous, but we were always conscious of the fact that our actions had the potential to either boost or diminish our reputations, and we went the extra mile to make sure everything our company did was handled in the right way. The danger is that you'll become too wrapped up in what the public thinks of you, relying on it for external validation. But as long as you have a healthy sense of self, maintaining that public-facing identity and that reputation can earn you a great deal of social currency.

And that currency will be of considerable value, because one of the sweetest advantages of starting a company in your twenties is that when your business is twenty-five-plus years old, you'll still be young enough to pursue a second act in life. You'll get to your early fifties—yes, it will happen, and it goes fast like a dream—and you will still be (relatively) young and employable. Fifty is the new forty, if you're healthy and eager. With the value of your equity stake giving you a stable foundation to stand on, you won't need to scramble and take any job just to pay the bills. You can take a pause, maybe a sabbatical, and reflect on your true dreams and desires. Then you can move on to a whole new career in any number of fields, and another twenty-five-year run could easily be in the cards for you. Your options are wide open. In addition to being able to look back fondly on something meaningful that you've created, you get to live your life twice, all because of the gift you gave yourself in your twenties by making something out of nothing.

9.
Control

When I was eighteen years old, the universe slapped me hard, twice, in a very short period of time. The first slap came when a buddy of mine and I traveled down to Maryland to see some Jerry Garcia shows. The first night we took Ecstasy. The second night, we did it again. The third night we hitchhiked up to Philadelphia for the next show, and that afternoon, as we were walking in to the venue, I turned to my buddy and said, "So what are we going to do tonight?"

"I already dropped some acid," he said.

"Ooh, give me a hit," I replied, and I took a dose, not even thinking about the fact that I hadn't slept the night before or that I was terribly dehydrated. I had no conscious, deliberate thought of *What is my intention?* or anything like that. I just took it.

As soon as it kicked in, my body shut down. I walked around the concert for the next eight hours having a really, really bad trip. If I look back now, I probably had a panic attack and I couldn't settle. I had a lot of anxiety, and you don't want to have anxiety when you're on LSD. It's a powerful substance, and I wish I'd known that it has to be taken with the proper intention. You have to know what you want to get out of the journey, because once you start, good trip or bad, you're fully committed for the next eight hours.

I had taken LSD on two previous occasions, and at the time I felt like they'd both been mind-expanding in a positive way, but the truth is that taking LSD in any frame of mind before you're twenty-five is a risk. The chances of having a bad trip are real, and the lasting effects are real too. Your brain is still in the process of being wired, and you don't want it to be rewired in a way that isn't naturally intended.

Three weeks later came the second slap. I was back in Toronto with another friend, and we went out one night to a gentlemen's club—or strip joint, as we called them back in the day. At the time, the legal age to get into a place that served alcohol was nineteen, and I was only eighteen, which is why I had a fake ID that I'd gotten from my sister's boyfriend.

At some point during the evening, despite the fact that I was already drinking underage in a place I wasn't supposed to be with a fake ID I wasn't supposed to have, I decided it would be a good idea to go outside and smoke some hash; I wanted to get high to deal with the anxiety that I was still feeling after the bad LSD trip. So I turned to my buddy and said, "Do you want to go get high?"

"No, I'm good," he said. "I'll stay." My buddy was smart; he went on to become a lawyer. I went by myself, which was not too smart at all.

Out in the parking lot, I got in my mom's Toyota Celica and I was hotboxing in the car when I heard a knock on the window. I rolled it down, hash smoke poured out of the car, and standing there were two guys in plainclothes who identified themselves as police officers.

"What are you doing?" one of them asked.

"Nothing," I said.

"Can you step outside?"

"Sure."

I climbed out of the car, and they eyed me with justified suspicion.

"Do you have any drugs on you?"

"No," I lied.

"Empty your pockets."

I emptied my pockets, and what they found was literally nothing more than half a gram of hash stuck to a quarter. One of them said something to me, and then he reached out and put his hand on me. I don't like being touched, so I tried to shove his arm away. The next thing I knew, they were throwing me up against my car, cuffing me, and tossing me into the back seat of their van.

So there I was, underage and high as a kite in the back of an undercover police van in the parking lot of a strip club, waiting for them to write me up a summons. Then they asked me for my ID. In my wallet, I had my real ID and my fake ID, and I got the stupid idea to give them the fake ID, thinking somehow I'd avoid getting in trouble that way. I gave them the fake ID, they wrote up the citation in my sister's boyfriend's name, slapped me with the ticket, and went on their way. Once they were gone, I went back into the strip joint and told my buddy what had happened, and he was beyond happy that he hadn't come out back with me.

The next morning, feeling guilty, realizing I wasn't going to get away with anything, I came clean to my parents. To their credit, they were understanding and supportive and cool about it, while still being firm and forcing me to face the consequences of my actions. My dad took the fake ID, cut it up, and flushed it down the toilet. Then he drove me to the police station in Richmond Hill and made me confess that I'd given them the incorrect information, at which point I got charged again, this time with a public mischief charge for using a fake ID. I had to go to court, where I pled guilty, and the judge gave me a conditional discharge and sentenced me to some community service. Fortunately, in Canada, your record gets expunged after five years.

My mother went a bit further. She was upset because she was sure that I had a drug addiction problem, so she forced me to go to a rehab place and have an interview with an intake counselor. My friends were smoking every day at school, and I was only smoking on the weekends, so I knew that I wasn't an addict. But I went just to make her happy and put the whole thing behind me. Still, it was true that at that point in my life I was more or less off the rails, pushing the limits and not focused on school, and I was lucky that the universe took me to the edge and then gave me a pass to try a different route. I said to myself, *If you continue getting high and don't focus on the important aspects of your life, you're going to stray.* I knew if I kept taking unnecessary risks, the universe was just going to keep knocking me down, and I was smart enough to realize I needed to put my energies toward the more positive aspects of my life. But it did ruin my last year of high school because I was still carrying around a lot of anxiety from the experiences I'd just been through.

If you put me on a therapist's couch and started digging, it wouldn't take long for you to learn that my core, root-level drive in life stems from the fact that our family was never stable financially. I was always the kid in the cafeteria line mooching off my friends, asking them for some spare change to buy some extra food or snacks. My situation always felt precarious thanks to the lurking, ever-present trauma of our history. My grandparents having to uproot their lives, flee from the Communists in Bulgaria, and start over from scratch in Israel. My parents creating a whole life for us in South Africa, only to abandon that and resettle and start over in a new country. There was a deep-rooted fear of scarcity that started with them and got transferred over to my siblings and me.

Our first ten years in Toronto were comparatively stable; there was always food on the table, and the electricity wasn't getting shut off. Still, it was always apparent to me how hard my parents were working to keep us afloat. Looking back, I have so much compassion for what my mother and father endured on their journey. They were deprived of so much because of the times they grew up in, and they were always doing their best to provide for us with the tools they had. Amid so much chaos and instability, it's a miracle they were able to give my sisters and me as much as they did. They gave me a foundation I was able to build on. They gave me the ability to see and understand risk. And seeing their resilience in hard times taught me that anything was possible. At the same time, our circumstances meant that there was always a sense of scarcity, never abundance.

I had always been aware of the fact that everything could disappear at any moment. Then, when my father's business closed, my fears became all too real. The big, bold neon-colored message to me was "Don't put your life in the hands of other people." Then, on top of our financial insecurity, my parents' marriage ended, which only cemented the feeling in me that I had no choice but to chart my own path and take control of my own life. Those were my high-school and college years, my formative years, and they were a time when the ground kept shifting under my feet. I learned to deal with it in the only way I knew how to: by asserting as much control as I could over my own destiny, by working compulsively to make my own way and do for myself. One of the greatest blessings you can have in life is clarity, having a sense of purpose, knowing what you want to do and which direction you ought to take. As a child, I'd been blessed with that. From the age of eight, I knew I wanted to be in business. Whether it was selling products or developing buildings on empty lots, I loved to dream about all the creative possibilities of what I could do as an entrepreneur. When we launched the Earth Buddy, consciously, that excitement and energy was all that was driving me. But I know now that just below the surface, as a result of the anxiety and scarcity I'd grown up with, I was also being driven by a fear of being dependent on anyone else, and a need to control my own destiny no matter what.

||

When you're young, the same openness to the world that makes life so dynamic and so much fun can also lead you to struggle. Being open leaves you vulnerable. Your emotions are bigger. The instability of life can feel overwhelming. You can try to escape that instability, mask it and hide it, as I did for a while with drugs, or you can face it head-on, by taking control.

It's clear, in hindsight, that much of my need for control came from an unhealthy place, and it has taken many decades of therapy for me to grapple with and understand how the events of my childhood shaped who I am today. The truth is, you can probably take any successful person in any human endeavor, and if you dig deep enough you'll find some wound or tragedy that person is trying to leave behind. Still, even though the desire for control can come from an unhealthy place—and even though it has led many people to an unhealthy end—wanting to have a say in your destiny is inherently a positive thing. You're getting out of the passenger seat and into the driver's seat, giving yourself a sense of agency you didn't have before.

Starting a business is not just about having an idea for a new product or service. You might be able to tap into the zeitgeist and see the white space. You might have an inspiration for something that the market is demanding, and having that spark is an essential first step. But just because you have it doesn't necessarily mean you should strike out on your own. And, if you do, your choice can't be based on how useful you think your idea would be, nor should it be based on how successful you think you might become. Because all of that is unknowable at the start.

The real questions you have to ask yourself are: *Do I want to be in business for myself and accept all that comes with it? Is being an entrepreneur, with all its risks and rewards, the life that I want to lead? Am I committed to this? Do I have the creativity, drive, work ethic, stamina, and integrity to go the distance?* Entrepreneurship, in other words, is not just a job. It's about wanting to create and control your own world. It's a life path that you choose. It is its own goal, in and of itself.

When Anton, Ben, and I sat down to draw up a mission statement for the company, we deliberately made it as broad as possible. It was less about the specific products we wanted to sell and more about the lives we wanted to lead. We made general value statements like "We want to design and develop our own products and sell them globally." "We will entertain new ideas wherever they come from." "We will always do the right thing even if it's tough." "When our partners and inventors are making lots of money, so are we." We also went step by step and didn't think too far into the future. We delineated the "why" up front and then filled in the "how" as we went along.

We also knew what kind of life we didn't want to lead. Anton and I had both watched our fathers struggle with small retail operations, and we knew we didn't want to be dependent on people coming into a store to buy what we were selling. The carpets and furniture my dad was selling, none of it was his own merchandise. He was a middleman, always buying from someone else, his profit margins dependent on whatever price they quoted him. He was never in control.

At Spin Master, we determined from the start that we would never put ourselves in that position. We would design and develop our own products and ideas. We would own the patents and brands and trademarks. We've since branched out into licensing toys from Monster Jam, which we don't own, but in our core business, we create everything ourselves, and we don't worry about who sells it to the end consumer because that's not what we do. Over the years, when people asked us "Where is your company going?" or "How big do you want it to be?" we didn't have an answer other than "We will build it as big as it can be, which is yet to be determined." Which was our way of defining the type of life we wanted to live. We wanted to build a global, long-term business that was diversified enough to weather all kinds of ups and downs and, eventually, be able to operate under its own steam, allowing us to step back and live other lives while still reaping the rewards. In other words, we wanted control.

ONCE WE WERE UP AND running, my need for control manifested itself in every aspect of the business. I personally signed every single check that the company wrote for the first ten years. I personally signed off on all the product costs for the first fifteen years; not one product that we manufactured went into production until I signed off on the final cost of goods. I would meet with the team every Wednesday, everybody would bring in the products, and we'd talk about the costs, where we were at, and where they needed to go back down and look at the margins.

Since I was the one hitting "Send" on the wire transfers, I controlled our cash flow by setting our payment terms with vendors, sometimes extending the payment terms out. I negotiated the bank terms as well, making sure we were a debt-averse company. We could have grown faster and been bigger, but I didn't want to take on the debt to do that, because taking on debt means ceding control. I made sure I had input, along with Anton and Ben, on all the major hiring decisions, and together Ben and I stayed closely involved in the development of every product, and every commercial we made to sell every product.

Reading the above passage, for some people the term "control freak" might come to mind, but I was never that, exactly; I'd maybe put myself one notch below. A control freak is someone who can't delegate because they never trust anyone else to do anything. That's not me. It does take me longer than the average person to arrive at a place where I can trust other people, but once I reach that place of trust, I'm good.

A control freak is also someone who's tossing and turning every night, racked with anxiety from trying to control things that cannot be controlled, plotting contingencies to account for worst-case scenarios that, in all likelihood, are never going to happen. I always had a healthy fear of uncertainty and scarcity, but I never lost sleep over it. In life and in business, you never know how something is going to turn out. You have to accept that you have very little control over outcomes. What you can control is the commitment you make to the goal at hand: how you're going to spend your time, who you want spend your time with, how long you want to invest yourself. I always understood that and accepted it, and it was because I knew I had no control over the outcome that I invested so much in controlling every conceivable step of the process. And I think I never lost any sleep because I knew we were always putting in the work and doing the best we could, and beyond that I looked at the unknown as a gift.

I can recognize, however, that my drive for control manifested itself in negative ways as well. Namely in that I didn't have enough fun. I could never sit back and relax and enjoy the wins. It was almost a superstition: "If I enjoy it too much, it's going to go away." I did have that baked into my DNA somewhere. I still have it, but now I'm cognizant of it and I've worked on it so that I can actually enjoy what we've built and what I have.

The need for control can be unhealthy when it manifests out of fear or insecurity. In the early days of Spin Master, a lot of my drive for control came from precisely that. But over time, hopefully, you grow and evolve, you quiet the voices of fear inside you, and you find that you want to exert control for a more constructive and more rewarding reason. Namely, to bring your work and career more fully in alignment with your personal gifts and talents and your own sense of what gives your life purpose and meaning.

WE ALL HAVE DIFFERENT MOTIVATIONS and needs, different dreams and desires, and starting your own business allows you to work and structure your day to suit your individual personality. You do that, first and foremost, by being in control of how you manage your time. Time is the one asset that everyone shares equally. We all have the same twenty-four-hour day, and we all get as many years as we're lucky enough to have. That's it, and perhaps the single greatest reward of running your own business is deciding how your most valuable resource will be spent.

When I was seventeen, working as a telemarketer selling cable subscriptions, I had to come in at a certain time, follow a script, be told what to do. I would sit and watch the clock as the hours dragged on. It felt like time wasn't moving at all. I knew I never wanted to have that type of work experience again. Frankly, I'd already had enough of it in school, when most of my time was spent on a schedule that someone else had set. That rigid experience was especially difficult because of my learning disability. I had to spend more time in class, more time studying, all to meet the benchmarks of success that were set for people who didn't have my particular challenges or my unique talents. Deep down in my DNA a part of me was crying out to march to my own drum. Luckily, I didn't need to spend ten years in a cubicle to figure that out. Having a sense of freedom was important to me; I knew I was never going to settle into a job that felt like high school, where I would spend all my time on another person's schedule.

Before you get married and start a family—if that is a decision you make—the time you have on your hands is immense. You have your nights, late afternoons, and weekends to do as you please, and when you own your own business, no one will tell you what to do and how to do it. You'll control when you come in and when you leave. You'll decide which meetings to attend, how long you want the meetings to run, and what areas of the business you want to focus on. When you want to take a break, you take a break. When you want to take a holiday, you take a holiday. You'll be in charge of everything from how you want to dress to whether or not you're going to sneak a nap in the middle of the day. (I used to sneak naps in my car in the middle of the day.)

The nine-to-five rhythm is a holdover from the Industrial Revolution, and it feels especially arbitrary in the wake of the digital revolution. We always had a philosophy that, within reason, you come work the hours you need to get your role done; we were never watching the clock, never cared what time people showed up or what time they left. (We also didn't care about the way people dressed. Long before every office went casual, we were already there. When we opened up our Los Angeles office, people were coming in in shorts. Then one day someone came in with flip-flops, and I was, like, "Okay, that's one step too far.")

For me personally, despite its challenges, running Spin Master was a gift after so many years of arbitrary schedules. I am not a morning person. I preferred to start later and end later, while Anton and Ben generally started and ended earlier. For the first ten years, I was in the office by 9:00 A.M. and leaving by 7:00 P.M., plus a lot of

Sundays. It was intense. Once I could manage it, however, I started coming in at 10:00 or 10:30 A.M., to give myself time for morning meditation, running, and yoga; having that time for myself before the day took off and got away from me was critical for my health and well-being.

I was also in control of how much time I spent away from my desk. So much of the real magic in business comes from outside the office. That's where the world is happening. That's where you're out of your comfort zone, meeting new people, seeing new things, gleaning insights. "If you go, you learn," I've always said. "If you go, you get." When you're building something, you're constantly connecting the dots and putting the pieces of the puzzle together, and I took every opportunity to go to meetings with buyers, to go to trade shows, to set up new offices or visit new factories. I was constantly on the road—Mexico, Chicago, New York, Hong Kong—gathering knowledge, making contacts, planting seeds, looking at new product ideas. If I took a business trip and wanted to extend it a few days for personal travel, explore those countries and neighboring cities, I was free to do so. I set the agenda. Looking back, I only wish I would have taken even more liberties with my time away, because it was always so rewarding, both personally and professionally. However you choose to use your time, the most important thing is that you have the freedom to show up the way you want to show up, and that's priceless.

BEYOND CONTROLLING YOUR TIME, starting your own business empowers you to shape the environment and the culture in your organization to bring it into alignment with your particular talents and gifts. When you read the history of great musicians and how their classic albums came together, one near universal constant is the lengths they went to carve out and control their environment. That was true for Bob Dylan and the Band and where they went to go and set up and write their music. It was true for the Beatles recording at Abbey Road or traveling to India. Controlling your journey is necessary to get the inspiration that keeps the flywheel of creativity going. Everything else stems from that.

We all have certain skills we are gifted with when we come into this world, inborn abilities and personality traits that define who we are. What is your gift? It may take a while to figure out, but when you know, you just know, because you feel most like yourself whenever you're doing it. You step out onto your school's track for the first time, and you can run like a gazelle. You pick up a guitar for the first time, and it just feels natural in your hands. The chords and the progressions, it all makes sense.

You've still got a long way to go. You've got hours and hours of diligent practice ahead of you before you reach a technical mastery of whatever it is. But the positive feedback loop of enjoying it and wanting to do more of it happens almost right away. There's no friction. It's effortless. You know you're using your gift when you can lose yourself in something and the whole idea of time falls away. You sit down to the task, and the next thing you know you look up and hours have gone by. You're in the flow state. Your energy level peaks and stays high. You have the ability to channel ideas and influence people around you in a positive way because those people are now your mirror; they're reflecting back to you the energy you're putting out into the world. Simply put, it's you when you're being your most authentic self. Whatever that is for you, that's your gift.

Sadly, some people never get the opportunity to identify their talents when they're young. No one ever showed them the right door to open, so they don't learn until later in life that what they love is travel or photography or cultivating a garden, and only then are they able to try to align their lives and careers with their gifts. Others of us are lucky enough to know in our bones from a young age what we're meant to do, and whatever hardships I may have endured in my youth, in that respect I was one of the lucky ones. Thanks to my parents, I grew up immersed in the world of business and commerce. I saw what made it exciting. I saw that what made a good business thrive, more than anything, was people. Business, at the end of the day, is nothing more than humans interacting with other humans. How people organize themselves, interact, and collaborate—that's what defines what any particular business is, and that's what I loved about it.

I went into business knowing I wasn't employable in most traditional fields because of my dysgraphia. I probably could have held a job in sales, and given my passion for real estate I might been successful doing that, but for the most part I knew I'd need the freedom to do things my own way. I'd spent all of my high school and college years stuck at a desk, taking three hours to do work that the other kids could do in less than one, bending my brain to force it to work within the confines of how other people wanted it to work. It was excruciating. But from the day we started Spin Master, I did the opposite. I designed my day to work the way my brain worked, and it was liberating.

When I come into the office, I'm scheduled in meetings from the moment I arrive until the moment I leave. I never take lunch breaks. I've only gone on five business lunches in my life, and I mean that literally. I can count them on one hand. I never go out to restaurants, and I never sit at my desk and eat by myself. I've eaten every single lunch of my career in a meeting. Once I'm going, the meeting cadence is back-to-back-to-back-to-back-to-back-to-back, just this crazy flow of one meeting giving way to the next. Which works for me because of the way my brain functions. I don't like to take notes, I don't want to write memos or talk over Slack, and the way I assimilate information best isn't through reading. It's through face-to-face conversation and dialogue. So that's how I've always structured my day.

Through all the years we were building Spin Master, I loved forging new partnerships and collaborations, sharing my vision, getting others to believe in it, seeing what opportunities we might explore together. Whenever I was in a meeting and I had a thought or an idea that I needed to share with this person or that person, I would turn to my assistant say, "So-and-So is joining the meeting. Find them." Sometimes I'd page people over the intercom, pulling them out of other meetings to come and join my meetings, which would start with two or three people and maybe end with eight, all of us going around the table, improvising. It was like being in a jam band of ideas, and the rhythm was always high. I could put in ten-hour days of meetings like that and not get bored for a moment. I created a living, breathing flow of information, because that's how my mind processes information, and the creativity in my mind was unleashed. The ideas and thoughts that I'd struggled to express on the page in school, now they were all free to come bursting out of my mind, ready to be implemented to help the business grow.

Controlling my environment at Spin Master also meant controlling who I was able to meet with and what information I was surrounded by. In a world with so many distractions, controlling the information that flows into your brain is critical to shaping decisions to move your business forward, and for me, having the ability to do that was a gift. The word that comes to mind is "idiosyncratic." Given the idiosyncratic way my brain works, if I had been forced to spend my whole life working in a structure and on a schedule dictated by someone else, conforming to their culture and environment, I don't think I ever would have achieved anything close to what I have now.

Like me, you know your own idiosyncrasies, the way you need to work in order to maximize the talents and gifts you've been given. Whatever culture you create will begin to take on characteristics of your personality, and you'll be able to mold that institution to maximize your productivity, to amplify your strengths and surround yourself with people whose strengths make up for your weaknesses. (Because you will never be great at what you're weak at; it doesn't work that way.) The most important thing is to work in a way that matches who you truly are. There are tons of business books out there that will tell you a million different tips and tricks for the best way to succeed. But what none of those books have is an understanding of who *you* are. The truth is that there is no right way or wrong way to run your business. There is only what's right for you. The results will back it up, and that will point the way forward.

Ultimately, the big question you have to ask yourself is not just *Am I putting my talents to use?* but *Am I putting my talents to* good *use? Have I aligned the use of my gifts with my true purpose, with a goal that I find meaningful and worthwhile?*

The reality of this world is that you can be a very smart, very gifted individual who gets paid to use your talents for something you don't believe in at all. You can do that and still achieve stellar results and attain great material success. On the surface, you may appear to have it all, and you may even tell yourself that you're more than satisfied with the life you've led. But deep down you'll know that's not true. Your soul will know that it's not properly aligned, and that frustration will manifest itself in unhealthy ways, whether it's anxiety, boredom, procrastination, or something worse. You'll end up creating workarounds to make yourself feel happy even though you're not.

Your true purpose can be anything that excites you, anything that impels you forward. It's a thing you believe *needs* to get done. Somewhere in the world, there's a hole that has to be filled and you're the one who's meant to fill it. That could be something you need to do for yourself, for your community, or for the whole of society. It might be working with children or the elderly. It might be making music. It might be developing cutting-edge technology with AI. There is literally no limit to your choices.

When it comes to living a purposeful life, there are many different paths to take. Public service and the nonprofit sector both offer meaningful opportunities. But in my experience, starting a business is one of the most dynamic and powerful ways to go about it. Business is creativity in motion. It's an expression of what you care about and how you want to see the world. When you start your own business, you begin to make the change you want to see on that very day. You decide what product or service you're going to provide based on what you believe the world needs. You decide which customers you want to benefit from those products. You decide how you're going to treat people, from the wages you're willing to pay, the hours you expect people to keep, and the range of benefits you're going to offer. You decide how you want to treat the environment. You decide if you're running a company that won't tolerate financial kickbacks or sexual harassment. And if more businesses were created, there would be more diversity in the business world, fewer large corporations, and more real engines for innovation, which would create the most jobs and spark the most ideas for new business in the future. Simply put, when you start your own business, you're not just protesting and petitioning for progress. You are the progress.

Staying true to your talents and your sense of purpose takes courage above all. Most of us waver. We let conventional wisdom and prevailing societal norms blow us off course. We're surrounded by well-intentioned people who genuinely want the best for us, but in trying to protect us they often nudge us onto the safer, more predictable path, picking apart our dreams and pulling us away from our truest selves, doing us a fair amount of damage in the long run.

The safer route may be safer in the short term, but over the course of a lifetime it won't feed your soul. It won't fulfill you. It gives you the paycheck, the house, the nice car—the material things—but does it give you that spring in your step?

WORKING FOR YOURSELF, TAKING CONTROL of your life, is the ultimate form of freedom. It is the freedom to dictate your time, the freedom to express yourself, the freedom to create—the freedom to be who you want to be. Which, of course, should not be taken as the freedom to be free of any obligations to anyone or anything. Freedom doesn't mean having carte blanche to do whatever you want. If you have partners, you'll have obligations to them. If you have employees, you'll have obligations to them as well, very serious obligations. Having people whose livelihoods and families depend on your ability to make payroll—whether it's five people or five thousand people—is an enormous responsibility. But the key thing is that those are responsibilities and obligations that you have freely chosen, which makes them completely different from the burdens of being put at a desk and told what to do. You have what I call a tethered freedom, but as long as you love what you're tethered to, you're good.

It's also true that when you're trying to grow a business you will always be short on people to do what needs to be done. You will constantly be wearing multiple hats and performing multiple roles. You will need to be able to switch gears again and again, as if you were running an endurance obstacle course. It's your baby, so you'll always be the one taking the late-night calls and the early-morning meetings. You'll need to have a whatever-it-takes type of work ethic—within ethical bounds, naturally. There will be moments when you're working *all* the time, far more than you would clocking in to a regular nine-to-five job.

But the reality is that the definition of "work" changes when you're passionate about what you do. When you're not in love with what you're doing, or who you're doing it for, that's when a job truly becomes a grind. But when you're the one deciding how your time is spent, and you're spending it in service of a dream or a passion that you truly believe in, then work becomes something else entirely. It's almost unfair to call it "work," because it bears little resemblance to what we traditionally think of when we imagine punching a clock for someone else. When you control your own destiny, you have a different life energy driving you.

Are there costs? Sure. When you're in your twenties, you can spend your time partying or you can spend that time building your life. It is a choice, and there is a trade-off. I will never forget the time I traveled to Thailand with two good friends over the Christmas holidays. We were having a blast, the kind of fun you can't have later in life once family and middle-aged responsibilities have crept in. But then a work issue came up. I needed to go to Hong Kong to interview a woman for a position; we were looking for a new general manager for our office there. I had to beg off and leave just as the other guys were heading to Laos to travel up the Mekong Delta. They begged me to join them, and I was tempted, but I didn't waver. I went on to Hong Kong as planned. To this day, my friends still talk about the rest of that trip and how much fun they had, how incredible the river was and the gestalt of it all . . . and I missed it. On the other hand, we ended up hiring the woman for the general manager position and she helped us keep the momentum of the business going.

At the end of the day, finding the right balance between work and fun is a challenge for everyone, whether you own a business or not. The important question is who decides what that balance is going to be. Will it be you or someone else? In the end, one of the best parts of being your own boss is having the ability to combine the two. Is your trip for business or pleasure? Why should you have to choose? Once Spin Master was more established, we started throwing an annual party at the International Toy Fair in New York. I'd always invite friends to join me. They'd hang out and have fun, and I'd stay over in Manhattan with them an extra day or two. Because I could. I didn't have to ask anyone's permission, nor did I ever feel like I was doing anything wrong. When you own your own business, the same goes for everything you do. The person you end up being most accountable to is yourself. You get to decide, guilt free, how and where and when you want to spend your life, to bend it and mold it as you see fit.

UNLEASHING MY CREATIVITY, MANAGING MY own time, mitigating financial instability—these were my core rationales for wanting to exert control and have agency over my life and career. In that sense, for me, having control was an end in itself. But the final thing to understand about control is that it is also a means to an even greater reward.

From the moment you're born, you're set on a journey of growing up, leaving your home, and entering the world. As a baby, you rely on your parents for everything. But then you walk to school on your own for the first time. You get dropped off at the mall alone with your friends. You get your driver's license and take a road trip, paying for the gas with money from your first job. With each independent step, you're accomplishing things you might never have thought yourself capable of. With each success, each achievement, you're developing a stronger sense of self-esteem and self-worth.

Building your own business is the ultimate form of independence. It's a test of your character that you'll never experience in the nest of your parents' house or in the nest of a job at someone else's company. Once you begin, the training wheels are off. There are no more interviews, no more final exams, no more performance reviews where you have to meet someone else's criteria to tell you whether or not you're good enough. You will create and sustain something that was not there before, and your own success or failure will tell you if you have what it takes to stand on your own. Whatever happens will be because you made it happen, because you took a risk—a risk that maybe people around you didn't think you were capable of taking. The sense of self-worth that comes from taking on this monumental task is truly invaluable. It is the ultimate workshop of personal growth—and if you're not growing as a person, I can promise you that your business won't be growing either.

Because of my parents' emotional negligence, I learned to be independent when I was young, perhaps too young. There are healthier ways of teaching your kid self-reliance than by leaving them at hockey practice with no idea how to get home. Later, because of my parents' divorce and my falling-out with my father, I was pushed out of the nest quite abruptly. And again, there are healthier ways of doing it. But the reality is that those hardships forced me to develop the agency and self-reliance that everyone needs to have.

Today, at fifty-four, I don't run the business day-to-day anymore; I am at the point where we are trying to see if the business can continue to grow and prosper without the founders at the helm. As a founder, I can spend 30 percent of my time on those areas of the business where I can contribute best, and then spend the balance of my time elsewhere, giving me even more control over my own path. It's allowed me to pursue other personal development goals, like writing this book, setting up a foundation to help kids with learning disabilities and to help the homeless get off the streets—and potentially launch me into more public service work.

There's a difference between dependence and interdependence. It's true there's no such thing as a "self-made man." We live in a society, in communities and in families, where we all need to look out for one another and rely on one another; as you've seen in these pages, I would not be where I am without the help of countless others. But even as we recognize our interdependence, it's vital to have the sense of self-worth that's necessary to stand on your own, to not be needy and incapable of doing for yourself. Naturally, you don't have to be an entrepreneur to have self-esteem and independence. But that independent path, if you choose it, if it's the right path for you, offers an unmatched opportunity to be in control of your own destiny—to challenge yourself, test yourself, and, in the end, become the self you were always meant to be.

10. Painting Your Masterpiece

Jimi Hendrix started playing professional gigs when he was nineteen years old, then rocketed to fame with his debut album, *Are You Experienced,* at the age of twenty-four. The Beatles put out their first album, *Please Please Me,* when Paul McCartney and George Harrison were only twenty and John Lennon was just twenty-two, with Ringo Starr being the senior member of the group at the ripe old age of twenty-three. Mick and Keith were only twenty when the Rolling Stones made their major label debut. The Who's Roger Daltrey and Pete Townshend? Only twenty-one the day *My Generation* hit the shelves. Billie Eilish? Two Academy Awards before the age of twenty-three. Then you've got Leonard Bernstein, who started conducting in his twenties and became the youngest person ever to lead the New York Philharmonic.

And it's not only great musicians who start young. Steven Spielberg was twenty-six years old when he directed *Jaws* and only twenty-four when he directed his first feature film, the made-for-TV hit *Duel.* That's the same age Francis Ford Coppola was when he made his first motion picture, before going on to get hired for *The Godfather* when he was twenty-nine. Famously, Orson Welles was a boy genius of twenty-five when he produced, directed, and cowrote *Citizen Kane*, often considered one of the greatest films, if not *the* greatest film, of all time.

There are painters and writers too. Picasso painted *Les Demoiselles d'Avignon*, turning the entire European art world on its head, when he was twenty-six. *The Persistence of Memory*—that Salvador Dalí painting of the melting clocks in every college kid's dorm room, one of the most recognizable paintings in history—was produced when Dalí was twenty-four. In the early 1980s in New York, Jean-Michel Basquiat and Keith Haring both brought street art into the mainstream with major solo exhibitions when they were, respectively, twenty-two and twenty-four. Ernest Hemingway published *The Sun Also Rises* at twenty-six. F. Scott Fitzgerald penned *The Great Gatsby* at twenty-eight. Charles Dickens's first serialized novel, *The Pickwick Papers*, hit stores when he was twenty-five, and Mary Shelley started writing *Frankenstein*, one of the most enduring science-fiction/horror novels of all time, when she was only nineteen; it would be published soon after she turned twenty-one.

I could go on. And so could you. Because it is universally accepted and understood that artists are capable of doing amazing, incredible work at a very young age. And I'm not just talking about young people making some fun, enjoyable paintings and stories. I'm talking about era-defining work that takes the cultural zeitgeist and turns it on its axis, blowing away the old world and ushering in something completely new. When Nirvana's "Smells Like Teen Spirit" debuted on MTV in September of 1991, the hair-metal scene of the '80s imploded in an instant, and the alt-rock Gen-X '90s were born. On the day that happened, Kurt Cobain was twenty-four, Krist Novoselic was twenty-six, and Dave Grohl was just twenty-two.

Which is not to say that artists don't continue to do great, era-defining work well into their later years. Many do, producing compelling films and novels that build on decades of well-honed craftsmanship and a lifetime of accumulated wisdom. But even those works, as accomplished as they may be, rarely contain the same spark or vitality that accompanied their earlier successes. There's a propulsive momentum driving young artists that the public feeds off of and responds to, and that momentum almost inevitably mellows with age.

So why is that true? Why is it that with artists, age, experience, and maturity are never considered prerequisites for success? Why do we encourage young artists to take on the world while telling young entrepreneurs that they should wait and get a few years' experience under their belt? Why is it that we universally acknowledge the genius of youth in art but never in business?

"Well, because that's art," you say, "and not business."

I disagree. I believe that business is an art, and given what we understand about youthful creativity in other art forms, we would do well to regard it as such, because our failure to do so means that we, as a society, are wasting an enormous amount of talent.

||

Growing up, I was always someone who appreciated art. I loved music, especially. As a teenager, it was a big part of my life. Listening to Bob Dylan for the first time opened me up to the world. Getting high to Led Zeppelin or the Grateful Dead was mind-expanding, quite literally. As it does for so many people, music helped put me in touch with the deepest parts of who I am, and it has been and continues to be a huge part of my life. I've also always had a deep appreciation for good design and good architecture. By my early twenties, I was getting more into painting as well, and in our early offices I had three Rothko prints behind my desk.

As much as I loved art, however, I never considered myself an artist and harbored no secret ambition of becoming one. I loved listening to music but had absolutely zero talent for creating it on my own; I lacked the dexterity to play an instrument, and I didn't have much in the way of a voice for singing. Because of my dysgraphia, I couldn't paint or do anything like that. My passion was always for business. Everywhere I looked I could see opportunities, and I would think about them and dream about them. I especially loved real estate and even at eight years old I would drive past old buildings or open lots and think how cool it would be to develop and build something new and exciting there. I loved the idea of building something, of creating something out of nothing. Still, even though I found business to be endlessly creative, through all the decades I spent building Spin Master, I didn't think of what I was doing as "art." Recently, that changed. When I took a step back from the day-to-day affairs of the company and began to reflect on what my partners and I had built, I realized that what we'd created *was* a work of art. I was an artist, and I'd painted my masterpiece.

How did I come to that conclusion? I suppose you have to start with the basic question: "What makes something art?" There are probably a million different ways to answer that question, but one of the most fundamental has to be that art is a form of self-expression. If you have a point of view about something, and you seek to express it through some medium, whether it's words or music or pictures, then you're engaged in the process of making a work of art. If you think about some of the truly great businesses that entrepreneurs have built over the years, from Ford to Apple to Nike, in their DNA and the way they operate you can see that they have a clear point of view about what the world should be, and the way they're run is in service of expressing that idea.

Another important question to ask is, "*Why* do artists do what they do?" Why do they create? Why do they spend hours toiling away on a sculpture or a song lyric that the world might never see or hear, and that offers little hope of paying the mortgage? The answer is that they have something inside them that needs to come out, an idea or an emotion or a vision that they have to share or express. When you're an artist and you're in the zone or in a state of flow, you're wide open. You're taking ideas and energy from the universe and channeling them through yourself and onto the canvas or the music sheet or whatever medium you're working in. It's a clean, open, flowing transmission of thoughts and ideas. Which is part of the reason why the work of young artists is so dynamic and exciting. They're assimilating, digesting, and transmitting information at an astonishing rate.

What I've learned is that the same thing is true in business. When you're building your own company, you're waking up every day and you're taking all these ideas from the universe, everything that's bubbling around in your subconscious, and you're putting it all into this entity called a business so you can send it out in the world to see if it stands up on its own. Which is no different from the way a writer pours themself into a novel and then offers it up to the world, hoping that it resonates and connects with people. And that's art. It may not be like the classical art forms that we associate with the term, but I believe that it's art all the same.

In terms of what people traditionally define as an artist, the closest analogy to running a business would probably be conducting a symphony orchestra. Your medium isn't oil or paint or chalk but other human beings. You're finding them and identifying their talents and their strengths, bringing them together, drawing out their best ideas, and inspiring them to collaborate and work in harmony with one another. It's your job to stand there at that podium with your baton leading this large collective artistic effort in order to create something magical and beautiful. If you're putting something out in the world that has not been there before, if you're bringing something to people that makes their life better or entertains them or enriches their existence somehow, then I consider that to be art.

So why is it that young people are so remarkably talented in this arena? I have to imagine it's in part because they've just spent twenty-plus years growing up, observing the world around them, taking it all in. There is an energy and an insight that comes with having a fresh mind experiencing everything for the first time. All the channels are clean and open for you. You're thirsty for knowledge, for everything. You are a new soul, brought down to see the world anew, which is a powerful perspective to draw from and to project from. It gives you a completely different vantage point from the older generations, and with that you have the ability to innovate.

All those dreams and that new insight then comes to fruition in your early twenties, because once you're a young adult, instead of being a child or even a teenager, you now have the agency and the ability to turn those ideas into action. You can piece together the new elements, technologies, and movements of society because you're in the slipstream of the zeitgeist.

That was all true for me when Anton, Ben, and I started Spin Master at the age of twenty-three. Running a company is a creative enterprise. Running a toy company, even more so, because your task is to inspire hundreds of people to imagine and create new toys and games that will in turn spark the imagination and creativity of the children who'll play with them. Because Anton took on the task of sales, and because Ben was in charge of unearthing new ideas on the front end and then marketing them on the back end, everything in the middle, the development and manufacturing of the toys, fell to me. I was the conductor at the podium during that movement of the symphony, which I enjoyed and was well suited to. Because of my love for art and architecture, I had a good eye for product design. I used that talent to become an executive producer of sorts, making toys and TV shows. I couldn't draw the characters or design the products myself, but I had the ability to direct and orchestrate the people who could.

Over time, I also became the executive producer, the conductor, of the business itself, of Spin Master as a company. I excelled at that because my real talent as an artist—my true métier, if you will, as I alluded to in the previous chapter—is the meeting. Thanks to TV shows like *The Office,* bad business meetings have been parodied to death, and deservedly so. Those meetings are awful. The clueless, self-important boss droning on forever and the bored employees looking at their watches and checking their phones—the not-so-subtle message being that business meetings are a boring, unproductive time suck that drags everyone away from their desks, where they could be getting so much more done on their own. There's a whole trend toward streamlining those meetings, getting them over with, or getting rid of them entirely, replacing them with productivity apps, like Slack, that supposedly make you more efficient by eliminating the need to ever sit in a room with other humans ever again.

I couldn't disagree more. Good meetings are essential. A company, by definition, is a collective of people working together, collaborating, to do what no individual could accomplish on his own. Therefore, the interchange between people, and the quality of that interchange, is what makes a business tick. A good meeting helps people feel comfortable and lets them share their thoughts, sparking other thoughts in turn and raising up the energy level of the whole team. That's the magic, being able to bring out the best in everyone and create this fruitful, exciting exchange of ideas. The person leading the meeting takes a group of people and puts them together to spontaneously generate new ideas that no one individual in the room had thought about before everyone else entered the room—and there's absolutely an art to doing it right. Which is why I love a good meeting.

The moment I walk into a meeting, whether it's a boardroom of twenty people or an office of four, I turn on. I take on that role of conductor, orchestrating the discussion to draw out all the ideas everyone has brought to the table. I also become a bit of an actor, adopting my CEO persona. My energy and my level of excitement and passion spike way up. I'm like a performer in front of a packed house. I love being on that stage.

If my first trip to Hong Kong for the Sky Shark taught me that I had a talent for staying cool under immense pressure, it was when I first started traveling to Japan that I fully understood my talent for running a good meeting. Up to that point, being good in a meeting was something I was able to do so naturally that I never gave myself credit for doing anything extraordinary. When I was in Japan, however, the cultural differences were so stark. I didn't speak the language. I had to use a translator. There are also formal rules to a meeting in Japan that don't apply anywhere else. There's even a proper way to sit. Your company sits on one side of the table, and their company sits on the other side of the table—you never mix. The most important people sit in the center, facing one another, with everyone else fanning out to the sides in a descending hierarchy of power. Every meeting has a set schedule as well, a beginning, a middle, and an end, and you have to adhere to that structure and all the other rules without putting a single foot wrong—which I learned the day I put my foot hilariously wrong.

It happened when were in Japan trying to get the rights to a product called Aquadoodle, which is a large mat that comes with a pen that you fill up with water. When you draw on the mat, the image appears, and after five minutes it disappears. Then you roll up the mat when you're done. It was an amazing toy for a three-year-old because they can draw for hours but they'll never damage the floors or mark up your walls, because it's just water. The Aquadoodle had been a huge hit in Japan, with probably $40 to $60 million dollars in sales for Pilot Toys, which was a part of the Pilot Corporation, the hundred-year-old pen company. We wanted the rights to sell it in North America, and David Fuhrer, a guy we knew from the toy show, got us an introduction to Tak Abe, the general manager of Pilot Toys. We flew over, and they took us to a big potluck dinner and then out to a bar afterward. Everyone had a great time, so I figured we were on good terms and the big formal meeting the next day would go just as well.

When I walked into the meeting the following morning, there was this long boardroom table that sat at least twenty. The guys from Pilot were arrayed on the far side, all of them wearing suits, all of them with their Pilot pen neatly clipped to their lapels. I sat across from Tak Abe, and the meeting got underway. We started at around 8:30 and by 9:30 my blood sugar was crashing. Remembering that I had a banana in my bag that I'd brought from the hotel, I reached down, pulled it out, and started peeling it right there at the table. In a flash, David leaned over and whispered to me, *"Hey! Put the banana away!"* Barely a second later, Ben, who has absolutely no filter at all, blurted out, "What the fuck are you doing?"

What David and Ben knew, and I did not, is that there is absolutely no eating in a Japanese meeting unless food is brought out as a part of the predetermined schedule. Because I was looking down at my banana, I hadn't seen the reaction on Tak Abe's, face across from me. When I looked up, his jaw had dropped to the floor. I'd just committed the ultimate faux pas. It wasn't even like I'd tried to sneak a few almonds. It was a banana. There's no subtle way to peel and eat a banana.

But what was I supposed to do? The banana was already peeled. You can't put away a banana when it's already peeled. And I was hungry. So I ate the banana. As I ate, some assistant ran in with a garbage can, shaking like a leaf as he held out the can for me to put the peel in. Then he ran back out of the boardroom, no one said anything, and the meeting continued.

While some might have been mortified to have committed such a faux pas, I didn't let it bother me at all. In fact, I loved learning about all the idiosyncratic cultural differences of this foreign place. I loved learning how to navigate them and connect with people in spite of them. *This is so much fun,* I thought. *I'm really enjoying this meeting.* I loved it even more than the American meetings because it was such a challenge.

Indeed, in spite of my faux pas, in spite of the language barrier, I was still able to connect with everyone across the table. I was able to get people excited about our vision and get them to believe in us and develop a strong relationship with us. We ended up getting the account, and Aquadoodle was an amazing product. In four years, we did $150 million in sales. And every time I went back to Japan from then on, my nickname in the toy industry was "Banana Boy." It became a running joke, and everyone got a ton of mileage out of the story because it was so funny and so shocking at the same time.

What I'm able to do in a meeting, even with a translator and a cultural barrier, is facilitate. I walk in with good energy and excitement. I'll kibitz for the first five to seven minutes and set the tone. It's important to have fun when you work, and I love to banter about current events and learn about what's happening in other people's lives. Then we're underway, getting down to the issues at hand.

Once we're going, I'm able to read individuals in the room. People get nervous and reticent about sharing ideas; nobody likes to put themselves out there and get shot down. But my talent is being able to draw them out. I like working with introverts. A lot of creative people are introverted, I find. They've got great ideas, but you have to probe and dig to get to them, and that means making them feel comfortable. Then, once they get drawn out, they get swept up into the flow of things and they are out of their heads and into the discussion. Then I know when to move to the next person and draw them out, then move to another person, then return back to the first person and draw them all into a back-and-forth interchange. I let it run for a bit, then I bring it back, let it run, bring it back, and at a certain point I can let the room go and the conversation is moving under its own steam. It takes a while to boil the pot of conversation, and it's only when you get to the middle or close to the end that all the good stuff comes. A good meeting builds like a good movie. There's three acts: kibitz and introduce all the main players, hammer things out, and then come to a catharsis and a climax where together you've created an idea that didn't exist before you all sat down.

One of the main tasks of the conductor is to raise the energy in the room. Otherwise it's rote. When you raise the energy, people can feel your genuine passion for whatever the subject is that you're talking about. If you don't have that passion, everyone in the room is going to feel it. If you're phoning it in, then everyone else is going to phone it in too.

The other main task of the conductor is to take the ego out of the room. Everyone has to be treated equally, even though you're technically the boss. You need to remember that you're facilitating, not dictating. In fact, given the way it's perceived, the word "meeting" itself should maybe be retired. It's such an old, worn-out word, and the idea of meeting, in and of itself, doesn't mean anything. I almost prefer to use the term "gathering," which to me speaks to the fact that you're coming together for a meaningful purpose, to generate new insights that will propel the company forward. You're not just meeting. You're gathering. You're mind-melding. You're collaborating and creating.

A good meeting is one that no one wants to leave. If you run over and you're late, it's a good sign, a great sign. I have biweekly meetings with people and oftentimes they say, "We have nothing to talk about this week, so let's push it to next week." I won't do it. I've never canceled a meeting my whole career; I'm like a dog with a bone about it, and the meetings where people come in and say they have nothing to talk about usually turn out to be the meetings where the best ideas come out. And just like putting swirls of paint on a canvas, or writing musical notes on a staff, once you've orchestrated these human beings into coming together to generate those ideas, creating something new and innovative that's never existed before, you've produced a work of art.

NOT EVERYONE SEES BUSINESS AS an art. There are those who think of it as a game. To them it's all about the thrill of competition and beating the other guy. You give it all on the field and you either win or you lose, and somebody goes home with the trophy, that trophy being the largest market share or the biggest pile of cash. I've never subscribed to that outlook because I find it too manipulative in nature. It leans heavily into the negative perception that too many people have of business, that it's a heartless enterprise run by people who only care about profit and not about the impact they have on people's lives. But if people want to look at business from an uncreative point of view, they can. You can be uncreative, even unethical, and still be successful. That's true in the traditional art world as well. It takes a very talented painter to forge a Monet. There are plenty of architects who crank out run-of-the-mill buildings that don't bring anything new or beautiful into existence.

How you choose to use your talents really depends on how you want to be viewed in the world. If you are going to open your own business, it will involve organizing people and ideas and bringing things into existence; you'll have to decide which way you want to go. What type of culture do you want to have? What ethics do you want to operate by? Do you treat it as a game? Are you only interested in personal gain? Or do you want to do something interesting, creative, worthwhile, and fun? It's up to you.

I want to be seen as an artist who created something meaningful and worthwhile. In terms of the products we make, my work is easy to see. Every day I can look out across the world and see literally millions of children finding joy in the toys we've created. Every single day, those kids pick up something that we've made, and it sends them off into a flight of their own imagination, many of them dreaming up ideas that will make them the great artists of their own generation.

My real masterpiece, however, is not the products we make but the company that makes them. Together with Anton and Ben, I've built a business that, to me, is truly a work of art. Ask any of our employees, and they'll tell you it's a dynamically creative place to work. I always talk about a diversity of thought, and that's what Spin Master is all about. We're a creative meritocracy and always have been. Inside our doors, everyone has the opportunity to share what's in their head. We run on an organized chaos that is open to new ideas.

We're open to sitting with individuals wherever they come from, always looking to interact with people both internally and externally. We're always looking to exchange ideas and, through that exchange, to generate even more ideas that keep fueling the forward progression of the company.

In our business practices, we've built an impressive machine for innovation and growth. Anton, Ben, and I have always had a philosophy of "Never bet the farm." We took risks because we're a creative business, and when you're creating new things you never know for sure what the outcome is going to be. But we were always able to balance that risk on a stable foundation, so that no one failure would spell disaster for the company, which then set us up to take new risks over and over again. We've built up a repetition muscle that gives us an ability to continually try to create new things.

Most importantly, we've built a place where reputation and integrity matter. By holding ourselves to the highest ethical standards, we've created a flywheel effect. People know that if they come to us, the company will always do right by them. Spin Master will partner with them and will always treat them right in every interaction while doing its best to put out the highest-quality products we can. As a result of that, we've engendered strong goodwill across the industry, which brings in more people who want to share more ideas and do more business with us.

THE OPPORTUNITY TO BE AN artist is a gift. The opportunity to create an extension of yourself that will live beyond you is a gift. I would also argue that being an artist is a responsibility. When you have a powerful imagination and the conviction to see the world differently, it can be difficult to have the courage and the confidence to stand up and articulate your ideas, especially when you're standing up to the older generation to say how we ought to regenerate the world after the mistakes that they've made. But young people are gifted with a new and exciting vantage point for a reason. The world needs to change and grow and evolve, and for that to happen, young people have to be able to look out to the horizon and see what older people have become blind to. If you have that vision and that imagination, you have a responsibility to share it with the world, just as your parents' generation has a responsibility to trust you and encourage you to step forward.

Ultimately, I think, we fail to see business as an art because business is seen as buttoned-down, sober, practical, analytical. Whereas art is seen as the opposite. Art is a world of feelings and intuition, emotion and sensation. No one looks at art and thinks it's a rational pursuit. But I would argue that business isn't a rational pursuit either. You have to be a bit crazy to think, *I've got this brilliant idea that nobody else has thought of, and the world needs to see it and share it.* That's no less true just because your inspiration is to create something people will buy and use rather than buy and hang on a wall. Building a business relies as much on inspiration and intuition as carving a sculpture; it is the act of creation with monetization attached to it. Senses and feelings are not rational, and every truly great business starts with something that somebody feels, an idea that starts welling up in you long before you get to the nuts and bolts of cost projections and manufacturing inputs. And, just like Bob Dylan or John Lennon or Dalí or Picasso, only the person who has that irrational inspiration can bring it to life.

We are all artists. Every one of us has the ability to be creative in how we live, what we do with our time, and how we give back to society. At no time in our lives is that more true than in our twenties. Those years are a wellspring of creativity, and we would do well as a society to redefine business as a creative, artistic endeavor, because like it or not, business is the basic driver and renewal engine for large chunks of society. The universe was created to create, and business is a wonderful tool for creation. Seeing the marketplace through that lens, we might start to give creativity the value it deserves.

Plus it's just more fun. It's fun to look at business as an art form and a platform for creativity, rather than as just spreadsheets and profit and loss statements. Seeing creative possibilities and being able to shape them is an art. Whatever business you're in, you're putting something out into the world that you're asking people to spend money on. How you came up with that idea, and how you bring that idea to life, those are artistic, creative questions.

Musicians often talk about where their music comes from, how they are merely a vessel for inspiration that comes from somewhere deep inside them or is bestowed on them by the universe. The people who come up with brilliant innovations in business are no less creative, and we should give them every opportunity to share their inspiration with the world. Because it's one thing to be able to paint or sing, to have an idea for an image or a lyric, but then there's the next step: making it real, taking it from the purely intellectual to the practical and material. You may not be great at it right away. In fact, you probably won't be. But that's okay. You'll get better. You'll learn the skill of how to do it, practicing over and over and over, to the point where you become a craftsman, capable of taking inspiration and turning it into something real that exists in the world. That takes time. It takes practice, mentors who are willing to help, and the ability to fail and get up and try again—and nobody has more of those resources than young people.

11.

The Inverse Risk

In 2000, I took my first trip to Japan. At the time, Japanese youth culture was just starting to explode in the West. Over the previous decades, shows like *Speed Racer* and *Astro Boy* had been slowly establishing a foothold in North America. Now, thanks to the rise in global trade, the popularity of Japanese video game systems, and the free flow of information online, the zeitgeist was shifting and accelerating dramatically. From Pokémon and Digimon to Dragon Ball Z and the Tamagotchi, Japanese shows and toys were becoming global phenomena. Sensing an opportunity, I went looking for toys that I could bring back and distribute in North America.

One of those toys, Beyblade, had just been developed by the Takara toy company. Beyblades were customized spinning tops with cool zip cords to wind them up. Kids could do battle with them in this plastic arena, and the winner would be whichever top knocked the others out. When Takara's team showed it to me, I thought it might have potential, and I brought it back to the guys in Toronto. They were not impressed. "Spinning tops?" they said. "Not so cool." So we told Takara we weren't interested.

Then, when I went back to Japan six months later, I met with the Takara team again and asked them what was going on with Beyblade. "Oh, it's great," they said. "We're making a TV show around it."

"You're making a *TV show* around it?"

As soon as I heard the words "TV show," that really grabbed my attention. As anyone who's been to a Toys "R" Us knows, licensing characters from TV shows and movies is a huge part of the toy business, and one we were keen to get in on. Over the course of seven years, we'd built our company and reputation with our own original toys, and now we felt like we were established enough to go to other companies and get them to trust us with their brands. We'd started pitching ourselves to the big North American brands like Disney and Marvel, but every time we bid we'd never win. The license would always go to Hasbro or Mattel. But I thought if we could license a brand-new Japanese show, something like Beyblade, we might be able to slip in and find the opportunity that had eluded us thus far.

"Well," I said to the Takara team, "if there's going to be a Beyblade TV show, maybe we would be interested after all."

"Too late," they said. "We just did a deal with Hasbro."

The moment they said that I felt slighted, even a bit hurt, that they hadn't told me about the show from the beginning. It was like they had tried to sell me a car but hadn't bothered to tell me about the car's coolest feature. But the deal was done, and there was nothing we could do about it except move on. Then Takara and Hasbro launched Beyblade, and it went on to become a massive phenomenon, selling millions of units worldwide and turning into a billion-dollar, multi-generational franchise. I made a mental note that we needed to start working on creating our own Beyblade at some point in the near future. After all, if we could create our own TV shows, we could just license the toys back to ourselves.

The next year we took our first trip to MIPCOM, the animation trade show in France for the broadcasters who buy syndicated shows; when you went, you'd spend two or three days watching hours and hours of animated shows people were trying to sell. We weren't a broadcaster, and we weren't there to buy anyone's shows or sell anything of our own, but we wanted to learn about what made a good show. Since we didn't have anything to sell, we just met with broadcasters and made friends and educated ourselves on the whole industry. We did that for five years, so we were more than ready by 2006 when fate brought us together with Sheldon "Shelly" Goldberg. Shelly, in his fifties, was a real toy-industry character. He'd been around working as a rep for inventors for years, but he'd never really had any big success at it. Then, through our inventor relations team, Shelly brought us an idea from Aldric Saucier, a twenty-three-year-old who had never invented anything in his life.

The concept couldn't have been simpler. It was a marble. Marbles are one of the oldest toys in existence. They've been around since before ancient Rome and, like chess, marble games are played in different cultures and countries around the world. But nothing about marbles had changed in decades, if not centuries. Perhaps there was a way to make them new and exciting again? Aldric's idea was to put a small action figure inside a marble. You would open up the ball, and inside would be this little action-figure guy. That was his concept. He didn't even have a prototype for it yet; the idea was laid out in a bunch of sketches. Ben Dermer—a young guy we'd hired out of college as a product demonstrator who'd go on to become our vice president of inventor relations—looked at it and connected with it right away. "There's something here," he said. "No one's done an action figure in a marble before. It's super innovative." So we licensed it from Shelly and Aldric and started doing some prototyping.

Initially, the best we could do was a literal translation of the drawing. We made a marble that you peeled open, and inside was an action figure that you then had to peel out. Nobody was thrilled by it. You still had the shell of the marble attached on the backside with the action figure on the front, and we were like, "Yeah, it's okay, but it's not great." Fortunately, by that point I'd made maybe twelve or fourteen trips to Japan, and in that time I'd developed good relationships with the toy companies over there. Realizing we needed some extra help, I said, "Why don't we go to Japan and see if we can find a partner? They love miniature things over there, and they're good at development."

So I took the prototype and flew to Japan. My first pitch was to Bandai Namco, creators of Pac-Man, Tekken, Gundam, the Mighty Morphin Power Rangers, and countless other media and video game franchises. They looked at it and said it wasn't for them. Then I went to Tomy Toys and gave my pitch to them. They said the same thing: "Thank you very much, we're not interested." Then I took it to Isao Kokubun, president of Sega Toys and a legend in the Japanese toy business. He speaks not a stitch of English, but he loves toys. He looked at it and got it right away. "It's great," he said. "We'll partner with you."

I left the prototype with Sega, flew home, and came back three months later to find that they'd absolutely nailed the concept. They'd already built a prototype too. With the model we'd made, we'd put the figure inside the ball; they were separate elements you had to manually transform. With Sega's, the marble itself turned into the figurine. They were one and the same. You rolled it and it literally popped open and transformed on its own. They also had a whole gameplay system worked out as well, which the original inventor had never even thought about. You would roll your marble onto a card. Inside the card was a strip of metal, and thanks to the springs and magnets inside the ball, when it hit the card it would pop open and transform to do battle. It was so well thought out. There was a whole point-scoring system, everything. They'd even come up with a name: Bakugan, which means "exploding universe."

All it took was one demonstration and I was sold. It was like watching the Sky Shark fly. I was like, "Wow, this is really magical." The way that it popped open and transformed all on its own, and the fact that you could put it back into a ball and transform it over and over, that was the pixie dust. It was exactly what we were looking for.

On the spot, I turned to Mr. Kokubun and said, "What do you think about doing a fifty-two-episode animated show together?"

"It'll cost twelve million bucks," he said. "Do you have six?"

"Let me think about it and get back to you."

I got on the plane, went back to Canada, and ran it by the guys. Six million was a lot of money for us to invest on our own at the time. So we decided to partner up with a company called Chorus, which owned the largest children's TV network in Canada. We pitched them on the idea. They loved it, and agreed to come in for 25 percent of the budget, which offset our risk on such a big investment. Having them as a partner also guaranteed that we'd have at least one place in the world to broadcast the show; since we'd never sold a TV program before, we had to be aware of the prospect that we might not be successful in syndicating it. I flew back to Japan and told Mr. Kokubun, "Okay, we're in. Here's our six."

Together with Sega we formed a consortium. They would produce the show in Japan through their animation division, TMS, and we would make the toys. Sega would sell them in Japan, we would sell them outside of Japan, and we'd share revenue across territories. We sold the show, *Bakugan Battle Brawlers,* to the Cartoon Network in December of 2007, which was a crazy last-minute bit of luck, since we'd already shipped all the product for a spring 2008 launch—and it went on to do what it did.

Bakugan took off like a rocket. It was at least ten times bigger than Air Hogs and Flick Trix. It was like taking someone who'd only ever built houses and suddenly they're building a skyscraper. We had multiple factories going at the same time, manufacturing and shipping around the world. We had licenses going out in other categories. Manga adaptations, guides, cases, clothing, video games for Nintendo—you name it. We organized live events and tournaments. The fans took the toys and the shows and the characters and made them their own, writing fan fiction online, customizing their figures, building their own battle arenas.

The kids had a level of passion for Bakugan that I hadn't seen before, and it was largely driven by the show, which wound up airing in 140 countries around the world. Air Hogs and Flick Trix were fun toys, but they didn't have stories. Thanks to the show, Bakugan had a story. It had characters, the hero Dan Kuso and his Dragonoid battle partner Drago. It had mythology and lore, all of which fired the imaginations of the kids who played with the toys. They could lose themselves in the epic tale of heroes and villains and fantastical creatures for hours. By the time Christmas of 2008 came around, we couldn't keep them on the shelves. It was insane. In that first year alone we did close to $300 million in sales. The following year, in 2009, we were outselling both Transformers and Star Wars.

Then, three years later, we fumbled the ball. After four seasons, the show's storyline had run its course, ratings fell off, and the toy sales quickly followed. Unfortunately, the economics of making the show on its own without having a robust toy line to back it up were not great; the money we made from the show itself didn't cover the cost of making it. So with the toy line going down, we opted not to continue with it. In hindsight, I think it was a mistake not to keep it going. When you look at something like *Pokémon*—they've never missed a season, and it's grown into this massive business. Ultimately, we would take a different tack. There's a theory in the toy business that every seven years you get a new generation of kids, so every seven years you've got a window to reboot an existing franchise or brand, and that's what we did. We relaunched it for another three-year run from 2018 to 2021, and our plan is to relaunch it a third time with a feature film in 2028. So the toys have stayed popular, and it's worked out over the long haul. But the initial failure was an important lesson for us at the time. When people love something, they want it to stay consistent and familiar. But while staying with that consistency year after year, with each new season you have to make it feel exciting, fresh, and new. It's a tricky balancing act, and this being the first show we'd ever done, we didn't pull it off.

TRYING TO REPLICATE THE SUCCESS of Bakugan, and thinking we'd learned from our mistake, we produced three other shows. All of them failed. At that point, we went back to the drawing board. I asked myself what was it about Bakugan that had resonated with kids, and for me it was the idea of transformation. The chance to become someone else—especially someone more powerful or more capable—is a compelling idea for young people to play with. At that time, the market for preschool kids, ages two to five, was wide open. There hadn't been a big hit or a new idea in that category for years, and no one had ever done anything for preschoolers like I was envisioning: a show that was dynamic and exciting and adventurous with the idea of transformation at the center of it.

I went to our entertainment team—there were four of us on it at the time, myself, Jenn Dodge, Matt Wexler, and Adam Beder—and I had them send out a brief to the top creators in the business, asking them to come up with a concept that delivered on the broad idea I'd laid out. We got a whole bunch of different takes back. Some people had actually done thirty-second animations with characters transforming, all kinds of stuff. But there was one submission by Keith Chapman from England, the creator of *Bob the Builder;* I'd always wanted to work with him. His concept was Robbie and the Rescue Dogs, about a kid and a bunch of different dog characters, different archetypes, who all went on rescue missions. Only there was nothing in it about transformation: zero. Basically, he'd just ignored our brief and pitched us the show he wanted to pitch.

Still, it was a good story idea, and we realized we could add the idea of transformation back in ourselves. We thought it would be cool if we could put backpacks on the pups, and then the backpacks could transform. We could also make doghouses for each character, and the doghouses would transform into their vehicles. It turned out to be a great combination. Keith had brought us a great story, and we'd added in the transformation play pattern based on our toy experience. Once we had that, we said, "Okay, let's go."

We went to a young animation company in Toronto, Guru Studio, and we started doing the character development with them. That's when we decided that we weren't going to make them dogs but puppies. Every kid on earth loves puppies. Once we had that, the rest of it started to fall into place. Robbie became Ryder, the ten-year-old boy with the courage and the know-how to be the leader of the team. All the different pups started to take on their own distinctive quirks and personalities. Someone on the team said, "Hey, wouldn't it be fun if all the pups had their HQ up in this tower and they'd go up in the tower and slide down it in every episode?" So we created the tower and fit it into the narrative of the story.

Then we did something that, to my knowledge, had never been done before. Most of the popular kids' shows you know, particularly the ones that come out of Japan, always started out as the toy first, or the video game, or the playing cards. *Pokémon* started as a video game. *Bakugan* and *Beyblade* and *Transformers,* they all started as toys. Then, using that concept, someone else would go off and create a show. Nobody ever developed them at the same time. So instead I went and got a toy designer, Eric Tscherne, who worked on Hot Wheels, and I gave him the animators' concept art. I told him, "Draw over the animators' designs." I took him off developing physical products and started him working on animation. So he took what the animators had in terms of the look and feel of the vehicles, and started iterating off of them, taking the look and feel closer to what he would have done to make the physical toy.

The animators got a little miffed.

"Why is this toy guy drawing over our designs?" they said.

"Let's create a fusion between the two," I said, "and we'll see what happens."

So then the animators started drawing over Eric's designs, and he kept on drawing over theirs. The result was this marriage of inspired toy design from a professional toymaker, mixed with beautiful character design from professional storytellers. Over the course of the process, we brought in writers, a director, and a producer, and the creative process became this dance between these different creative forces, all of them jamming together to create a show.

We were taking our learnings from Japan and mashing it up together in a classic preschool television show. We were a hybrid, doing both at the same time, which was utterly unique. No one had ever fused the two creative art forms of toy and character development into making a show for preschoolers. At some point we went through a brainstorming process to come up with a name, and I honestly don't remember how it unfolded or who ultimately came up with it, but what I do recall is that the first time I heard it I didn't love it: PAW Patrol. The logo and the iconography were great, but the name, to me, sounded a bit harsh for preschoolers. But boy was I wrong. I'm just glad I was smart enough to go with the team.

Once we had the whole concept for the show and its characters fleshed out, we took it and pitched it to Cyma Zarghami, the president of Nickelodeon. They bought it. We launched it in August of 2013, and even before the toys went on sale the following summer, retailers were being bombarded by parents asking, "When are the PAW Patrol toys coming?" If you went online, you could see pictures where people had made their own decorations for PAW Patrol birthday parties.

Once the toys and merchandise hit the shelves, PAW Patrol took off, achieving a level of success that dwarfed anything we might have imagined. Within a few years, the show was airing in more than 170 countries and had been translated into more than 30 languages, reaching hundreds of millions of households worldwide. Our action figures, play sets, and merchandise were flying off the shelves. We had PAW Patrol sheets and blankets and pillows, PAW Patrol pajamas and T-shirts and backpacks, PAW Patrol plates and toothbrushes and sippy cups. Soon, Ryder and his pals had jumped off the television screen to join live touring shows and appear in dedicated PAW Patrol sections at theme parks. They would later star in two feature films.

By 2015, the franchise had grossed more than $1 billion. By 2018, it was grossing more than $1 billion per year, and as of this writing it's generated more than $10 billion overall. Within a few short years of its launch, PAW Patrol was the top preschool toy franchise not only in the United States, Canada, and the United Kingdom, but also in Australia, Mexico, Spain, France, and Italy. And according to one 2019 survey, PAW Patrol had become the leading brand for children up to six years old anywhere in the world, beating out Elmo, *Frozen*, and even Mickey Mouse.

Through every new iteration and phase, we've worked to keep the franchise fresh, exciting, and new without sacrificing the consistency and familiarity that viewers expect. Knowing we didn't want the show *PAW Patrol* to lose steam the way *Bakugan* did, we went into it with a deliberate mindset. "Let's make this last for five seasons," we said. Then, once we hit five, we said, "Let's get *PAW Patrol* to ten." As we got closer to ten, we changed it again. "PAW Forever," we said. That was the mission statement, and now we're at year thirteen. Even as new shows like *Bluey* have found their own blockbuster success in that same category, we're still going strong. At a certain point, PAW Patrol became a permanent, indelible piece of the cultural fabric. Like Barbie and Pikachu and Kermit the Frog, PAW Patrol is now a part of how kids grow up in nearly every country in the world. As I look back from the age of fifty-four, that is an amazing, astonishing, mind-blowing thing to have accomplished. And none of it—none of it—ever would have happened if my twenty-three-year-old self hadn't jumped into action when my mom showed me an article from an Israeli newspaper about a novelty houseplant that grew hair.

And *that* is the inverse risk.

||

To understand the inverse risk, you first need a proper understanding of risk. As discussed in Chapter 1, risk is actually your friend. Nothing amazing happens in life without some form of risk, and it's not something to be afraid of. At the same time, what we often call risk isn't actually risk at all. It's resistance. Sometimes we approach a situation that isn't dangerous in the slightest, yet our defense mechanisms still spring into action. We get cagey. We doubt ourselves. We make excuses and pull back. It's because something inside us is making us resist moving forward. It can be tough to discern the difference between something that is actually risky versus something that we're resistant to or fearful of, and learning how to separate the two is something that only comes with experience and self-knowledge, which you only gain once you start doing. But one key difference is this: Risk is a sign you should be wary and step carefully. Resistance is a sign that you should move forward.

Resistance happens when you have the desire to do something, when you're inclined to do it and pulled toward it, but at the same time, some overthinking, overanalytical part of your brain steps in and says, "No." That resistance can come from any number of places. It could be the result of self-doubt. It could come from a need to conform to society's expectations, a fear of putting yourself out there only to be seen as a failure. But like risk, resistance is actually your friend, because it's telling you something you need to know. It's telling you, *Okay, there's something good that's happening here. There's something that I want to accomplish, some challenge that I have to face, and I need to push through this to get to the other side and try.* Because it is only by pushing yourself through that uncomfortable place that you'll actually grow and live up to your potential.

And what is your potential? You don't know. None of us do. We all have dreams and passions and inspirations, but none of us knows what we're truly capable of unless we're put to the test. None of us knows what rewards our choices might yield. We know what failure looks like, particularly in business: The product doesn't sell, the company doesn't take off, you liquidate and move on. There might be some black-swan event on the horizon, some worst-case scenario no one could have possibly imagined, but for the most part, failure is something you can game out pretty quickly.

The same isn't true for the upside. You have no idea how much magic awaits when you take positive, proactive steps to pursuing your passion. And you stand to lose it, all of it, if you don't have the faith and conviction to overcome that resistance and move forward in spite of it. That is what I call the inverse risk: It's what you lose if you don't take action. It's what you lose if you follow the conventional path because you don't believe in yourself. Simply put, it's the price of giving up.

The day we decided to make the Earth Buddy, I never in a million years imagined myself becoming the creator of a television show about marbles that transformed into mythical fighting creatures. We were very much about products and not at all about telling narratives or stories. I didn't even watch anime as a kid. *Speed Racer, Astro Boy*—those shows weren't a part of my vocabulary. Even after several years in the toy business, I had only the faintest notion of how big and important the Japanese toy market was or would become. For a long time, our hands were too full to think about that. We were so busy making the Sky Shark and our other products that we didn't have time. It was only once Spin Master got more than $100 million in market sales and had built out our manufacturing capabilities that I was able to lift my head up and say, "Okay, let's go see what else is out there." It was only then, around 2000, that we learned that Japan is the second-biggest toy market in the world, spinning out incredible, innovative products with the potential to cross over to North America. It was only after missing out on Beyblade that I decided to go to MIPCOM and learn about TV and see what we might do with it. I'd never thought about it before. It was almost too out of reach. And even once we were doing *Bakugan,* if you had asked me then if I imagined doing a show for preschoolers? I'd have told you the thought never crossed my mind. Because it hadn't.

The day we decided to make the Earth Buddy, I never could have imagined how magical it would be to see so many people come together from around the world to make these shows happen, nor could I have imagined how much joy it would give me to see it. One of the hardest things to convey to people is the number of moving parts and the sheer amount of human effort needed to get something like Bakugan or PAW Patrol off the ground. They're both intensely creative and highly technical endeavors that require a perfect symphony of individuals working seamlessly together in a moment in time, and on both of those shows, everything was perfect. The attention to detail was magnificent.

The thing that was consistent on both of those projects was that the people involved loved what they were doing. No one did it with the expectation of a huge payoff. Nobody was phoning it in, and that fueled everyone and elevated everything. We all want to find meaning and purpose in our work, and to see so many people find that opportunity through me was immensely rewarding. To have served as the conductor of that perfect a symphony orchestra was fulfilling to me in a way that I never would have imagined at the age of twenty-three. That's the beauty of making your own way in the world. You're writing your own story as you go, and you don't know how meaningful and consequential it's going to turn out to be.

But the day we decided to make the Earth Buddy, the thing I never in a million years could have imagined was the joy I would feel in seeing kids immerse themselves in the imaginary worlds I'd helped to create. With Bakugan, I would see the kids playing with them, trying to collect all of them. They knew every detail of the backstory. They knew the stories and the characters better than I did. We were the *Pokémon*, the *Frozen,* of that moment in time. A friend of mine who works for *Pokémon* told me that for a while they were nervous that we were going to permanently elbow them aside. When you capture the hearts and minds of a whole generation of kids for four years, it's fulfilling beyond anything you might have dreamed, and then to have *PAW Patrol* surpass what *Bakugan* did was even more rewarding.

PAW Patrol succeeded because it resonated with kids. It connected to something deep inside them not just because it was about puppies, but because of its core themes and ideas. The reason that young people play is because play is how you learn to be an adult, which is why it's so important to show them a world built on decency, compassion, and putting others above yourself. In every episode of the show, one of the pups uses their special skill to help solve a crisis, teaching children the importance of teamwork, community service, and helping others. Kids love to envision themselves having valuable skills and know-how and being called on to step in and save the day, and these toys that I helped create turned into one of the building blocks that the next generation is using to grow and become themselves.

Sometimes I stop and try to calculate just how many kids that is. In America alone, there are approximately 4 to 5 million kids per age cohort. The show is most popular with ages two to five, so that's anywhere from 16 to 20 million of them at a time. Every year you add another 4 to 5 million, and the show's been running now for ten-plus years. Then you take that number and expand it globally, and now you're up to about 400 million kids. I figure the show has at least touched 250 to 300 million of them. That's a lot of humans, all of them shaped in some small way by something that I did. I think about it quite often now. I never thought about it once when I was twenty-three. Never even imagined it or wished for it, not for one second.

BAKUGAN DIDN'T HAPPEN FOR US until year fourteen. PAW Patrol didn't happen until year nineteen. It took us that long to achieve the highest potential of what we could do as a toy company. To walk that path for nineteen years, through some serious ups and downs, took an incredible amount of dedication and faith. Like a musician playing gig after gig after gig, we honed our craft, producing toys, launching a new line every year, producing line extensions, one after another. With that constant repetition, we honed our intuition and our taste and our skills. We built up our confidence and our belief in ourselves, infusing the company with the kind of dynamic energy that's contagious, drawing the brightest, most talented people in the industry to join us. And all that effort took nearly two decades to come to full fruition. There is no way that I or anyone can see that far into the future. At twenty-three, you don't even know who exactly you're going to be that far into the future. You don't know how much magic you'll create in the future, nor do you know what you'll find meaningful once you get there.

What you do know is that you have an idea, an opportunity, the boundless energy of youth, and what feels like all the time in the world. You have your inborn talents, your idiosyncratic temperament, your sense of purpose, and your convictions. And if you have all that, the biggest risk you can take in life is not to bet on yourself.

Because when you don't bet on yourself, it's a betrayal. It's a deep, deep betrayal of yourself. It robs you of the life force that could be propelling you forward. Instead of unleashing that energy in the right direction and enjoying the compounding effects of success building on success, you get a negative compounding effect that drains you and drags you the other way. You start by suppressing yourself, which then leads to suppressing a bit more and a bit more and then you start to shrink and shrivel away. That's what the inverse risk is, really. It's the betrayal of self. Because if you're doing something you're not meant to be doing, how do you expect to draw any energy from it? That's not how it works.

You'll never find yourself in perfect alignment 100 percent of the time. Everything in life involves some measure of pragmatism and compromise. But you can't ever let that stop you from being in the right channel and moving in the direction you need to go. You want to stay in the positive feedback loop that comes with never betraying yourself. Because that's how you unlock the energy you have inside you. That's how you unleash your imagination. That's where the most magical and unpredictable things happen, and that's when the universe will take you to heights you never dreamed possible.

Acknowledgments

would like to give my thanks and gratitude to all the people at Spin Master, those who helped our company take flight, and those who continue to bring our magical products to life; also, to all the companies and individuals who supported Spin Master and believed in what we were putting out into the world. To my partners, Anton and Ben, for believing in my vision and the potential of what I was able to contribute. To my younger brothers, Adam Beder and Matt Wexlor, for jumping on board right out of school and helping bring some of the most beloved characters into the world. To Mark Segal, Jeff Cohen, C. W. Yuen, Winifer Chung, and Evangeline Saldana for their rock-like support and guidance over the years. To my sisters, Michelle and Maskit, for all their years of support. And to my parents, for bringing us to an amazing country, Canada, a place where one has the ability to reach their full potential, and where all opportunities and dreams are possible.

I would also like to thank Tanner Colby for helping write and bring my stories, thoughts, and ideas to life. He guided me and showed me the way and the art of writing a book. Byrd Leavell, my agent. It was love at first sight. Thank you for taking me on as a client, believing in my ideas, and making the sale to Crown—after nineteen out of twenty publishers turned us down. Kevin Doughten, my editor, who also believed in my ideas and stories and guided us along the way. Jess Scott and Margarita Lapidus, for keeping everything moving forward. Kris Jackson and Dave Sarrafo, for helping with the artwork. Yael Vizel, Sean Sade, Mika Orr, Christina Miller, Shimon Rosen, Franck Azoulay, Raphaela Schneider-Friedman, Jack Bensimon, Scott Reid, Samantha Nutt, and Amanda Shuchat, my good friends who took the time to read this manuscript and give me notes with love.

And finally, thanks to Anne Lamott, who wrote *Bird by Bird,* a beautiful book about writing a book.

Appendix

Now that you've reached the end of the book, I hope that you're inspired to start thinking about new and innovative ways to bet on yourself as you head out to face an uncertain and ever-changing world. I also hope that you'll keep this copy close at hand as a resource to refer back to as you continue your journey. With that in mind, I've included this appendix, which breaks down and summarizes the core ideas of each chapter.

In addition to these main takeaways, I've also included some space with each chapter for you to jot down your own notes. As I said in the book's introduction, this is not a how-to, nor is it really even a business book. I've simply used my life as an illustration of certain universal principles that are true for young people all over the world. Your path will look completely different from mine, and it's up to you to determine how these universal principles apply to your situation. What does your risk tolerance look like? What older people do you have rooting for you? When you look around, what waves do you see coming in the zeitgeist? What kinds of white space do you see that other people are missing? You can jot down those answers—along with any other thoughts, ideas, and inspirations you may have—and use them to define your own vision and craft your own mission statement, giving yourself a true north to which you can always return when challenges arise and life tries to pull you off track.

Part I: Start

Chapter 1: Risk

1. Risk is directly correlated to what you have to lose, and in your twenties you don't have that much to lose. You have fewer assets to put on the line, and a near-infinite expanse of time to work with. Take the plunge while it won't cost you that much.

2. Passion de-levers risk. When you're passionate about what you do, you naturally bring so much energy and enthusiasm to the task at hand that you lower the chances of failure out of the gate.

3. The "safe" path offers plenty of risks of its own. Risk is everywhere, and sitting in a classroom or a cubicle for two years while life passes you by may pose as much risk as striking out on your own.

4. The way we evaluate risk is inherently biased and flawed. The downsides of taking a risk are staring you in the face. The potential upsides might be more than you can possibly dream of—you can't make a meaningful comparison between them before you even start.

5. The single greatest benefit to confronting risk is developing the ability to confront risk. Once you get the stomach for facing it and the muscle memory for dealing with it, you'll be able to handle risk like a pro.

6. Following your dreams may feel like a big gamble, but you're taking an even bigger gamble when you fail to believe in yourself. The greatest risk is a life unlived. Go live yours now.

Thoughts

Chapter 2: Everyone Is Rooting For You

1. The secret asset you have as a young person is that everyone is rooting for you to win. If you take yourself seriously, people will almost invariably treat you with enthusiasm and respect.

2. The drive to help the young is a hardwired instinct. It's human nature. As a young entrepreneur, you will always have that incredibly powerful force working in your favor.

3. When you ask an older person for help, you're not just taking a favor. You're giving something to them in return: a chance to repay a debt to the people who helped them, a chance to assume the status and respect of being a village elder, and a chance to feel young again by letting them share in the energy and enthusiasm of youth.

4. When older people are rooting for you, the benefits go far beyond cheerleading. You'll catch breaks on everything from payment terms to deliverables. You'll get a pass on your mistakes, and second chances when you need to learn and try again.

5. The help you need is coming from every direction, from friends and family who have experiences to share, and from competitors and industry stalwarts who want you to succeed. To get their help, all you have to do ask for it. Then ask them again, and ask them again, and ask them again.

Thoughts

Chapter 3: Partnership

1. When you start a business, you can go it alone if you want to, but you probably shouldn't. The right partner will help you sharpen your ideas, bring complementary skills to the table, and bring out the best you have to offer. Together you will be able to build something greater than either of you could attempt on your own.

2. Finding a partner is like dating, and your twenties offers a much bigger, more diverse, more interesting pool of prospective people to choose from. At that age you'll also get a clear, unvarnished view of who they are, where they came from, how their families raised them, and what values they possess.

3. When you search for a partner at a young age, you're more open, less jaded, and a little naïve—and that's a good thing, because those are the qualities you need to remain open yourself to establish the bond any good partnership requires.

4. As a young person, you're not fully formed yet, and neither is your prospective partner, which gives you the ideal opportunity to grow into something even greater with each other.

5. You and your partner have to share the same work ethic, have the same risk tolerance, and have the ability to mind-meld. Even more important are shared values and trust. Without that solid foundation, you will not succeed.

6. You will fight and argue and drive each other up the wall. But the hard-fought process of forging that partnership will, in the end, make you into one part of a happy, healthy collaboration—and that is a goal in and of itself, just as much as the products and services you create and whatever profits they may bring.

Thoughts

Part II: Build

Chapter 4: The Zeitgeist

1. The zeitgeist is the cultural climate of the times, the defining spirit or mood in fashion, music, consumer products, or politics. It's the wave of "what's new," always shifting as new ideas and technologies upend everything that came before them.

2. Like a surfer searching for the perfect wave, you can learn to feel what's coming simply by observing the world and connecting the dots about how people spend their time. And wherever young people are gathered, by definition that's where the zeitgeist is taking shape, allowing you to see it more clearly than those who aren't as close to it anymore.

3. It's not enough to be able to spot changes. You have to be open to embracing them. And once you spot a wave, you have to act fast because others will see it too. You want to launch yourself early enough to ride the wave, but not so early that you can't get traction—and not so late that the trend has become obvious to everyone.

4. Surfing the zeitgeist doesn't always mean chasing the obviously trendy thing, like the internet in the late nineties or AI today. You can use technological and cultural shifts to reinvent and redefine any established industry.

5. Countless business titans have been wiped out by failing to see the future coming, and the constant movement of history creates a decisive advantage for younger entrepreneurs who can exploit new niches by tapping into changing tastes, desires, and cultural norms.

6. Catching the zeitgeist is the ultimate growth driver. It's more powerful than advertising and completely free to anyone who wants to use it.

Thoughts

Chapter 5: The Power of Not Knowing

1. There is an incredible amount of power in not knowing what you're doing, simply because you can't see the roadblocks ahead and so you don't know what's impossible. When you have no self-imposed limits, you'll go further than you ever imagined.

2. Ignorance is part of what allows you to see what I call the white space, the unfilled opportunities in the marketplace. It's just a matter of identifying them, creating something innovative to fill them, and reaping the rewards.

3. Knowing too much can be a hindrance. All that information clutters your mind, makes you overthink, and impedes taking action. History is full of things that "couldn't be done." Inevitably, those problems were solved by someone too ignorant to know it couldn't be done.

4. "Not knowing" can also mean "a different way of knowing." Intuition counts for as much as rational analysis. You always need to balance your intuition with practical research, but you should never discount the power of being passionate and following your instincts.

5. When you're young, the market isn't the only thing you don't know. You don't truly know yourself. You have no idea what incredible things you're capable of, because you haven't been tested yet. It's only when life forces you to dig deep that you discover you have the strength and qualities necessary to succeed.

6. Work is only interesting and rewarding if it's challenging you to grow and learn as a person. Therefore, by definition, you almost have to start from a place of ignorance for your endeavor to be fulfilling. The magic of any undertaking comes from taking a leap into the unknown. Even as you grow and mature and develop a mastery of your craft, the key to success is to stay out at the frontier where you're always learning and growing.

Thoughts

Chapter 6: Luck

1. Luck is not the same as chance. Chance is random. It's a fluke. Luck is what happens when you create an opportunity for yourself, have the ability to see it, and have the confidence to actualize it.

2. Luck is what manifests in your life because of the hard work you're putting out into the world. Whenever we say someone is "in the right place at the right time," odds are it's because they did something to get themselves there.

3. Luck typically manifests in your life through other people, through friends and family and colleagues; they're the vectors that bring opportunity your way. But you don't get it through networking or transactional relationships; you get it by building meaningful bonds through shared experiences, by focusing on others' happiness and fulfillment. And you can exponentially increase your own luck by surrounding yourself with other lucky people who carry good karma from powerful webs of meaningful connections.

4. Networking alone isn't enough. You need the ability to see opportunities and the confidence to act on them. "Überluck" is when you understand the opportunities life gives you and choose to capitalize on them rather than let them pass by.

5. Because luck comes from your own doing, it's an endlessly self-generating resource. Even failure can be a form of luck. Any failure that doesn't kill you gives you the opportunity to learn valuable lessons that will lead to bigger wins in the future. Whether you're succeeding or failing, as long as you're generating forward momentum, you're still creating luck.

6. Doubt is the antiluck. It kills momentum, and once you lose momentum your luck evaporates. You're out of the mix when opportunities come along. When something feels right, when an opportunity comes along, don't take too long to act on it, because luck exists only in the moment.

Thoughts

Chapter 7: Failure

1. There are two types of failure in business. Systemic failure is the failure to run a competent organization, which is unacceptable. But the failure that comes from trying your best and falling short is nothing to be ashamed of. In fact, it's a gift.

2. It's best to fail when you're young because you don't have far to fall. Plus you have plenty of runway and energy to start over, and whether you decide to try again or take a different path, you've given yourself the gift of removing a potential regret from your bucket list.

3. It's good to fail when you're young because the world is more forgiving of your missteps. As long as you own your mistakes, people will cut you some slack. You'll also gain the reputation of someone who can cope successfully with failure, which is a vital skill to possess.

4. You need to experience failure young because that's when you need to learn from it. You learn to take failure seriously but not personally, tackling it head-on without letting it crush your confidence. The more you fail, the less catastrophic each failure seems, and you develop the resilience that only comes with being knocked around by life.

5. One of the most important elements of running a successful business is momentum, and failure creates its own momentum. Even as you're falling and flailing, you're still moving and generating energy. Some products work, some don't, and no one setback is the end of the world. The key is to keep moving, keep products flowing, and not stagnate, because proper failure becomes an essential element of progress rather than a setback.

6. A good test of whether you're on the right path is to ask yourself, *Do I enjoy failing at this?* Building any business involves stumbles, setbacks, and challenges, but if you've found your true calling, your losses will be as interesting to you as your victories, because they give you the opportunity to grow at doing what you love.

Thoughts

Part III: Reward

Chapter 8: Equity

1. The moment you have an idea and begin to will it into reality, you own 100 percent of its value. That is equity. It's the gift you give yourself by starting something out of nothing.

2. At an age when you're being driven by the boundless energy of youth, having equity gives you a way to channel all that energy. Owning a stake in what you do gives you motivation, a sense of purpose, and a clear direction for your life.

3. The seemingly boundless energy of youth *will* get used up and dissipate over time, and *someone* is going to extract the value from your labor and convert it into equity for themselves. The question is: Do you want to keep that return on your efforts, or do you want it to accrue to someone else?

4. Equity is the repository that allows you to store the value of your youthful energy before it tapers off, allowing you to continue to tap into it and to keep it growing for decades into the future.

5. Always invest, and reinvest, in yourself. Take home the minimum salary you need to be comfortable and secure, and leave as much equity as you can in the business. The ability to cash flow your own operation and take your own risks will save you from the downsides of taking on debt, whether from the bank or from outside investors.

6. When the time comes to reap the rewards of the equity you've built, the decision you make is entirely yours. That said, be mindful of all the intangibles that maintaining your equity stake can bring you, like an identity, a platform, and an ongoing place in the conversation.

Thoughts

Chapter 9: Control

1. Becoming an entrepreneur is not about having an idea for a product or a service to sell. It's a decision about the life you want to lead. You have to want to create and control your own world and be willing to take on the responsibilities that come with that choice.

2. To be a successful entrepreneur, you don't need a plan. You need a philosophy. The day you begin, sit down with your partners and define your goals as broadly and as simply as possible. Let that mission statement be the North Star that guides you, and then fill in the details along the way.

3. Perhaps the most fundamental reason to own your own business is to have the ability to control your time, the one asset you can't buy more of and that you'll never get back. When you own your own business, you decide when to come in, when to leave, and what priorities you want to pursue in between.

4. Beyond controlling your time, when you work for yourself you'll be able to control the culture of your environment, molding it into an extension of your own personality in order to maximize your productivity, unleash your imagination, and dedicate your talents to a life you find meaningful and purposeful.

5. Working for yourself is the ultimate form of freedom, but it is a tethered freedom. You will still have obligations—to your partners, to your employees and their families—but they will be responsibilities that you've freely chosen, not burdens imposed on you by someone else.

6. Control isn't just an end in itself. Being in control of your own business is the ultimate test of your character. You'll create something from nothing, and the sense of self-worth you'll gain from that monumental task will be truly invaluable.

Thoughts

Chapter 10: Painting Your Masterpiece

1. There are many ways to define art. It is a means of self-expression, a process for artists to learn more about themselves, and a powerful engine for creation. If you're engaged in any of those endeavors, what you're making is a work of art, and that makes you an artist.

2. The classical art form that is closest to running a business is conducting a symphony orchestra. Your medium is other human beings—you're finding them, identifying their talents, and inspiring them to work in harmony to create something magical.

3. Young people make great artists for so many reasons. They're immersed in the zeitgeist, learning and growing at an astonishing rate, and observing the world with fresh minds. And, as young adults, they have the agency to act on their ideas for the first time.

4. Art is perceived as emotional and intuitive, while business is too often portrayed as buttoned-down and rational. But starting a business isn't a rational enterprise. Building a business relies as much on inspiration and intuition as carving a sculpture, and only the person with the inspiration can bring it to life.

5. The opportunity to be an artist is a gift, but it's also a responsibility. When you see the world differently, it takes courage to stand up and articulate your ideas. But the world needs to evolve, and if you have that vision, you have a duty to share it. Ask yourself: *Do I want to be someone who's only interested in personal gain? Or do I want to do something interesting, creative, and worthwhile?*

6. Everyone has the ability to be creative in how we live and give back to society, and at no time is that more true than in your twenties. As a society, we should take advantage of that by recognizing business as the creative, artistic endeavor that it is.

Thoughts

Chapter 11: The Inverse Risk

1. The inverse risk is what you stand to lose if you don't take action. It's what you lose when you follow the conventional path because you don't believe in yourself—it's the price of giving up.

2. What we call risk is often just resistance. It's when we approach a situation that isn't dangerous at all, yet we still doubt ourselves, make excuses, and pull back. But where risk is a sign to be wary and step carefully, resistance is actually a sign to move forward, because it's telling you there's something good happening that you want to accomplish.

3. While failure can be gamed out quickly, you never know the upside of something until you try it. You don't know your true potential until you've been tested, and you have no idea how much magic awaits you when you pursue your passion.

4. Life is long. Your biggest successes may come years or even decades from now, and there is no way that anyone can see that far ahead. You don't know how much magic you'll create along the way, nor do you know what you'll find magical and meaningful once you get there. You don't want to foreclose on those possibilities before they even have a chance to happen.

5. When you have a dream and a sense of purpose, the biggest risk you can take is to not bet on yourself. When you don't bet on yourself, it's a deep betrayal of yourself. To unlock your energy and unleash your imagination—where the most magical things happen—you need to stay in the positive feedback loop that comes with never giving up on yourself and moving in the direction you're meant to go.

Thoughts

ABOUT THE AUTHOR

Ronnen Harary is the cofounder and chairman of Spin Master, the global children's entertainment company behind PAW Patrol, Bakugan, Melissa & Doug, Rubik's Cube, and Toca Boca. He has built brands that define modern childhood. Driven by a belief in the power of play, he founded the Toy Movement and supports philanthropic initiatives through the Ronnen Harary Foundation, bringing toys to children in underserved communities and expanding the reach and role of play worldwide.